THE

A story for anyone who ever felt that life wasn't fair!

BY
DONNA FERGUSON

1993 Donna Ferguson, Newport Beach, CA 92660
2012 Republished in Memory of Donna Ferguson by:

Onesimus Publishing
Post Office Box 1644
Wildomar, CA 92595

ISBN: 1481065084
ISBN 13: 9781481065085

Cover Art "Imagine" by Brenda Hoddinott
Used by Permission of the Artist
http://drawspace.com

Printed in the United States of America

Acknowledgements

*It is with deep affection and gratitude that
I acknowledge Betty and Herb Hawkins
for making it possible to share the secrets
of a little girl's heart;
but the name of the One to Whom this book is
dedicated is for the reader to discover.*

Prologue

If, as Shakespeare suggests, "All the world's a stage," and we are merely players on it, how many of us would choose the roles into which we were born? Would we not prefer to play the hero, the philanthropist, the humanitarian, or to run with the rich and famous? Would there be any treacherous bit players or unhappy endings?

Like it or not, some of us are born more advantaged than others. And while we usually equate this advantage in financial terms, it is really the emotional economics of our family that set the stage of our lives. These scripts – written long before we even make an appearance – are inherited from our ancestors, and the ancestors of others who occupy our stage with us.

When we inherit a script of abuse, we also inherit the director of the unfolding drama of the rest of our lives. As children we have no control over the situations that confront us; rather, we simply learn to adapt. We often cannot distinguish between appropriate and inappropriate behavior, and are well into the second act of our lives before we begin to understand the script we are playing to, and recognize the identity and the character of those who share our stage.

The dysfunction of an abusive childhood teaches us to wear a mask, to pretend to be something we are not, to hide our feelings so we may be accepted by the rest of the cast.

Recovery from abuse is painful at best; and it takes courage. But, paradoxically, the failure to rebuild our broken self only results in an even more broken self. We think that if we can just find the right answers the pain will go away – if we can just put the blame in the right place, we will stop blaming ourselves. We search for formulas that don't exist; chase after false solutions to bypass the discomfort of recovery. And in so doing, we tighten the snare that keeps us at the mercy of a dysfunctional script, unaware that we could, by choice, restrict its terrible impact on our broken lives.

What we need most from our world is understanding and resolution – and a willingness of this world to turn a compassionate ear toward the child inside of us – the child who is trying so hard to tell us the things we need to hear.

For generations we have called ourselves the land of the free and the home of the brave – but for countless millions, the reality is that we have become the land of the victim and the home of the abused. How long and how many casualties must we endure before we dare to confront the evils that place our children at risk and threaten even their offspring?

It is well past midnight – and all is not well. It is time that we take off our masks, repair the damage and stop passing our wounds onto the next generation.

If you have been an abused child, in reading the script of life inherited by Dorian you will most certainly discover some of the hidden fragments of your own life, and meet players who shared your stage. And if you choose to rescript the destiny of your inner child, you can find encouragement and confidence in the unfolding of the new script Dorian chose to live.

Chapter 1

"I forgot what little girls were supposed to be made of.
I would never forget what they were used for."

He was too good looking for his own good. Everyone said so. He was well muscled, a half head taller than most men, endowed with a dark mustached Hollywood Mystique women fawned over. He walked with the authority of a man who knew he was exceptional; stood with an air of importance. Cobalt blue eyes and a dazzling, ready smile gained him easy recognition. When he entered a room the place bristled with his presence. His voice was rich, deep, articulate, and when directed in anger could set me trembling.

An engineering degree was useless in the thirties. He was caught in the backlash of the times. We lived on relief and on the extra money he made painting portraits. Patrons climbed the stairs to our flat above the drug store; posed in the big chair Mummie covered with fabric she said "would make do." She did the wash in the bathtub; hung the clothes over the fire escape. We shared the bathroom with four families.

My mother, Elizabeth, had a delicate Swedish colouring in direct contrast to my father; a doe-like mistrust of others and was described as "aloof" and "somewhat different." Her gentle ways lent her a refinement lacking in other women living in the building, but her personality could change abruptly when my father stumbled up the stairs, drunk and abusive, her sweet temperament turning to rage because he drank our precious "extra" money.

Graham was his most frightening and punishing self when he was drinking. It was on such an occasion that he tried to cut my ears off, and he would have, too, if not for Mummie. I saw him hide some candy in the cupboard, and when he wasn't looking, I climbed up on a chair and wolfed it down. When he caught me with chocolate all over my face he made me confess, and then pushed me to the floor, put his knee in my back and held me by the hair. The blade of his knife was sliding up my neck. I was hysterical; begging him not to take my ears.

Mummie jumped on his back, knocked the knife out of his hands, and ordered me down the hall to lock myself up in the bathroom. That was the night I heard her say she couldn't take much more of him.

Marian came to have her portrait done. She was fair haired, like Mummie, and had enough money for "extras." We only had enough for "the bare necessities." Marian and my father passed secret smiles between them; there was always an uneasiness about Mummie whenever Marian was due for a sitting.

I was frightened by an argument one afternoon, and scurried under the kitchen table and watched through the fringe on the table cloth as Mummie told him he was disgusting. He knocked her to the floor. She cradled her face in her hands, whimpering.

How could he betray her; put her in the family way again, when all the time he was sleeping with Marian as well? How could she look for day work with another child on the way? How did he intend to provide for his family?

A sense of foreboding told me there would be no kisses or promises from him this time.

We lived on the street bordering Chinatown in Vancouver, British Columbia, Canada. Women on the other side of the city hired women from our side to clean for them. Whenever we were "low on cash" Mummie did "day work." I looked after my brother, Duncan. He was three years behind me. Mummie taught me how to use the stove; how to mix Campbell's soup and water in the pan. I waited for the tiny blips to collect at the top of the soup, telling me it was time to pour it and test it for Duncan. We were told never to leave the building, and never, ever to step out on the fire escape. I opened the window; we sat on the ledge and dangled our feet over the people going in and out of the drug store.

On November 27, 1937, three days before my seventh birthday, Marian's portrait was finished. Graham wrapped it in brown paper and said he was leaving to deliver the painting. Mummie waited at the kitchen window until he caught the street car before she pulled down the shades. Then she moved the rocking chair in front of the stove and sat down.

"How would you like a new game tonight?"

We were delighted. She could pick games out of the air when she wanted to amuse us.

"Tonight we'll take a journey to a far-away land."

"But how will we get there, Mummie?"

"In a magic rocking chair! Come on you two – up you come – one on each knee. I'm going to tie us all up together so you'll both be safe until we get to the far-away land."

She hooked some belts together and secured us in the chair.

"What's the name of the far-away land?"

"Some call it Heaven; some call it the Promised Land. Do you remember what I told you about Heaven, Dorian?"

"That's where the angels live. And they have silver wings and silver dust about their heads."

Her face was colourless, sad. "How would you like to meet an angel?"

"Oh, yes," I squealed.

"I have another surprise. Look in my pockets."

Her apron pockets were crammed with salt water taffy. We could have all we wanted, but first we were to promise to sit still without fussing until we reached the far-away land. We promised.

3

We were eager to eat the candy, and gobbled it down, adding a new piece before we were done with the first, until our cheeks bulged with contentment. Then the fun ceased. My jaws were tangled, sticky; my head throbbed. I felt the impending need to vomit and tried to climb down.

"Mummie, stop rocking the chair. I'm gonna be sick!"

"Hush, Dorian," she scolded. "You promised not to fidget! We'll be there soon. Here – have another piece of candy. That's a good girl."

I wrestled my face out of her hands.

She was trying to force the candy into my mouth.

We never had candy.

Candy was too expensive. Now there was too much candy.

Why tonight?

"Mummie stop rocking. I'm getting sick."

She paid no attention; she was singing her favorite song, "The Isle of Capri." Her body weighed heavy against me, yet her voice was from another room. Duncan was slumped asleep in the crook of her arm, the kitchen full of the suffocating smell of gas.

"Mummie! Let me go! I'm gonna throw up!"

She didn't answer. Her arms went limp, releasing me. I fumbled with the belts and slid from her lap, determined to get to the bathroom. The black and white squares on the linoleum rose up to meet me. A checked mask covered my face. There was no more air; no more light. It was deathly quiet.

My next awareness was that of a doctor bending over me. "It's much too soon to tell if either of them suffered any brain damage; only time will tell," he said. His face was distorted as if in a dream; his words out of step with his mouth. My father stood in a separate dream at the foot of the bed. His face floated free from his body and came to rest above my head. I noted four vivid, fresh red welts on the left side of his face where, I remember thinking, "Mummie must have scratched him again." I heard him say Mummie was gone. Mummie was dead.

A clock above the door said exactly ten o'clock. Duncan was encased in a cellophane tent in the next bed. When I looked again he was gone. "Moved to another wing of the hospital," they said, but I didn't believe them. I was sure he was dead along with Mummie. And just as sure my father had something to do with what happened to her. The stripes on his cheek worried me; his face was clear when he left to deliver the painting. I would have remembered. I always took notice when he and Mummie were fighting.

The nurse said I was very fortunate to be alive. If my daddy hadn't arrived "just in time" I would be dead, too. I was puzzled because he didn't save Mummie. He told her once that he wished he was rid of her, and there was something in the way people were acting that convinced me they were hiding something. It was all too dreadful to understand, far too painful to think about so I stopped thinking and feeling; put away my doubts and accusations along with the grief of living without Mummie and Duncan and shut the door to my mind. I was dazed; detached.

A social worker took me from the hospital and turned me over to foster parents. They were supposed to be a nice couple who knew how to take care of little girls. I was supposed to have a nap every afternoon to build me up so I could go back to school. I rarely napped; never got back to school.

Whenever the lady of the house was away, her husband took me to his bedroom to show me "what grownups do" in the magazine he kept hidden in the back of the closet. I was afraid of the pictures of naked women tied to beds and hooks, at the appearance of men with clenched fists towering over them. They were hurting the women with whips and chains. I saw knives. Guns.

Grownups did horrible things to each other.

He did horrible things to me.

His wife felt my forehead when she came home because I was sick to my stomach and didn't want supper. I made myself very small by hugging my knees, and pressed my back close to the wall. Then I barricaded myself in front with the pillow. He feigned concern, but his expression was a stern reminder that if I ever told on him "something worse" might happen. The indelible imprint of "something worse" from his magazines silenced me. My body burned with the memory of hammering, searing pain; a crushing weight pinning me face down on the bed.

He used his magazines every time he used me. I had to pretend it was a bad dream because bad dreams, however excruciating they might be, were easier to escape than daytime terrors.

One day his wife came home unexpectedly and caught him.

He said it was my fault – I asked him to do it.

I was plucked from the bed and slammed to the floor.

The social worker was very disgusted with me – not sure anyone would take me. People didn't want nasty little girls. My hand hurt. She was squeezing it much tighter than she needed to. I felt thoroughly shamed; guilty as charged.

What was it that little girls were supposed to be made of?

Sugar and spice?

Everything nice?

Not all little girls.

Certainly not this little girl.

My second foster father was "delighted" to have a little girl in the house again. His wife was not as delighted – something to do with the amount of the welfare check they were to get for boarding me. I was painfully void of comfort and protection against this new place and people, and filled the need with a pair of bed pillows walled tightly to my sides. As long as the pillows were next to me I would know who, or what was there in the middle of the night. I don't remember how many nights the shadow hovered over the bed, or the exact night it descended upon me. I do remember the sickening stench and taste of him, his hard, insistent hand forcing my jaw; gagging; a towel wiping my face; and lying frozen in the bed clutching my pillows.

I forgot what little girls were supposed to be made of. I would never forget what they were used for.

❧

Graham came for me in August and on the way to his flat he talked about the "new lease on life" he was enjoying with his wife, Marian. It was a very nice flat, with much more room than we had above the drug store. Marian had her own sewing machine and made me a blue and white cotton dress with sprigs of white rick-rack here and there. She even put a pocket on one side and gave me a penny to keep in it, "for good luck." Graham was pleased with the new dress. He wanted me to look especially nice when I went to visit the McGregor family in Calgary, Alberta, and a few days later he took me to the train station.

I was terrified at the sight of the locomotives; great iron Cyclops sprawled over the tracks. I clung to his hand, anticipating the dangers of a temporary home, cringing at the prospect of an unknown family and the steam-belching beast that would deliver me into their hands. The last few days had been so pleasant; so pleasant that I thought his temper a thing of the past. He flashed his dazzling smile at Marian, then at me. Now that I was whining, tugging at his trousers, I knew otherwise. But it didn't discourage me. I pestered and pleaded, in hopes he would give in at the last minute and let me stay in Vancouver.

"Not many girls your age will ever have a chance to travel across the Rockies all the way to Calgary by train."

"I don't want to go to Calgary. I want to stay here with you!"

"You'll like the McGregors, Dorian. They live in a big house; two stories; and in the best part of town."

He turned toward the porter and lowered his voice for a few minutes. Then a luggage tag with instructions tied to a piece of twine was dropped over my head, where it was to remain until I was safely delivered to the McGregors.

"P-L-E-A-S-E, Daddy! I want to live with you!"

"And you can someday; but not right now. Marian isn't used to children."

"But you will come and get me someday – won't you?"

"Of course!"

"When?"

"I don't know," he snapped. "As soon as I'm able. We'll leave it at that!" He tempered his voice when I started to cry.

"Maybe Christmas – if you're good."

He turned away abruptly and would no longer look at me. He palmed some money to the porter, grabbed me under the arms, hoisted me onto the train and hurried down the platform without another look or word. I was about to start after him when the porter whisked me into the coach, rattling on about a contraption he was going to make into a bed for me. He plunked me at a window, patted my head, and tried to reassure me.

"Now don't you worry none. I'll take care of you. I promised your Daddy."

My face was pressed to the glass as we inched out of the station; the city faded. The sights and sounds of travel rose to a montage of terror until the monotonous, hammering, ca-chug-ah-chug, ca-chug-ah-chug of the locomotive tuned into he-doesn't want-me, he-doesn't-want-me and I gave in to tears.

Somewhere in Vancouver my father was laughing with his beautiful new wife. They were happy. I wanted to be happy with them. But I was going on an adventure, transported by a steel reptile snaking its way through mountain tunnels, bellowing as it consumed the miles. I cupped by hands over my ears to drown out the mournful wail announcing the small farming communities clustered along the Canadian Pacific Line. Passengers settled into their sleeping quarters; the lights dimmed to a faint iridescent glow at intervals the length of the coach. Alone, frightened by the sounds of my journey, I welcomed the flutter of the curtains as travelers visited the restrooms and wondered where they were going on their "adventures."

The isolation of the upper berth, combined with the rocking coach, brought back the stifling, suffocating anxiety of the night Mummie died. I wanted to sleep, to shut out the harrowing sense of abandonment, but remained in a state of alarm, bolting in the berth when the train slowed, shuddering when it returned to full speed. As soon as the porter started "good morning" his way through a line of people parading to the restrooms, I put on my dress, smoothed down my hair, and waited for a lift down.

I returned to the window to acquaint myself with the province of Alberta; Calgary began in the late afternoon. The porter replaced his pocket watch, satisfied.

"We'll be right on time today."

"It looks a lot like Vancouver," I told him.

"Yep! All cities look pretty much the same on the outskirts. Ever been to Calgary before, young lady?"

"No sir."

The train was still creeping into its stall when the porter scooped me up and eased us onto the platform. We proceeded toward a uniformed gentleman engaged in conversation with a second, serious-looking gentleman linked arm-in-arm with a diminutive, brown haired companion. Cecil McGregor tipped the porter. Beatrice McGregor escorted me to a glossy black car. She called out the streets and points of interest, and as we started over a bridge flanked with lion statues, she raised her hand toward a street hugging the rim of a hill. We were almost home.

The house was as grand as Graham said it would be. Beatrice mentioned it was Colonial. The yard was marked off by a row of trees on one side, a trellis blooming shades of pink and lavender on the other; two-storied elegance with deep green shutters was set off by the greenest of lawns being tended by a young man with a white hanky covering his nose and mouth. My mind took hold of the moment: was I being kidnapped by bandits? How could I be sure these people were really the McGregors?

Once I was inside the house, the luxury of my third temporary home commanded my full attention. The dining room table was set with flowers and gleaming silver, the likes of which I had never seen, and plates without chip or crack, each one matching the other. Beatrice pulled out a chair and ordered me to "skootch" up to the table. She seemed pleased to have me there. Cecil was reserved, letting Beatrice take charge. Their son, Bill, was a senior in High School. He played rugby and, according to Beatrice, was their star player. He explained the hanky over his face: working in the yard aggravated his hay fever. He was cordial, but appeared to be putting on an act of acceptance – the way a woman might if her son brought home a garter snake and asked her to hold it for him until he found a box to keep it in.

Beatrice gave me a tour of the house just before bedtime. I was to have the front bedroom. A green and maroon paisley satin comforter was folded at the foot of the bed. Delicate curtains flounced around five windows. Two overlooking the rim of the hill onto downtown Calgary framed the lions on the Centre Street Bridge; those on the outside wall were patterned with the willow trees that divided the McGregors from the Cameron family next door. Elaborate "B's" embellished sheets and pillow cases.

Beatrice gave me one of Cecil's undershirts to sleep in. "First thing tomorrow you and I are going on a shopping spree. What do you think of that?"

"I've never been to one of those."

She chuckled. "Well then, it's high time! Cecil can drop us off on his way to the office. You'll need a complete outfitting. We'll even get you a pair of patent leathers. Would you like that?"

I guessed I would, but having no idea what patent leathers were, I sat on the bed, minding my manners while she told me how I was going to be her little girl from now on. I discounted her remarks. My father was going to come for me like he said he would, yet rather than be rude and tell her she was wrong, I yawned to indicate I wanted to go to sleep so she would leave.

I sat in a daze on top of the comforter. Under any other circumstance I would have been infatuated with the place. After the house quieted down, I listened for noises, fretting over the two men in the house. It never mattered how nice the women were in the temporary homes; men were evil. I needed to hide before I could sleep. I made a bed out of the comforter and pillows and curled up on the closet floor. A ribbon of reassuring light slipped under the door from the lamp on the night stand.

Beatrice opened the door in the morning and called for Cecil. He wanted to know what I was doing in the closet. I couldn't answer him. He left shaking his head, urging us to "get down to breakfast" if we wanted a lift downtown. He wasn't going to wait for us if we weren't ready to leave when he was. He had a lot of important work waiting for him at the office.

I put on my blue and white dress and listened to Beatrice's explanation of Cecil's important job at the oil company. He was the manager, and well thought of by company president, Ben Whyte. She was extremely proud of the way Cecil worked his way up from the oil fields into management. She said Cecil was a very punctual person; he didn't like to be kept waiting.

My dresser drawers grew fat with shopping expeditions. I stood at the closet door, counting, and thrilled to the feel of the slick patent leather shoes Beatrice said were only for Sunday best. I asked for more hangers because the nighties were too pretty to fold away in a drawer. She was quickly transformed into a fairy godmother in my eyes. Although Graham sent me away for awhile, at least I was with a kind and generous woman who seemed to enjoy my company. This was nothing like the other temporary homes.

Cecil had little to do with me and gave no indication of how he felt about my presence in his home. Bill told his rugby buddies I was a "royal pain in the neck," but I was good for snitching cookies when they practiced passes in the backyard. Beatrice would never scold me for eating too much of anything; even cookies. I needed "fattening" and was given every opportunity. Bill's friends were much more accepting of me in the beginning, but he gradually paid me more attention, until one day he said if anyone picked on me I was to let him know. I told my new friend Leona Whitherspoon, "Having someone who'll look out for me is the best thing that's ever happened to me so far!"

We celebrated my eighth birthday the first of December. Cecil asked Beatrice to take it easy with the presents; Christmas was just around the corner. I was filled with excitement over the reunion with my father. There was no discussion of his visit; his name was never mentioned. I decided it was just an adult game; not saying anything; not wanting to spoil my surprise. It was a time of great secrecy. Mysterious bundles were smuggled in; many whispers over the list Beatrice insisted I write for Santa Claus, even after I told her there was no such person. I wanted Graham for Christmas, but said nothing about him.

Christmas morning presented me with an overwhelming abundance: dolls with handmade outfits from Beatrice's bridge club, skates, a sled, books, games, boxes upon boxes of trinkets Cecil termed "unnecessary." Beatrice was particularly proud of a silver locket with a fancy "D" engraved on the front.

"Something to hand down to your own daughter someday."

I wore a green taffeta. Beatrice fussed over my hair with the curling iron. Graham would surely say something about how nice I looked. I planned how it would be when he arrived; when Beatrice told him how good I was; planned his smile when she told him what she told everyone else, "She is such a helpful child." She would brag on my behavior; he would say he was proud of me. I had lived up to my end of the bargain.

The chimes rang with guests arriving for the traditional Tom and Jerries. I answered the door, each time expecting to find Graham standing on the porch in one of his dazzling smiles. He lied to me; he'd lied before.

On December 25, 1938 I huddled under the paisley comforter, swaddled in rejection, listening to the howling north wind; a requiem for my father played on iced willow tree flutes. Graham was never coming to Calgary; he would never share his life with me. I was part of him, yet he chose to pass me on to someone else. I felt secondhand, second class; worthless, like a garment he no longer took pleasure in owning. I fought with the striking mustached face, the godliness of one I so desperately needed to be important to. I wanted to forget; erase him from my heart; stop the pain of knowing he was lost to me forever. I needed him. As much as I feared him, I longed for him. He was my god. Only the promise of Christmas enabled me to endure the months in Calgary without him; none of Beatrice's efforts had trained my heart away from him; presents were no match for him.

Now I knew he never intended to come. He didn't want me. He wanted Marian. My eight-year-old self hoped she turned sour on him. A flash of rage and jealousy conjured a figure of Marian; the brutal feelings of rejection and replacement were as a spotlight upon the man who stood at her side with his face turned away from me. My father was to become my ghost of Christmas past, stepping into the light whenever conditions were right for his coming, with Marian at his side. They haunted me from the shadows; always sensed; engaging me in an emotional dance of now-you-see-us, now-you-don't.

Beatrice was puzzled by my sudden lack of enthusiasm for the presents I was so taken with Christmas morning. Cecil attributed it to too much excitement – too many mincemeat tarts during the holidays – and prevailed upon her to dose me with castor oil.

Chapter 2

*"Youngsters are a lot tougher than we give them credit
for. They get over things a darn sight easier than we do!"*
".... I certainly didn't feel very tough."

When Cecil asked me what my New Year's resolution would
be I shrugged, not daring to divulge it was to put the memory
of Graham behind me and substitute Cecil in the sacred
place. I concocted a story (one I would keep to myself) of
how my real father died in a tragic accident. Someday I could
tell people there was a very good reason he never showed
up. It wasn't that he didn't love me; he was in Heaven with
Mummie and Duncan.

Winter yielded to spring; the perennial purple crocus
nudged their stubborn heads through the last remaining
patches of snow, and with the subtle warming of Alberta,
a new father ascended the throne. Until the spring of '39 I
allowed him a peripheral existence; now my eyes wooed him
with scrutiny.

Most of what I managed to learn about Cecil was gathered
from discussions from Beatrice's bridge club. When it was her
turn to host a group I was never restricted from the run of the
house, and occasionally invited to share in dessert. The ladies
spent a good deal of their time discussing husbands.

Beatrice said it herself: Cecil was moody, a pessimist, but she knew just how to manage him. Before learning the difference between a pessimist and an optimist, I assumed that black moods went with grownups. Graham was moody, so was Mummie. Beatrice was my first encounter with optimism. I'd seen her finesse Cecil out of his moods. Conditioning from earlier years warned me to move more quietly through the house, and hold my tongue at mealtime when Beatrice applied her skills.

Cecil never gave clues. It seemed just a matter of chance as to whether or not he would acknowledge me. I kept out of his way when he wasn't looking at the bright side of things – felt decidedly better when he was. I delighted in his occasional reference to me as "squirt," regarding it as a precious potential of what might ultimately come to pass between us.

Cecil's hairline was receding before Bill was born. A sizable area of scar tissues he called "proud flesh," started at the tip of his left ear and carried down his neck into his shirt collar; the result of falling with a sucker in his mouth when he was five. The stick embedded deep in his throat resulting in an infection which threatened his life. A second fall from a horse at full gallop left him with an impaired left arm set in at a 60 degree angle at the elbow. All the McGregor boys were somewhat pigeon-breasted, but he felt his was the most pronounced. He made sport of his bad left side, turning his body whenever Beatrice was taking snapshots. All in all he was not to be compared to the likes of Graham, but if he would have me as his daughter, I would accept him as my father.

Cecil set high standards for school, insisting he review all my test papers so we could go over all my mistakes together. He said it was natural for girls to have trouble with numbers, but if I put my mind to it there was no reason not to make a respectable showing for myself. He confessed to some reservation over my stepping right into the second grade with only two and one-half months schooling prior to my mother's death, but when they were through testing me he agreed with the principal, relieved to learn my brain had suffered no residual effects from the gas. Cecil always took his studies seriously when he was in school; I should do the same. There was great pleasure to be gained when I presented him with a good grade; equal shame when I didn't. If I was going to succeed with him I would have to succeed in school.

School was not as disagreeable for me as for some, but as soon as we were dismissed I felt an urgency to get back to Beatrice, to know that things were still right at home. While my classmates dallied and detoured, I ran much of the way, slowing to a walk only when a stitch in my ribs put some sense into my stride.

Beatrice prepared special afternoon teas on Friday. After a change of clothes and a good hand washing, I readied myself in the sunroom. She gave tea time all the pomp befitting a visit from Grandmother McGregor, and I'd heard how particular she was about afternoon tea. The good china was laid out on a tray between us on the window seats. Two lumps per cup at the very most was the rule. A delicious schedule of scones, oatmeal cookies with pockets of raspberry preserves, and baking powder biscuits served with lemon curd or maple syrup alternated to make Friday afternoons an occasion to contemplate on the way home. Beatrice baked on Friday in preparation for the weekend when she and Cecil had their private afternoon teas in the sunroom. She added just enough tea to my cup of warm milk to convince me I was participating in a genuine afternoon tea, which, according to Beatrice, was something the McGregors took great stock in.

"You can tell a great deal about a woman, or a man for that matter, by the way they take afternoon tea."

If somebody was going to judge me, they would not be able to find fault. According to Beatrice, it was a major *faux pas* to be caught with crumbs or preserves on the lip of the cup, so I practiced drawing the napkin ever so lightly across my mouth after each bite before raising my cup. I worked at crooking my little finger just so, but not enough to appear snooty. Beatrice did not care for snooty.

The ambiance of the sunroom set it apart from the rest of the house. Veridian garden tapestries reflected from windowed walls, with rose chintz blooming the full length of two sides of the room. Sun spots cavorted over an oriental carpet. Cecil's books were housed in glass-cased bookshelves; one shelf set apart for his back issues of National Geographic. He said, "Help yourself" to the back issues; "Hands off" to the more current issues. I was partial to the room, and spent considerable time sitting cross-legged on the carpet, toasting my back in the sun, traveling the world in Cecil's back issues.

The house was a mansion in my eyes. Oversized rooms, traditional staircase and hardwood floors I could stocking-skate over made me wonder if we weren't some of the "filthy rich." The grounds triggered my imagination. I crawled on hands and knees under the bushes, pretending to be one of the small creatures living there, and climbed each of the eleven willow trees, seeking the most comfortable cradle. When Beatrice expressed concern when I started taking books into the trees with me I assured her I wouldn't do what Bill did: I wouldn't fall and break both my arms in a "single mishap."

Bill took it upon himself to see to my musical appreciation. Saturday mornings we stretched out on the floor head to head in the living room and listened to the Metropolitan Opera. He was well schooled in classical music and sang along with the baritones. I could tell he enjoyed showing off.

A frequent complaint of Cecil's had to do with "those pesky dandelions taking over the front lawn." Seeing another opportunity for approval, I pinched off the tops before breakfast and gave him a count as to how many I'd managed to intercept before the wind could scatter their seed. Beatrice doted on her peonies; proud of the bushes she put in when they took over the house in 1934. I ran to her one afternoon shouting that we had fifteen peony bushes and every last one was covered with ants.

"Where there are peonies, Dorian, there are bound to be ants. Haven't you noticed any in the house?"

"Where are they?"

"In the bouquets! Take a look. I'll bet you'll spot one or two."

"And what should I do if I spot any?"

"Squish them! We can't have ants taking over the house!"

"How do I do that?"
She rubbed her thumb and forefinger together.
"In my fingers?"
"Yes, and be quick about it. They bite!"
I decided to ignore ants altogether.

❧

Beatrice wanted my portrait added to the mantle and felt my very first family portrait was somewhat of a historical event and merited a special dress. Cecil complained that I had plenty in my closet that would do nicely, but she insisted. Beatrice curled my hair; the photographer rouged my cheeks and lips. I was enshrined in a crimson organdy with white ruffled collar and cuffs and brass buttons marching down the front. I checked my resemblance each time I passed through the living room, much preferring the one in the gold frame to the one in the bathroom mirror.

Bill had his portrait taken to commemorate his graduation from high school about the same time. I was extremely proud of the fact that Beatrice saw fit to put us side by side on the mantle. I idolized Bill, placing him before Cecil, or Beatrice. It was his roguish charm, the same dazzling dark good looks - so like Graham's - I am sure that caused me to trail after him. I wept bitterly when he went off to California to begin college at Berkeley.

Beatrice wasn't herself for a long time after Bill left. Nobody was, because the very same day Bill called to assure us he was settled into college, Great Britain joined with France in declaring war on Germany. Cecil moved the Philco from the living room into the kitchen so we could listen to Winston Churchill on the BBC during supper. Nobody spoke at the table; Cecil was extremely grim. Beatrice blew her nose as if she had come down with a cold. I was sent to bed early, very concerned, fearful, aware that something terrible was going on, and that it was likely to continue for a long time to come.

On September 10th Cecil announced, "Things will never be the same again." Canada was at war with Germany.

When his birthday came around at the end of May Beatrice said it would do everybody good to get their minds off the war for an evening and planned a dinner party. She was complaining of a "dilly of a headache" the morning after. Cecil told her to go back to bed, reminding her, "Champagne always gives you a headache."

The house was unusually quiet when I got home that afternoon. I called out to Beatrice, but there was no answer. I continued calling, room to room, but the house was dead. I remembered her headache and ran upstairs to see if she was still resting. She was on the floor – face contorted – lips twisted in soundless effort. One trembling hand reached for the telephone. Saliva poured from the side of her mouth. Panic reached from her eyes to mine. A scream erupted from me, continued down the stairs, and across the grass to the Camerons' house. When I got back upstairs with Margaret Cameron, Beatrice was unconscious.

Cecil took the stairs two at a time, followed moments later by the family doctor and his nurse. Beatrice was paralyzed on her right side. She would take nourishment from the intravenous feedings hanging from the iron stand next to her bed. I was encouraged because the doctor was not going to move her to the hospital. And the familiar apparatus, like the one beside my bed the night Mummie died, made me think that if I got over what was wrong with me, Beatrice would too. Maybe a stroke wasn't as serious as it sounded.

Pressed into the banister, I kept watch from the top stair. Four days I perched; rising when the door opened, craning my neck for a glimpse, an answer. The white hill on the bed never shifted. Bill arrived the same afternoon the priest came, and I was packed off to spend the night with Leona Whitherspoon.

When Leona's mother entered the bedroom the following morning, I expected a scolding for making too much of a ruckus because she had already warned us that Mr. Whitherspoon liked to sleep late on Sunday.

I listened to what she said – watched the words like machine gun rounds fire from her teeth.

I was not going to cry.

Beatrice was not dead.

When I got home Cecil would tell me it was all a mistake.

"Get dressed, dear, your father wants you home right away."

Cecil was waiting on the lawn, his left arm tucked into his side. We entered the house without looking at each other; without speaking. The dreaded cape of reality settled over me at the sunroom. Familiar faces gathered in shock along the window seats. Anna, Beatrice's once-a-week house-keeper, smothered sobs in her apron and made one pot of tea after another. Cecil poured the scotch and rye for those who needed it. I jumped to his orders to fetch Mr. so-and-so's hat; Mrs. so-and-so's coat.

The cruel day had ended. I paused to look at the empty bed; all traces of Beatrice had been erased; her favorite rose coloured spread replaced by the "spare" covering from the linen closet.

I limped to my room and shut the door. Bill was in the bedroom that backed up to mine; his grief penetrated the walls. I heard Cecil say good night to John Cameron; sensed him taking the stairs slowly, painfully. I wanted to run to him, but needed to distance myself out of grief. We were alone; isolated; each dealing in our own way with the heinous loss.

I stroked the comforter. No more Beatrice. Beatrice was gone; just like Mummie. I was as a small gray rabbit, held in a steel-toothed trap, my spirit shrieking because there was no escape from the tortuous teeth – struck down by an immense power – crushed again by that ugly someone who dealt out such madness to small things. My eyes and throat burned dry, and unable to cry, I crammed the pillow into my mouth, bit down, and moaned.

❧

The teeth of the trap tightened. A facsimile of Beatrice lay in a satin lined box at the mortuary. Did I want to kiss my mother goodbye? "No thank you." Beatrice's mother wiped her eyes, offering consolation to Bill who continued to sob openly. Cecil's mother was between Bill and Cecil, stoic, patting their arms. I could feel the light brush of Cecil's suit coat on my arm, and sat silent, clutching my own cold hands, straining for breath in rapid, shallow effort against the grief lodged in my throat.

I watched Cecil as they gave her to the ground, his face in spasm, upper teeth pressed into his bottom lip, then, covering his face, he broke. A handful of dirt scraped the casket; grief tore at my heart, still I offered no tears.

My eyes were stayed on Cecil when we left the grave site. Even at nine years of age, I could discern that something was gone from him; something more than colour or vitality; he was as dead to me as Beatrice. At the time I had no idea how accurate my perception was. He died the day Beatrice died, but it would be 21 years before he took his place beside her.

People came to the house after the funeral and stayed on to sip drinks and lament the unfairness of life; the cruelty of separating two people who were sweethearts since the 8th grade. How could he manage without her? Anna maneuvered sandwiches and small cakes onto Beatrice's silver trays. I helped pass them around.

Someone said, "What an unusual child; I hear she hasn't shed a tear."

Someone else said, "The child is in shock; two mothers dead in less than four years."

I took to my bed that evening, heavy in the knowledge that life was something one learned "to make the best of."

In the days immediately following the funeral, I rambled about the house, feeding on memories stored in frames, monograms; taking stock of the jars of preserves we canned right after I arrived from Vancouver, deciding we should save them for special occasions to make them last; to make her last. I made repeated visits to her closet to lean against her clothes – to catch the last remaining scent of her, and pleaded with Cecil when he said, "It's time we put her away once and for all." He marked the boxes with a "B" and had John Cameron give him a hand down the stairs with the heavier cartons. After they stacked everything in the basement, Cecil invited John to a cup of tea and a smoke. They talked about world affairs; and me.

"Say McGregor, how's that girl of yours doing?"

"She's doing fine, John, just fine. Youngsters are a lot tougher than we give them credit for. They get over things a darn sight easier that we do!"

Cecil spoke with some degree of pride; evidently I had accomplished something worthwhile in being a lot tougher than anyone gave me credit for, and I knew Cecil wasn't one to spend compliments freely. He was wrong about two things. I wasn't over Beatrice, and I certainly didn't feel tough. But if I was to remain in his good graces, it made sense that if he thought highly of me on any count it was going to work in my favor. While Mother McGregor was with us he was going to make a decision about a number of things – and I was one of them. I was braced for any indication of what my fate would be; hoping against another "adventure."

Chapter 3

"I certainly didn't want to go through life with the wrong answers; not when it came to a matter as serious as God."

Alma McGregor was the walking definition of a grandmother, a fraction under five feet with a pronounced posture and an aura of competency about her. The firm set of her jaw suggested a woman vaguely perturbed about things in general. Her salt and peppered hair was roped into a tidy knot at the nape of her neck; ringed with tortoise shell combs. She pinched her cheeks when company was coming, and everything about her smelled of violet sachet; from her knee length bloomers to the embroidered hanky that lived in her purse.

She presided over four daughters-in-law with the authority of a matriarch; a visit from "Mother McGregor sent them into frenzies of closet straightening. Her husband "went to be with the Lord" when her youngest was two years old, leaving her with four sons. The general store, in the small ranching community south of Calgary, had been in the McGregor family for two generations. She would not break with tradition just because she was a widow, and told the boys they would all have to pitch in. It would take everything they had to run the store and manage the cattle ranch eleven miles east of town. She set her mind to hold onto what was rightfully

25

theirs, and managed to preserve the family inheritance. The ranch was eventually disposed of, but the store remained in the family, currently in the hands of her youngest boy, Clarence. Cecil was the eldest; she said he had the best head for business.

Alma agreed to stay on after the funeral to watch after me and give Cecil time to make some important decisions. It was then she told me we were actually related; she was my natural father's second cousin and arranged my adoption. If I liked, I could consider her my grandmother, although technically she was my third cousin, making Cecil my fourth. The revelation filled me with pride. I was an authentic family member. She emphasized the importance of cousinhood in Scottish families, and I seized mine with childish gullibility, trusting it to ward off future unpleasant acts of fate. Alma had first-hand knowledge of my natural mother's death, and not the least put off by my questions.

"Your father had a drinking problem…he was well, what we call a ladies' man. Good looking men sometimes get into trouble that way. I think she was concerned about providing for her children. She was expecting another one, you know. Sometimes life is more than some people can handle. Some are stronger than others…some more cowardly. Oh, not that I think she was a coward. Not at all! She was troubled with depression…or so your father told me…but it would be expected…with so many problems!"

Alma held me captive with the details: how Duncan and I were pulled out of the flat after Graham returned home, smelled gas around the doorway, and got the druggist from downstairs to open the door. Mummie was dead in the rocking chair; Duncan and I unconscious on the floor. She astounded me with the news that Duncan was living with a family in Vancouver; that she actually saw him shortly before Beatrice died.

"And all this time I was sure he was with Mummie. He's alive! How wonderful!"

"Yes! And Mrs. Peterson is a lovely woman. Your brother is well cared for."

I immediately settled it within myself that Duncan and I could meet someday, but Alma's inferring connection between cowardice and suicide left me sorting two trains of thought; one hinting that Mummie might have been a coward, the other that depressed people were not to blame. The end result was that of a nagging paradox in the shadows to scapegoat her death for things that would never have happened if she had never turned on the gas.

Bill returned to his studies in California; Alma took over the spare room, setting up her closet in mercantile fashion: every day dresses segregated from Sunday outfits, shoes arranged according to use, undergarments displayed in the drawers as if she were expecting customers.

"Life has to go on," she said. We went about our days avoiding comparisons of how it used to be. I was torn between resentment over the presence of this woman in place of Beatrice, and a growing affection and need of her. Cecil was withdrawn, and prowled the stairs to the liquor cabinet at night. Alma turned in her bed, sounding the bed springs, to let him know she was awake and aware of exactly what he was doing.

Cecil defended his drinking. "Mother! I'm not going to rack and ruin just because I have a few nightcaps. It's the only way I can get to sleep. And I'll use it as long as I need to!"

He took his liquor to his room on the weekend. Alma could be heard "tisk, tisking" at the sight of an empty rye bottle when she did his room the next day.

"Alma's famous health balls" traveled with her in a tin canister embossed with a picture of the King and Queen of England. She doled them out every morning, "two apiece to keep us fit." Cecil always declined. If they were that good for me, and they were tasty, I saw no reason not to eat them in quantity. Alma said she wasn't going to punish me for gluttony – God would do that. The health balls were nothing more than ground figs and prunes held together with a little honey.

Anna continued her weekly cleaning, leaving the house heavy with Johnstone's paste wax; Alma and I shared routine chores the balance of the week. Monday nights we lingered over the dishes with Lux Radio Theatre, always anticipating next week's production. There was always a preview of what was coming up; just enough to get hooked. Alma referred to the Bible nightly. Now that she was "in charge" of me, she was going to see I became "grounded" in the Word of God. He was important; so important we had to pay our respects once a week in a front pew as close to the pulpit as she could arrange. I found it difficult to follow most of what was delivered from the pulpit, and entertained myself by holding beauty contests in my head with the ladies in the choir.

Cecil didn't go to church. He had no use for traditional religion, saying, "Heaven and hell can be right here – especially hell. You don't have to die to get there." She flushed at his opinions, but never contradicted him in front of me, telling me privately that I was to rely on the Bible, and gave me a small Confirmation Bible given to her in 1880-and-something. It was crinkled at the edges, some of its pages were missing, but knowing the value she placed upon holy things I felt endowed by the gift in spite of its decay.

Homework and Bible study were carefully monitored and I entered training to become a "well-rounded young lady": knitting, crocheting, embroidery and the tedious task of darning stockings. Alma had her own system for repairing stockings. If I did it her way, the mend would be easy on the feet, an important consideration when your feet were as tender as Cecil's. He was plagued about the feet and ankles with patches of raw flesh and doctored for psoriasis with an old herbal doctor in Chinatown. He took me with him once when he ran out of medicine. One of the side rooms was guarded by two fierce coloured dragons clinging to a pair of black panels, and when Cecil passed through them, I was sure a secret ceremony was taking place. He came back through the dragons holding a thin blue bottle with a skull and crossbones leering on the label, and entrusted it to me on the drive home.

Cecil treated his feet once a day whenever his "condition was acting up." He poured a scant tub of bath water and asked me to fetch his blue bottle. Twelve drops of potion turned the water to milk. He sat on a stool at the tap end of the tub and swished, twenty minutes, while he read the paper. Sometimes I'd stay with him, sitting on the toilet seat cover. If he folded up the paper, I knew it was our time to talk; and I was always behind on what I wanted to talk about.

"Grandma says if we don't watch it, we could all end up in hell!"

Cecil peered over his spectacles. "My, that does sound serious. A thought like that could darn near scare a person to death!"

"It does! I have nightmares!"

"I'm not surprised."

"And when I wake up, I pray to God to forgive me of my sins, even if I can't think of any I've sinned."

"I don't want you getting any foolhardy notions into your head about going to hell."

"But Grandma says…"

"Rubbish! Nothing but rubbish!"

"She said I'm to fear God; showed me right in the Bible. And Reverend Crawford talks about it all the time."

"I've never thought too highly of him – I wouldn't take everything he says to heart. Use your head, Dorian. Does it make sense that God would want you to be afraid of him?"

"Well – I certainly am!"

"Fear, in the Biblical sense, refers to respect."

"Like what I'm supposed to do to my elders?"

"Exactly!"

"And that's all there is to it?"

"As far as I'm concerned it is. If you respect God you'll do what you're supposed to do. I suggest you pay more attention to growing up and less about what's going to happen to you when you die."

"But what does happen to us?"

"You're too young to understand."

"Why do grownups always say that?"

He chuckled. "I think you know why."

"Because they don't like to be bothered?"

"Partly. Partly because we don't always have all the answers. We don't like to appear ignorant."

"Could you just tell me where you *think* Beatrice's gone to?"

"You might look at it Ben Whyte's way. He says she's gone home; back to God."

Cecil spoke of Ben Whyte as if he were the last word on any number of subjects, and I gathered that he looked up to Ben Whyte as much as I looked up to Cecil.

"Does Ben Whyte know a lot about God?"

"I expect he knows as much as anyone."

"Then there's no chance Beatrice could be in hell – is there?"

"Absolutely not!"

"Have you ever been afraid of God?"

"Not that I can remember."

"Do you love Him like the Bible says you should? With all your mind and all your heart?"

"With my mind, yes, many times."

"What times?"

"When I'm out on the lake, casting for trout, or just sitting out on the porch late at night having a smoke, looking up at the sky wondering if there's not somebody on another planet somewhere doing what I'm doing – wondering about me. When you consider the universe you have to marvel at it; at the One who set it all in motion. Mother always told us when we were youngsters that the stars were God's footprints. I like that analogy. Anyone who says there's no God is a damned fool. That's one area where mother and I have no argument, but I've also spent a good deal of my life being angry with God. What do you think of that?"

"I'd be afraid if I were you."

"You've never been angry with God, Dorian?"

"Is that allowed?"

The sharp clap of laughter brought his mother to the foot of the stairs. "You two minding the time up there? It's almost half past seven."

He went on laughing, gripping the side of the tub. "Whoo-weeh! That felt good. I can't remember when I last had a good laugh. Now – where were we?"

"Being mad at God."

"Only dogs get mad – people get angry. So you've never been angry with God?"

I shook my head. "I wouldn't dare!"

"You will be. Everyone is at some time or another. You'll rarely hear anyone own up to it though."

"When it happens to me, I'll come and tell you."

"You do that. Now, hand me a towel and run downstairs and warm up the radio. We don't want to miss Amos and Andy."

On my way to the living room I was wondering how long it would be before we would have our next talk; when I could ask him another pressing question: did Satan really go about like a roaring lion seeking whom he can devour like Alma said he did?

The most important people in my life held separate, and more often than not, opposing views on what I understood to be a very critical subject. I knew better than to pester Cecil, but stayed primed for the chance to pry him for answers to the more bothersome questions.

"If Heaven and hell are right here, which one are we in right now?"

"Since Beatrice died, we've been in hell."

"If Heaven's right here too, why can't we just go get her back?"

"It doesn't work quite that way. It's difficult to understand something this deep. We all look for answers, Dorian, and the time is coming when you'll be doing your own soul searching. In some respects, that's exactly what you're doing now. What I think doesn't sit well with mother, but if the truth were known, we're not so far apart as she might think. Perhaps when I'm more her age I'll see it more her way. Do you understand what I'm trying to tell you?"

I nodded and lied with one gesture, more confused than before, but willing to take him at his word and await the day I found my own answers. But there was always the nagging question of who was right; who should I believe in the meantime? And what if I never found the right answers? I certainly didn't want to go through life with the wrong answers; not when it came to a matter as serious as God. Either Alma knew what she was talking about or Cecil did, and there was no way to know which of them was on the right track. Either hell was a real place or it wasn't, and it could make a big difference, if I ended up with the wrong answers. After much nine-year-old deliberation, I decided religion was like a lot of other things; something I'd have to learn to make the best of.

Alma was with us four months. She was worn out and longed to return to her home in Vancouver. Cecil commended her for standing by us; we never would have made it through without her. He was going to arrange for a housekeeper as we needed somebody around to look after us. That meant I was staying!

On her last night, Alma took longer than usual with the bedtime ritual that served as a reward for good grades. We sat together on the bench in front of the vanity mirror. I took out my braids; she dismantled her combs and hair pins. After our customary 100 strokes with the brush, I gathered her waist length hair into a pile on top of her head, and adorned her with pearls and broaches from her jewelry box, building a crown for the queen who was attending a royal ball. On this particular evening she removed her engagement ring and slipped it on my finger. I knew she cherished the ring from the way she pinned it to her apron when she worked in the kitchen.

"This will be your ring someday. I'll make sure it gets into your hands long before I go to be with the Lord."

She addressed the future. Courage was not a trait exclusive to men; I would have to muster up a fair amount of courage myself until Cecil got adjusted to being without Beatrice. She alluded to his moodiness, and said all her boys had the same tendency, as did their father. Melancholia, she called it; being out-of-sorts. Beatrice was good for Cecil because she had a knack of handling him. Blending her explanation with what I'd picked up from Beatrice's bridge club gave me fresh insight into the confusing man who held the key to the rest of my life. Like a coin portraying two faces, he could flip into a jovial teasing mood, engage me in a fake boxing match, call me "squirt," and draw me in with his humor. Then just as I was snagged, revert to his stern manner, speak in lecturing terms and go about his affairs as if we weren't living in the same house together. Now that I understood this as his out-of-sorts side, it would be just a matter of recognizing which face he was wearing, act accordingly, and learn to keep him "in-sorts" the way Beatrice did.

"You come from good stock, Dorian. You'll do well enough with your life; it's in your blood to be strong. But never forget, no matter what your father says the Bible is the infallible Word of God, written under inspiration of the Holy Spirit. If you learn to live by God's principles, nothing you come across in life will get the best of you."

If I wanted to, I could sleep with her. Tomorrow night she would be sleeping on the train. I didn't feel as safe anymore. I didn't like goodbyes, and it seemed that life was full of them.

Cecil took us to lunch at the Paliser Hotel as a sendoff for Alma. We stayed with her until the very last "all aboard" before starting home.

"Will she really come back for a visit like she said she would?"

"You bet your life she will. And when she does, the first thing she'll want to know is have you been reading your Bible?"

"I promised I would!"

"Then see that you do."

"But you said it was all rubbish!"

"That is not what I said at all! I said it was rubbish for you to worry about going to hell at your age."

"When do I start worrying?"

He chuckled. "I don't think you'll ever have to worry about going to hell – not if mother has anything to say about it."

"But the Bible is God's Word, isn't it? Like she said?"

"I don't contest what's written in the Bible; it's how people interpret the Bible that gives me trouble; get 10 preachers and you'll have 10 different opinions. Mother has her opinion;

I have mine. Ben Whyte has another. He tends more toward the middle of the road. I tend to lean the same way."

"You told me once that Ben Whyte knew a lot about God."

"And he does."

"How come he knows so much?"

"He's a student of theology."

"What's theology?"

"Look it up in the dictionary."

Cecil also believed everyone should find their own answers to words, and rather than provide me with definitions, he sent me to scavenge from the big dictionary in the sunroom. If I had to hunt it up myself I'd be more apt to remember it.

After reading the definition for theology I was all the more confused. Then I went back for the word nuisance; something Cecil accused me of. Upon learning I was turning into "an obnoxious, annoying and offensive person," I was deeply hurt. It was no less encouraging to discover that muster was the act of collecting. Where did one go to collect courage?

Chapter 4

"The strapping unearthed previous shameful events, and I was never able to bury them again."

Margaret Cameron was not entirely sure she wanted the job. "I've thought it over. I'll give it a try! I'm not obligating myself right off! Understand?"

"Sounds fair enough," said Cecil.

Margaret was in her late 40's, as tall as Cecil, big-boned and awkward. She plodded, head down, watching her feet; a hump was forming between her shoulders. Her tightly permed hair glared bright red, and freckles splattered her face and arms. Cecil said, "She's a pitiful sight of a woman, but she's perfect for us."

Cecil was of the opinion that Margaret had long since missed her chance for a husband and family of her own. She lived with her parents and a black cat, O'Brien, named after a young man she was once fond of. O'Brien was one of those arrogant, elusive cats very few could win over. He was spending more time at our house now that Margaret was working for Cecil. She displayed annoyance when I coaxed him into my lap. I got the idea she felt O'Brien was for her consolation, not mine, but I learned to sneak my time with him. We became fast friends and nosed around the yard together. He started following me up into the willows.

It wasn't that Margaret was so disagreeable that she couldn't be put up with; rather that her very presence was a sore statement that Beatrice didn't live here anymore; neither did Cecil much of the time. There was just too much that wasn't right now that Alma was gone and Margaret was in charge of me. She had a habit of running home "to see about something" after supper. I could see the Cameron home from the kitchen, but that didn't stop the premonitions from coming in the front door as Margaret was going out. The house expanded several times in size, and I had to run and switch on all the lamps. I never went upstairs when Margaret was next door.

Although I pitied Margaret, her appearance and lot in life, I was cruel in my avoidance of her, retreating to the sunroom to study rather than to the kitchen table the way I did when Cecil was home, which was less and less frequent since his promotion to general manager. Cecil turned down the position the first time it was offered. Now that he was "alone" there was nothing to keep him tied down; no reason he couldn't travel throughout the province to oversee the branch offices. When he was in town he kept company with the Rye bottle, or played cards at the Camerons.

Cecil appeared to be proud of his new responsibilities; grateful for the distraction. "The busier I keep myself right now the better I like it," he told Margaret. "I know you're holding down the fort for me here, and I appreciate the fine job you're doing." Margaret blushed under his praise. I knew she fancied him by the way she primped when he was due back in town, and decided that was the reason she continued to stay on. I dreamed of the time when Cecil and I could do without her. Maybe he could work in the Calgary office again. When I was older I would surely learn more about getting him out of his moods. Then I'd be the one to "fix" him – like Beatrice used to do.

❧

I was nearing the end of the fourth grade when Cecil told me about Maria Vincente, the head bookkeeper at the Lethbridge office.

"She's a beauty, squirt. I'm sure you'll like her. She's 35; close to becoming an old maid, but don't you let on I ever called her one. I don't know why she never married. You can meet her next week. I'm having a get-together with some of the staff from the Calgary office – some of the key people from the Lethbridge branch will be driving up to join us. I know you'll like her!"

Cecil recruited Anna to give the house a good going over and prepare some of her specialties to serve with the drinks.

Maria was beautiful. Her hair was black; black as Cameron's cat; worn in a fashionable updo. She resembled the sleek woman in the Saturday Evening Post advertisements for new cars. She had striking heavy-lidded, darker-than-brown eyes; "bedroom eyes," one of the men said. Another man slapped Cecil on the back and said, "Good for you ol' chap – you did all right for yourself."

They gathered in the foyer under the chandelier; everyone raised a glass to toast the soon-to-be bride and groom. A twinge of betrayal went through me.

It was only a matter of weeks into their marriage before I associated Maria's attitude toward me with Cecil's attitude toward her. If things were going well between them, she drew me into her confidence, inviting me to the bedroom to watch her put on her face. I wasn't going to be a child forever; it was important that I observe the falderal that went with womanhood. She was self-conscious about her nose to the extent of soliciting my opinion. Did I think it was too large? Did I notice the hook in it? I thought it a fine nose; classical; like the ones I'd seen in the paintings in my history books. If she and Cecil were at odds, Maria pouted and I kept out of the way. It was becoming more and more apparent that her prince was not as charming as he used to be; that Maria wasn't as gifted with Beatrice's ability to deal with an out-of-sorts man.

Maria wanted to put a few of her own touches on the house. She picked out a fabric so go with the rug and asked

Cecil what he thought about replacing the seat covers on the dining room chairs.

He was abrupt. "It took Beatrice months to complete the needlework on those chairs. We'll not change them! They stay as they are! Permanently!"

She appeared startled by his outburst, but tried again, asking if she could rearrange some of the furniture; add a few of her own things.

The furniture would stay where it was. In a last attempt, she insisted Beatrice's picture be removed from the highboy in the bedroom and brought downstairs to the mantle. He wouldn't hear of it. The picture belonged where it was. He simply liked things the way they were. He snapped his paper back into shape; she went back to reading her section of the paper.

The telephone sat on a shelf in the hallway outside the dining room. By laying on the floor with my ear to the heating grate in my room, I could hear conversations anytime I wanted. And I wanted to – every chance I got. Maria talked with her sister, Mary, who lived across town, several times a week.

"He's heartless! How does he expect me to live in this mausoleum? The only reason he married me was so I could keep his house and look after the kid. He doesn't love me. How can he expect me to share his bed with Beatrice's picture up there on the dresser? And that damned kid – she sneaks around and scares the willies out of me – always coming up behind me when I don't know she's there."

Now that I was aware of Maria's animosity, I sharpened my listening skills if she was on the phone to Mary or talking to Cecil. The living room was directly under my room; as long as the heating grate on the floor was open I could easily listen in, word for word. Cecil must have been smoking his pipe; she was probably thumbing through a magazine the way she did when she was upset: rapidly, smacking the pages together, glancing at the pictures without reading.

Maria was talking about St. Theresa's Home for Girls. Some of the girls were orphans, but they did take regular students.

It was economical; just the place for me until they had a chance to adjust to married life. She'd never been around children. I had annoying habits.

"She makes me nervous; always watching me. And she sneaks around. I never know when she'll jump out at me. I think she does it on purpose just to upset me. It's unnerving!"

"I find that hard to believe, however, I'll speak to her about making more noise around the house so you'll know where she is at all times."

Maria didn't respond.

This called for a remedy. A clearing of the throat might serve the purpose. It became a tireless habit; soon I was making the guttural sound when there was no need to. Maria could no longer accuse me of sneaking up on her.

Talk of St. Theresa's continued to filter through the grate. Cecil held his ground, seeing no reason to run up living expenses when I could live at home. I vowed to work harder to make Maria like me; to make her stop bringing up St. Theresa's and complaining to Mary.

"I won't be saddled with a kid that isn't mine, and what's worse is - she isn't even his. It just isn't fair. You know how long I waited for this marriage. Hells bells, Mary, aren't I entitled to some of the good life like everyone else?"

There was a pause. "You'd sing a different tune if you had to live with her! She's nothing but an irritating, fidgeting, nail-biting nuisance. And I swear, if she doesn't stop that incessant noise in her throat, I'm going to strangle her."

It was true; I was nervous. I did bite my nails; bit them raw. And as far as the throat clearing – what began as a device to make things better was making things worse. When I tried to stop the habit, I couldn't control the urge to do it.

Maria and I were rivals; and Cecil's loyalty to the vows he made when he acquired us was the trophy we fought for. I irritated her; kept her on edge. She controlled me; arranging my schedule to allow for little other than school, homework and chores, often extending the usual Saturday morning house cleaning until it was too late to join Leona and our neighborhood gang for the Saturday afternoon movies. Before I could leave for school I was expected to make all the beds, run the dust mop over the floors upstairs, and do the breakfast dishes.

I was old enough to iron now, and directed to come straight home from school "or else." I made excuses to avoid being at home, telling Maria I had to stay after school to study for a test when we weren't having one. She got wise and caught me, then screamed at Cecil, "This is the last straw – now we have a liar on our hands! What are you going to do about that?"

Cecil ordered me to my room and told me to remove my panties and lay face down on the bed. It wasn't the threat of the strap that terrified me. It was the loss of my panties – face down on the bed – waiting. I heard the slap of the leather, but more than the sting of the strap, it was the sting of fear and shame over being exposed in front of him. Cecil's strong right arm rose and fell. I rolled over the bed, from back to stomach, cupping my hands over myself in a frantic try for privacy and protection, trying to dodge the strap. It landed with vengeance, biting into my stomach and groin, across my hands as I tried to hide myself where I felt most threatened by the attack. I thrashed from side to side, screaming; the strap matched my every move.

"Are you going to stop telling lies?"

"I promise! I promise!"

I was on my back; Cecil's angry face above me. I let go of myself and reached for the strap to stop him, but it cut into my privates. I flipped onto my stomach and clung to the bedcovers until he put the strap away.

He had no idea of the severity of his punishment; no idea how I trembled in my bed over the horror of being exposed to a man again. He was back in the living room with Maria, attending to his evening paper while I tossed my head from side to side to shake off the experience. The strapping unearthed previous shameful events and I was never able to bury them again. The best I could do with them, and those responsible, was consign them to the shadows with Graham and Marian.

Maria told Mary I was disturbed; I was. Lying when there was no need to lie, and never knowing why; never able to answer Cecil when he asked me why, after I disobeyed Maria (which was in itself, a terrible thing to do) did I have to lie about it?

"Do you like to be strapped?"

"No!"

"Then why can't you tell the truth?"

I didn't know why.

Cecil was at his "wits end."

Maria had a sure cure for liars, and revealed her plan one Friday afternoon after Cecil left on a tour of the branch offices. If she really did have a cure, it would be worth it in the long run; I wanted to stop telling lies so I could rob her of grounds to send me away; to stop the strapping. I had to stop telling lies!

"Tell a lie," she said, "and you go to jail!" I was to remain in my room from 4 o'clock Friday afternoon until it was time to leave for school Monday morning, except for bathroom privileges. Under no circumstances was I to open the door if she was upstairs, unless she was in bed. She didn't want to see my "lying face" until Monday morning. Meals would be left outside my door.

I sat in the middle of the bed with nothing but hate to console me. Anger of such proportion it consumed the room, ran down the walls, flowed over the bed, drowning me. I bit the pillow and raged into the goose feathers.

I thought of ways to get even; the most vile thoughts ever to live in my head, I was sure. I prayed to God to save me from such wicked thoughts and opened all the windows to expand my prison and focused on the willows lined up outside the window, imagining them as a row of green-leaved people whispering in the yard. To pass the time we discussed what was wrong with Maria, and what I was going to do when I grew up. Life would be entirely different someday.

While Maria continued to correct my lying habits, I was lying to Leona, inventing excuses for missing the movies Saturday afternoons. After all, it was understood that "the gang," made up of a half dozen neighborhood playmates, always went to the movies together; it was the highlight of our week. When I did confide the situation to her, she crossed her heart and hoped to die, then ran right home and to tell her mother, who passed it on to Cecil as soon as he got back in town. He was embarrassed; shocked that Maria would go so far as to lock me up like a common criminal for two days. What would the Whitherspoons think? He knew how the women talked.

"Why do you do it, Dorian?"

"I don't know! Honest I don't. It's just that whenever Maria asks me why I didn't do something, or why I did do something, I lie. I can't help it! I don't lie to you!"

"Anyone can control what comes out of their mouth! And if you don't stop telling lies…."

From the time Beatrice died, I knelt at the dining room table each morning to have my hair braided, except for an occasional weekend when whoever was in charge didn't want to bother with it. Alma approached it as a duty; Margaret turned on the radio so it was less of a drudge. Maria was growing more and more resentful over our morning sessions, punctuated as they were with my yelps and hunched shoulders when the fine neck hair was braided too tightly.

"Why can't I wear my hair down, like Leona?"

"Because your father thinks braids are tidier."

On the rare occasion when my hair was loose I tossed my head, swished my hair, and fancied I bore a resemblance to the illustration on the jacket of Alice in Wonderland, and I even entertained the possibility I could be considered pretty; but only if my hair wasn't skinned back in pigtails.

Maria was working on my hair shortly after Cecil chastised her for keeping me prisoner in my room. I was acting up, as usual, squealing and pulling away. She slammed the brush to the table. "All right, Goldilocks, that does it! I'm not wasting another minute of my time trying to make you presentable." She beckoned me into the kitchen and picked up an empty jelly jar.

"From now on, you will deposit your allowance in here until you've saved enough for a permanent." She calculated the weeks. "About three months ought to take care of it."

"But I don't want a permanent!"

"You've been whining for curls, now you're going to get them. Then you can care for your own hair. Of course you realize you won't be going to the movies for awhile."

This was a calamity. Another three months without a single movie? Three months without a double feature? The fun of rehashing it on the walk home? Not only would I miss the main attraction, and the serial, I would be separated from the Centre Street Lions. The concrete cats were important to me. I'd go running ahead of the others, confiding my secrets; the anger I hid from everyone else; unburdening myself to the magical, mystical guardians of the bridge as we trooped to the theatre.

Thirteen quarters later my hair lay strewn on the floor, remnants of symbolic pride, leaving me with a garland of frizz; resembling a kinky-haired albino straight out of the pages of the National Geographic. And it had cost me a precious $3.25!

I was ugly! Maria had won again; she would always win. Cecil was always in another town, and when he was home he had little to do with me. I couldn't face him looking like this – of all the weeks for him to be home. And what would Leona say? I'd be the laughing stock of the school.

The solution was in the medicine cabinet. The next time Cecil laid eyes on me I'd be dead; gone to Heaven with Mummie and Beatrice; safe from Maria and the endless cycle of waiting for Cecil to come home; safe from St. Theresa's; from the shame of the shadow people. The skull and cross-bones on Cecil's medicine would be my ticket to Heaven. I removed the cap from the blue bottle, raised it to my lips, and ignited my mouth.

Dying was going to be painful!

Bolts of pain and regret took hold. My throat refused the fire. I crouched over the sink, gagging, spitting; hands under the cold water faucet. Splashing! Gulping! I'd botched it – still in the world – too big a coward to swallow the fire dancing on my tongue. I squatted in front of the sink, pressed my mouth against the cool porcelain, reached for Cecil's shaving towel and plunged it under the running water. My face was buried in the sopping towel when the door opened. Maria screamed. Cecil thundered up the stairs.

"What in the sam hell is going on in here? What's my potion doing all over the floor?"

I crouched lower, refusing to admit to anything.

Cecil wrenched the towel away and jerked me to my feet. "Open your mouth! Open your mouth. Damn it, Dorian, do as I say!"

I locked my jaws. He turned to Maria. "Leave us alone."

"If you swallowed it, you'll need to see a doctor. You weren't foolish enough to actually drink it were you? Because if you did…."

"Ugh ugh."

"Come on now, open up."

He peered into my mouth, cursed, trotted me into my room, and telephoned his dentist brother, Grant. He came back with a glass of whiskey and water. "Hold your nose and drink it down; it will help you sleep. What in the world ever possessed you to do such a thing?"

The following morning I woke charged with thoughts of the night before. My mouth was as a winter window caught in a morning freeze; teeth packed in white drifts that sloughed onto my fingertips. An angry tongue lay under a white crust and pink tracks marked my chin. Cecil consulted with his brother a second time, relieved that my incident didn't call for a physician. We could keep it in the family. A soft diet for a few days and I would be "good as new."

There was no further need to eavesdrop by the grate; my fate was sealed. The incident was interpreted as a play for attention. Cecil told Maria she might be right – maybe I was disturbed. The pernicious threat of another "adventure" kept me huddled under the comforter. I pulled at my hair in an attempt to straighten it, anticipating the ridicule awaiting me at St. Theresa's.

Leona couldn't take her eyes off my head the day she saw me in the front yard in my permanent. "Gee, Dorian, your hair looks – nice. I rather like it that way." Leona was schooled in her mother's perfect manners, never saying anything nasty to a person's face; I'd heard her say the very worst behind a person's back. Going away would at least spare me the embarrassment of facing my school mates.

The arrival of a package from St. Theresa's confirmed my enrollment. Maria handed me a roll of cotton tape on which the number 59 was repeated.

"You'd better get started sewing your number onto your things. Every pair of underwear, pajamas, sweaters; everything washable has to be identified. Then you can get started on these towels and sheets. It's the only way you can be sure of getting your own things back from the school laundry. Be sure to double your thread so they'll hold."

I sobbed into the comforter, stroking it like an infant caresses a security blanket. How bleak my bed at St. Theresa's would be without the comfort of my satin bond with Beatrice. If the human heart can actually feel the pain of its own distress; if what poets refer to as the wounds of the heart was my torment that mid-August night; it is a condition worthy of their poignant prose.

The news of St. Theresa's reached Leona through her father after a card game at the Cameron house. She was put out to think her best friend didn't even let her know she was going away.

"I was going to tell you. I'd never go away without telling you. It's just that I've been so busy getting ready."

I emphasized that it was a private school; how important it was to be exposed to this type of an education. It would round me out, so to speak, stealing Cecil's very words. I made a great to-do about learning French.

"I mean really learning, Leona, not just off the Corn Flakes box or waiting until eighth grade. The nuns speak nothing but French, so you see I'll come back way ahead of the rest of you!"

"When will you be back?"

"I'm not sure."

Chapter 5

"…Maybe Sister was right – maybe I couldn't measure
God's love by my circumstances."

The depot was as formidable as when I first arrived in Calgary.

"It won't take you long to make new friends at St. Theresa's," Cecil said.

"You're doing this to please Maria, aren't you? She doesn't want me around."

"You don't like Maria, do you?"

"Did she say that? Well, no, I don't! But only because she doesn't like me!"

"Maria doesn't like anybody these days – including me. And you can't deny that you've been extremely disobedient!"

I had no defense.

"Maria can be difficult, I know, but I've got to try to work things out with her; after all, she is my wife."

"But why can't I stay here while you do?"

Cecil was pacing. "Believe me. You'll be far better off where you're going. It won't be forever. It doesn't mean you'll never get to come home. Christmas holidays aren't far off. The school term will be over before you know it."

"And what happens after that?"

"We'll have to wait and see."

His manner and words were reminiscent of Graham's. As he cloaked his intentions with the privilege of living in the best part of town, Cecil hid the behind the benefits of private schooling.

Why did Cecil have to go and do what Graham did?

Why did he marry a woman who wasn't used to children?

I was crawling with anxiety over the separation and what was in store for me at St. Theresa's; the very real possibility of never seeing Cecil again no matter what he promised. I didn't need a luggage tag around my neck this time. I was old enough to speak for myself. The conductor knew all about delivering girls to St. Theresa's; he would see that I was properly turned over to the nuns. We boarded the train. Cecil asked a kindly faced woman if I could slide in next to her. This time it was I who would not look the father in the face.

He was striking a familiar pose as the train pulled away: the crooked left arm tucked tight to his side, the right leg extended, as if he didn't have a left side. He offered one last sparing smile, balancing a cigarette between his lips, and as he raised his right arm, I raised mine.

The kindly faced woman wanted to know if I was on holiday.

"I'm off to school – a private school – in Medicine Hat."

"Do you like school?"

With all the bravado I could gather I answered, "Oh, yes, especially this one. I'm going to learn how to speak French this year. The nuns speak nothing but French."

The threat of what awaited me in Medicine Hat brought a resurgence of the first train ride, the compounded effect of such harrowing proportions that I must have shut down, because in much less time than I expected it would take to cover 300 miles, I was in the hands of two women wearing black robes and white starched frames about their faces.

Sister Mary, a light, wiry young woman, and Sister Aloyious, brusque and heavy-set with a walk I found difficult to keep up with, led me to an old model Ford pitted with rust. Small homes and thirsty lawns dotted the streets of Medicine Hat, but victory gardens in back and side yards and vacant

Donna Ferguson

lots were well seen to. The last few blocks were steep. Sister
Aloyious had considerable difficulty with the gears.

St. Theresa's School was a threatening sight, squatting as
it did on the top of the hill. She appeared as a stern matron,
with a brick wall about her waist, spying on the town below.
She grew more and more ominous as we climbed the hill, and
when we stopped in front of what I was sure would be my
home for the rest of my school years, I wished with all my
heart I'd had the courage to swallow Cecil's potion.

Sister Mary took me three flights to a room furnished in
gray metal cots end to end in sets of six. The head-rails were
numbered; washstands completed the "Bedroom" allotted
each student. A large bathroom and combination dressing
room with individual storage slots was visible at the opposite
end of the dormitory.

I was introduced to Gabriel La Suer, a frail girl with a
serious face and signs of habitual concern between her brows.

"Where are you from?" I asked.

"From Montreal." She spoke with a French accent.

"Is this your first time?"

"Yes. My Grandmére is too old now, so I will live here."

"You have no parents?"

"My parents are dead. I've always lived with my
Grandmére until now. What about you?"

I shrugged, "I don't really have any either. My real parents are both dead."

"I'm sorry. Do you have any brothers or sisters?"

"Sort of – I had a baby brother once, but he lives in
Vancouver. I had a big brother too, for awhile, but he's in the
States. How about you?"

"No."

I put my clothes in locker 59. Gabriel and I spoke occasionally, still shy; uncertain about each other and St. Theresa's.
The entire student body gathered that evening at a single long
table in the English basement level, with very little conversation except for one or two girls working to establish a friendship. How abruptly life could change from one supper time
to the next.

Gabriel was given permission to sleep next to me until the girl belonging to number 58 returned to the school. I could hear my new friend sniffling after lights went out. I wanted to cry myself, but felt the need to be brave; after all, how would it look if I broke down and started bawling like a baby? This was definitely one of those times when it called for making the best of things; and being a lot tougher than anyone gave you credit for wouldn't hurt either. I slept poorly, churning on the cot. The hot dormitory air was laced with unfamiliar smells; strange noises invaded us from the floor above.

On the last Monday in August Gabriel and I rose to orientation week. The school director listened to our chests, tapped on our teeth, paraded us back and forth and poked in our noses and ears. He was old, disagreeable. I was pleased to have a legitimate excuse to stick out my tongue.

Tunics, blazers and tams were previously worn. Black stockings and white shirts were new. We brought a pair of black oxfords, understanding that as we outgrew our shoes we would exchange with each other. Uniform fittings consisted of little more than holding up a tunic while Sister decided to let it up or down. Every tunic bore signs of previous owners. If a girl was a little on the thin side or too plump for an exact fit, whatever came nearest to her size was what she got. In the end, some of us turned out better than others.

Sister Superior lectured on what she expected of us, leaving me to question my ability or willingness to measure up to the standards she would insist upon. We were assigned our chores; some to the kitchen, the school laundry, others would work outside in the yard. Duties were rotated once a month; everyone down to the youngest had something to do.

Sister Superior oversaw the school from the front office across from the parlor. The only high back chair in the nuns' dining room was reserved for her. She sat in the front pew in chapel and took Holy Communion before any of the others; when the priest welcomed us to St. Theresa's, blessed us and officially declared the school term in session, she was the only one who took tea with him in the parlor. I compared her station to that of England's Queen Mother – everyone giving way as she passed in the halls – standing at attention when she entered a room.

The nuns kept careful accounts in little black books, entering demerits for various breaches: talking in line, pinching or shoving, unacceptable table manners, spitting in the yard, or boisterous unladylike behavior. Talking after lights out, putting "things" (such as dead mice) in dormitory mates' beds and fist fights were more serious, and offenders were dunned pages of copying from the Liturgy of the Mass. If you were good enough (or crafty enough) a small gold cross was pinned on your uniform until the following week when they were collected for the next judgment.

Gabriel became a constant companion. She was timid, fluttery; a little bird of a person who needed looking after. She was visibly upset when she was sent back to her assigned cot after Emily Farnsworth arrived. How could anyone as beautiful as Emily wind up in a place like St. Theresa's? She was returning from a summer in Toronto with a favorite aunt, and before the war spent her summers in England on her aunt's estate outside London. Emily looked like someone who traveled abroad: mahogany hair, chiseled nose, extraordinarily long eye lashes. She had a way with her eyes, allowing them to rest upon you for a time, then gazing off, down, as if she would not allow herself to associate, even eye to eye, with those she knew she was superior to. When I compared my short, kinky hair with her flowing locks, she was definitely superior.

Emily was not well liked; there was much gossip about the fifth grade snob; I was too curious over her world travels to care and made an attempt to be friendly.

"Emily! Tell us about England!"

"It's a lot fancier than Canada; lots of uniforms and parades. And everything is hundreds of years old. Would you like to see my photographs?"

Gabriel and I shuffled snapshots while Emily narrated.

"Your aunt is very beautiful," I told her. "What's her name?"

"Agnes. Agnes Farnsworth. It's my middle name but I'm not overly fond of it. I am very fond of my aunt, though, so it's not quite so bad."

"Is your Aunt Agnes married?"

"Her husband was killed in the war. Not this one, the first one, and she says he is the only man she could ever love."

"I guess she'll be going back to England after the war?"

"That's right."

Later I asked Gabriel, "Isn't it romantic – the only man she could ever love?"

"I think it's rather sad; that means she will be all by herself for the rest of her life – except in the summer when Emily goes to visit."

"Well, I think that's real love: to love someone so much you couldn't love anyone else after they died, even if it meant you'd have to live by yourself. What an exciting life Emily will have after the war. She'll surely end up marrying a prince someday. Well, maybe not as high up as a prince, but nothing less than a duke, what with her aunt living in England."

Gabriel asked me if I thought Emily was stuck-up.

"No! She's just different."

I wanted to be as different as Emily, as pretty, with an aunt who could take me to England.

The school was a frightening place with intimidating caretakers. When thunder busters rolled across the sky, the darkened building held all the terror of a structure drafted by Dickens, and I gave in to Gabriel's pleas for company to the bathroom in the middle of the night knowing I would need to call upon her in time.

The nuns were distant, dark-garbed entities who floated an inch above the floor, with only an occasional rustle of rosary beads to warn us. They were ever present; ever judging. In the dim light of early evening we could suddenly find ourselves overtaken by a shroud of black; eyes and expression obliterated; a faceless, formidable instrument of God's decree. There were warnings about the evil one; protecting ourselves against his traps. The smell of incense from the first floor Chapel and echoes of Kyrie Eleison were a constant reminder of the need to guard our souls from Satan. Insecurity and fear hung like stale smoke in the corridors; visions to match Alma's description of a roaring lion that went about seeking whom he could devour easy to come by.

Our day began at 5:30 with the jolt of naked ceiling lights and the nerve-jangling summons of Sister Mary's cow bell. She walked between the rows of cots, spurring reluctant students with an extra flip of her wrist until all were on their knees, hands folded. After prayers we hurried to complete our toilette, make our beds, and get dressed before Sister started checking off demerits for "pokiness." We were required to leave the dormitory *en masse*; one girl could hold up the entire fifth and sixth grades and make us late to breakfast. The girl responsible would then be very unpopular because the entire class would be penalized with one demerit for not being in place at the table when grace was pronounced.

Those assigned to the kitchen for the month were excused from morning prayers, and dismissed ahead of the others to prepare a consistent breakfast of lumpy, scorched-flavored oatmeal, bread, and an occasional hardboiled egg. We inspected our bread on both sides, watchful for rodent feces.

There was always a sign of the school mice; they preferred the center of the loaf. Anyone making remarks about what was put before them was severely corrected; reminded that the Europeans would gladly trade us rations if given the chance.

Milk was served only if a $3.00 milk fee was paid in advance by a relative or patron of the school. Everyone was entitled to a portion with oatmeal; weak tea was provided for those not "paid up." I didn't understand why I wasn't getting milk, and asked if there wasn't some mistake.

There was no mistake! I wasn't paid up.

First I placed the blame on Maria, but later decided if Cecil agreed to send me away he probably had as much to do with it as she did. How humiliating to know I wasn't worth an extra $3.00 a month to them; how unsettling. The insult only confirmed my suspicions of what would be a repeat of Graham's performance. I never expected to see Cecil again; he would never have to explain why he was so miserly as to deny me milk any more than Graham would have to explain why he never showed up. Grownups were not required to explain themselves.

My reason for inferring to Gabriel that I had no parents was to cover my embarrassment at having an adopted father who would think so little of me as to send me away. If I admitted to that, I'd have to admit to Graham; how it happened once before. I couldn't tell my best friend how I was relinquished by two fathers in a row. What would she think of me? It also served as a bonding because she had no parents. I had to continue to cover up to have somebody to hang on to; to feel important enough to merit a best friend. And there was another reason: I couldn't assume the responsibility for the actions that contributed to my being there. It would mean it was all my fault again, and I couldn't carry one more brick of guilt.

Letters from Cousin Cecil always included my previous letter marked in red where punctuation, grammar or penmanship could be improved upon; misspelled words were circled several times. His choice of red ink was all the more belittling. No matter how much I poured into my letters I never produced a perfect specimen, and we were required to write once a week. When I handed in my letter for posting I could count on its return after Cecil graded it.

Sweet wafts of fresh baked biscuits and preserves trickled across our tables from the nuns' dining hall adjacent to ours, adding to my resentment over the inequity between generations. It was common practice among students to steal food from the nuns' pantry when assigned to the kitchen. I was anxious for my turn; longing for a chance to sink my teeth into the aromas we were subjected to. And the first place I was going to dip my hand was into the milk can.

Gabriel was concerned because my cousin didn't send money for milk and said she would share what she was getting. She poured half her portion into my cup and passed it back to me. Sister Luke intercepted it.

"Oh, no you don't. That's for Gabriel."

"But Sister, I want her to have it."

"Your aunt and uncle sacrifice to provide you with milk. You must drink it yourself."

"I was only sharing. Sister Joseph said we were to share."

Sister Luke returned the milk to Gabriel's glass. Gabriel, gathering gumption out of loyalty to a friend, confronted the nun.

"Didn't Jesus say we were to give to those in need? Dorian doesn't get milk so I want to share some of mine."

"That is not the correct interpretation as it applies in this case."

Taking courage from Gabriel, I recited, "Just exactly what is the correct interpretation as it applies in this case?"

"That will be quite enough, Miss McGregor! Any further conversation on the subject and you'll both be charged with six demerits!"

We said no more. Six demerits meant forfeiture of a most treasured privilege, and from my point of view, our only privilege. The owner of the town theatre offered a free movie one Saturday a month. Everyone assembled according to grades, and with four nuns as sergeants-at-arms, we marched down the tiers of wooden steps leading to the road into town. Anyone looking at the oncoming line of navy blue tunics must have had thoughts of a swarm of ants.

The school ran with mechanical precision; every moment scheduled. We ran with the same precision; mechanical school girls running up and down the stairs, all about the school. We maintained the hardwood floors in groups of four, lining up on hands and knees with buckets and bristle brushes working our way down the corridors, returning to rinse and dry with old towels. Sister clapped her hands, "Get your backs into it girls," and set the pace for the recitation of the rosary. We took liberties with the prayers when she was at the opposite end of the hall: "Hail Mary full of Grace, save us from this terrible place." We threw ourselves into the waxing, knowing we would soon be wrapping our shoes in rags, skating down the halls, polishing and sliding up the boards. Sister allowed us the fun of prolonged polishing. We giggled as we worked, tumbling into each other, ending in a heap of laughter. Some of the nuns were easier to work under than others.

Living with one-hundred-plus girls was smothering, and the regimentation required to keep things operating left me desperate for privacy. There was no place to hide except the bathrooms, and the nuns had a sixth sense as to who was where and for how long. I learned to hurry at night so I could steal a few moments at the windows before lights out. The view from the school, planted as it was at the brow of the hill with the town at its feet and a bridge spanning the river, set a scene similar to that of the view from the house in Calgary. Window time was a sweet interlude of idleness; a reprieve from the predictable portioning of my days. Ten minutes with nothing to do; nobody to account to; a time for dawdling and dreams. I was alone; my eyes on a creeping night sky; my mind on the house on Crescent Drive. I looked through the school windows into the living room where Cecil retreated behind the newspaper after supper in this chair beside the fireplace. Maria sat on the sofa, darning his stockings the way he instructed her, or going through her recipes. Foremost on my mind was always how Cecil was working things out with

Maria; whether or not I'd get a second chance to work things out with them.

๛

A careless tug of the curtains partitioning Sister Mary's sleeping quarters allowed me to intrude on her privacy as she prepared for bed one evening. I was surprised to see hair to the tips of her ears, being under the impression that nuns were required to shave their heads. She sat in front of an oval mirror and brushed her saffron hair with slow, deliberate strokes, fingering the strands, like one caressing secret coins held back from a dowry. She appeared as a Madonna, posed for the first faint wash of an artist's canvas, never to be completed, and unlike the others now that I had seen beyond their robes of chastity and service; more approachable, more of an ordinary woman.

She took part in softball games, always eager to turn the rope when we were jumping double-dutch, as long as she had her turn. It was then she hiked her skirts, jumped into the ropes and giggled like the rest of us. More often than not, the bottom of her skirts were dusty; her rosary beads askew; her shoes a sorry comparison to other nuns' glistening, even-heeled oxfords. I'd seen her pause at the front hall mirror, and although it appeared she was adjusting her headpiece, I suspected she might be admiring herself.

She stood apart from her sister nuns; otherwise I could not have loved her as I did. And I needed someone to love, someone to look up to, if I was going endure the place. My friend Gabriel was important to me, but I'd chosen the young nun as my surrogate mother, and I began to bond to her, manipulating my time to volunteer for extra duty after my regular chores.

We were working together in the Chapel. The setting prompted me to ask her why God took better care of some people than He did others.

"We are all precious in His sight."

"Then why does He punish us so much? He is very hard to please, Sister. I'm sure He has favorites. He doesn't punish His favorites."

"Wherever did you get such a notion?"

"What about some of us here? He took our parents away. He didn't give us anyone who wanted us. Is it because we have sinned?"

"Our students are not here because they have sinned – although each of us does – and when we do God always forgives us if we make our confession."

"But only the Catholics get to do that, Sister. I can't go to confession. The Priest can't forgive me – so what happens to me?"

"God knows in your heart if you've repented."

"Just the same, I don't think it's very fair of Him. Even though I don't do the really bad mortal sins, and even if I did, if I was Catholic I could go to confession and none of them would count – would they? Isn't that how it works?"

"Dear me, we are never to take that attitude."

"Gabriel understands everything the Sisters say about us. And she tells me. And Sister Luke said we were sinful. And she says other things – she declares the devil has already gotten his hands on some of us. Somebody told me once that I was wicked. Do you think I'm wicked? Do you think that's why God took Mummie away, and Beatrice, and everyone?"

"Hush child. You don't know what you're saying. God would never…."

"Then who does? Sister Luke said He has dominion over all creation – that means He can do anything He wants to. He could get us all out of here – back to our regular houses – if He really wanted to!"

"But Dorian," Sister Mary interrupted, "you don't understand."

"Let me finish," I demanded, stamping my foot. The smack of my shoe rolled over the Chapel walls. How could I have stamped my foot right in front of the altar? In His very own Chapel? Not more than 15 feet from where the Holy Eucharist is stored?

Sister folded her hands, looking from altar to crucifix, to the Virgin Mother; searching the plaster faces for direction. "Mon Dieu, Mon Dieu," she prayed.

"He doesn't care about us! He doesn't care about me! He's forgotten me – everyone's forgotten me." A cry unlike any I had ever uttered; piercing, primitive, filled the Chapel. A pair of black woolen wings engulfed me.

I wailed into her bosom; hidden in the sweet folds of her concern. Memories revived, now running loose, assaulted me: returning me to the kitchen with Mummie; flaunting the morbid irony of Beatrice's grave and Maria's victory.

Sister stood quietly until I was emptied and calm before walking me to the infirmary. Her eyes were tattletale pink although she spoke no sympathy.

"Will God ever forgive me for what I just did?"

"God loves you. He will forgive you. Now you put all those silly notions out of your head. I'll be back for you in an hour or so. Go on now, close your eyes and rest."

I was aware of a lightening within myself, and the weariness I felt at the time was a good feeling. Maybe Sister was right – maybe I couldn't measure God's love by my circumstances.

She continued to encourage me, repeating, "Things are going to be much better from now on." And they were, until I put a rock through the windshield of the school car after a playful snowball fight mushroomed into all out war, class against class, with an exchange of insults and snowballs packed with gravel. I was caught in the frenzy of the fight, throwing snow and pebbles as fast as I could get them into the air, intent on repaying a girl for her timely aim in my direction. I picked up what I saw as a pebble (Sister Superior would later describe it to Cecil as a rock which could have seriously injured a classmate) and directed it to a girl who was popping up and jeering from behind the car. The sound of breaking glass was remarkably clear above our voices. Everyone stopped.

Sister Superior, evidently a witness to the incident from her office at the front of the school, ran into the street. The evidence was sitting on the front seat of the car, entering smack-dab-in-the-middle of the right windshield. The girl came out from behind the car and pointed at me.

"She did it Sister! Dorian broke your window."

A spider web fracture fanned over the glass around a sizable hole. Sister maintained her composure, opened the car door and retrieved what I could never argue as a pebble, and tossed it into the air a few times. She remarked that somebody was going to have to pay for a new windshield. At the time I never suspected it might be me.

Demerits were to be expected; never such a scathing letter from Cecil. He had no other choice but to take the money out of my hide by not bringing me home for Christmas holidays; there would be no money for train tickets now that I'd turned into a hooligan and he was forced to pay for car repairs. As far as Gabriel and Emily knew, my cousin was going to be traveling. It wasn't that he didn't want to see me; he just wasn't able to have me visit this year.

"Please don't be too unhappy, Mon Amie. I will have a much better Christmas because you will be with me. My aunt and uncle cannot send for me."

Students embarked on holidays with relatives or local families who opened their homes at special times of the year; Gabriel was allowed back into Emily's cot. We talked long after "lights out" without as much as a single "shush" from Sister Mary. The nuns refrained from demerits; we could chatter in full voice at mealtime; our exuberance was overlooked when we chased up the stairs. Sister granted an extra hour of sleep, taking the consideration further by calling us by name rather than inflict us with her bell. The easing of rules brought a softer perspective of the nuns, but I passed through the twelve days of Christmas racked with anger over the traditional festivities Cecil and Maria were surely enjoying.

All resentments melted upon reading Maria's New Year's letter telling me what was really taking place in Calgary – certainly not a time of festivities around the punch bowl. Ben

Whyte passed away in mid December. The new president wanted his own man in charge of the branch offices so that left Cecil "out in the cold." And as if things weren't bad enough, Cecil's recent bout with depression, which she blamed on the loss of his job more than Ben Whyte's passing, had come to a very serious end. Cecil was suicidal. A substantial block of stock was due him when Ben Whyte's estate was settled, but until then Maria was gravely concerned about money. She might have to go back to work. She wasn't sure when, if ever, Cecil would be able to find a position. He wasn't sure life was worth the bother.

The suggestion of suicide set off an internal commotion, a siege of sick headaches, and cycles of belligerence and sullenness that sent Gabriel retreating to Emily. Sister rapped my knuckles with her pointer during class. "Pay attention, Miss McGregor." I couldn't; all my attention was on Cecil. My getting-by grades were nothing to be proud of; now they were deplorable. So much for learning French!

The Lenten Season was traditionally opened with a movie on the life of Christ. The film made a frightening impression on me; the potential for unsettling day and night mares. I agonized over man's cruelty to the innocent Jesus, and went to the Chapel early the following day. On my knees before a statue of Jesus, I contemplated the plan and purpose of God to the extent of my years and understanding. My concept of God had been of an all powerful Someone who observed the world from a comfortable distance. Now He was real: the issues of Heaven and hell took on a more serious certainty. I began toying with the possibility that God was not exempt from suffering, and while I did not fully understand why, I felt bonded to Jesus through my own suffering.

The gravity of what might be going on in Calgary, added to questions concerning my position on earth, motivated me to further reflect over who God was, and how that affected me. I grew religious in my visitations to the Chapel, arranging them when classmates were in the yard; when the Sisters were engaged in their own activities. I wanted God to myself; with no commingling of prayers there could be no misunderstanding what I transmitted to Heaven. I petitioned for Cecil's recovery and my return to Calgary.

In the beginning, knowing that Jesus belonged to everyone in the school, that everyone was of equal importance to Him, was taken as a dismal position, yet I came to terms with it. One could never enjoy an "only child" status with God, but for the first time there was Somebody in the shadows to encourage me rather than shame me. If one of the nuns took notice of me in the Chapel I accepted the praise for my spiritual initiative, saying nothing to anyone about any remaining doubts. I wanted proof that God actually knew how many hairs I had on my head; proof by way of answered prayer.

Apprehension over Cecil's condition began to manifest in premeditated acts of disobedience. We were reaching the end of the term when Sister Superior asked if I was competing for demerits, and scheduled me for an appointment in her office.

"I take no pleasure in this, Miss McGregor. It has been quite some time since I've made a decision like the one I am about to make. I am informing your father that you can no longer continue your residence here."

She pronounced sentence and waited, like a warden prepared for the pleadings of a prisoner banished to a more stringent location. I was on my way home. What great good fortune! All because I was a troublemaker!

"You have been very nasty, Miss McGregor; a poor influence on the others. I'm quite sure we can credit you with much of the food missing from the kitchen. It was you, was it not, who organized the raids on the Sisters' pantry?"

I studied my shoes.

"I thought so! And, coaxing Emily to drop out of line last Saturday! Unforgivable!"

Nothing terrible happened to Emily when she skipped out of line with me on the way to the theatre. We just snooped around town while the others went to the movie. Gabriel, too timid to follow, said she would try to cover for us. We knew it was risky; somebody was bound to notice and snitch on us; and they did. Emily said she acted on her own, but Sister Superior felt it was not the sort of thing Emily would be expected to do. "Out of character," she said, therefore, the blame could be placed solely upon my shoulders.

"Have you anything to say for yourself?"

"No, Sister Superior."

There was plenty I wanted to say, but with freedom so near at hand, it would be foolish to speak my mind. She might see right through me and reverse her decision just to punish me. If she only knew how thankful I was that she saw fit to pin the blame on my shoulders. There would be no reprieve. I backed out of the office, and with the click of the door, took off running, leaping into the air.

I was going home! And once I got there I was going to behave. I'd turn into a saint! Even Maria was going to be surprised at how helpful and obedient I could be. I'd never tell another lie. Cecil would never have to send me away again. I could help him get over his depression. By now he and Maria would surely have worked out their differences. If I was careful, things would go well. We could finally be a regular family.

There would be a price to pay for my behavior these last few months once I reached Calgary, but it would be worth it just to get back into the house on Crescent Drive. Part of that price was saying goodbye to Sister Mary, Emily and Gabriel.

Chapter 6

"Alma McGregor once told me that our bodies
were the temple of the Holy Spirit.
My temple was in ruins; desecrated."

I drew a sharp breath when I spotted Cecil walking toward me. He was thin, drawn, and fragile, and stepped gingerly through the crowd.

"You've grown some, haven't you?"

"I think so."

"Maria's fixing a special supper for us. Mary and Victor are coming over."

"I'm awfully glad to be home."

"I expect you are."

"Are you mad at me because I can't go back?"

"How many times have I told you that only dogs are mad? The word is angry, and no, I am not angry! We'd better get a move on. There'll be holy hell to pay if we hold up Maria's dinner. She's been at it all day!"

The promise of stuffed goose greeted us at the front door. Before I could land on the notion it was a welcome home dinner, Mary and Victor showed up saying how very thoughtful it was of Maria to give a special dinner in honor of their anniversary. Mary was pleased that I was there in time to help them celebrate. Victor contributed two bottles of his home-made red wine to the table.

I raved to Maria over the meal. It was outstanding. She excused me from the dishes so I followed Victor and Cecil outside to the back porch. They puffed cigars and debated Churchill's ability to lead the empire in a time of war. Everyone was exceptionally pleasant; nobody brought up my dismissal from St. Theresa's. Maybe my luck was changing, and in that case, best I not take advantage of Cecil's letting me decide when I should go to bed. I excused myself in plenty of time to give the grownups their privacy, then indulged myself in a victorious window-time, savoring the sweet sights and smells of freedom.

I tiptoed through the house early the next day. My picture was still on the mantle, along with Bill's; the ice-box stocked with three quarts of milk and a pint of heavy cream. I cut a slab of soft white bread, heaped it with preserves, poured a glass of milk and went outside. I was no more than settled on the back steps when Cecil was at the screen door.

"I'll get myself a cup of tea and join you." He balanced a cup and saucer on his knee, and told me of his illness. He was greatly improved. "Not completely, mind you, but definitely on the mend."

I spotted O'Brien crawling through the trellis. He bolted when I advanced, but once I crouched on the grass, he lifted his head and sniffed the air a moment, then trotted toward me with his tail high and nuzzled me.

"He remembers me! Whaddaya think of that?"

"I suppose you'll be back hanging in the trees together."

"Yep! We sure will!"

I kept Cecil under surveillance. He was still reserved, less given to humor, but outside of a considerable loss of weight, it seemed whatever ailed him was not as serious as it was; suicide was no longer a threat. I was still curious over a lack of righteous noise on his part over the way I left St. Theresa's. A second puzzle was continued tension between Cecil and Maria. The degree to which their marital difficulties were resolved became evident after John Cameron brought over a bag of green apples and suggested Maria bake a pie. Cecil liked it warm, served in a soup bowl, the crust mashed in with the filling, drowning in heavy cream. I lifted my bowl and took a deep breath. Cecil pondered the first mouthful, laid down his spoon, wiped his mouth and drummed his fingers on the table.

"Not bad, Maria; better than the last one." He turned in my direction. "Maria has been having trouble with sugar lately. It's either too much or not quite enough."

He turned back toward Maria. "Just a wee bit too tart this time; a touch more sugar and you'll be neck and neck with mother's apple pie."

I voted by devouring my portion, following up each bite with a complimentary and enthusiastic "Ummmm...."

Her napkin hit the table. "Hells bells, is there no pleasing you? I ran out coupons! Have you forgotten there's a war on?"

I kept my eyes in the bowl and shoveled the pie. Cecil made for the back door. Maria started upstairs, cursing in Italian. I kept my place at the table, fishing for every crumb, and raised the dish to my mouth to drain the last drop of cream. I could see Cecil through the screen door, half seated on the railing, popping paint blisters in the wood.

Evidently Cecil and Maria didn't work things out the way they were supposed to while I was away. Dissension grew throughout the day, topped off by a loud confrontation after I retired. Maria insisted he tell me something.

"You keep putting it off – putting it off – before you know it we'll be driving away and you'll be explaining everything from the car window as we go."

"Tomorrow," he hollered, "I'll tell her tomorrow!"

Suddenly tomorrow was a concern. Cecil was going to tell me something. Surely he wasn't going to send me away again. After all, it was he and Maria who couldn't get along. I'd taken great pains to be cooperative. I'd tiptoed around the house; all but bowed and scraped to Maria anytime she wanted. Maria and I were doing exceptionally well. That couldn't be it. But whatever it was, it was serious enough to cause an argument. Praying by the bed wasn't nearly as reassuring as kneeling in the Chapel.

The best way to wait for the news was in the willows. I was up early and midway up the tree with my back to the house calling O'Brien out of Camerons' yard when Cecil came outside to ask if I'd had my breakfast.

"I'm not hungry."

"I'll have Maria whip us up some pancakes."

"I'm not hungry."

"I've something to tell you."

I muttered a "here it comes" under my breath and dropped to the first large arm of the tree nearest the ground.

"It should come as no surprise to you that I'm still in a bit of a bind financially. They haven't settled Ben's estate, and I haven't worked in almost six months now. You remember the Harrisons? Well, Edgar found me a job. But it means Maria and I have to go up north to Dawson City for the next eight months to work on the Alaskan Highway. She'll do the payroll; I'll supervise the crews.

"Harrisons are building a house, and what a house they'll have when it's finished! It won't be ready for another seven or eight months, so we decided as long as they need a place to live, there's no use them paying to rent when they can stay here and look after you at the same time. We'll save money all 'round."

Cecil and Edgar grew up as classmates with both families involved in ranching; they worked in the oil fields together. When Cecil went with the company, he found a position for Edgar. They remained friends. During Beatrice's time we shuttled between houses for Sunday dinners. I never cared for the Harrisons; particularly their son, Peter.

I shot up the tree with O'Brien at my heels. "I don't want to live with the Harrisons. I hate the Harrisons."

"Dorian! Get down from there!"

I balanced myself and glared down at Cecil who was standing at the base of the tree clenching his fist. O'Brien was nearby, thrashing his tail as if to take his own stand against what Cecil was proposing. I was never coming down. I'd starve to death first. It would be better than living with the Harrisons.

Cecil started into the house. "You'll come down when you're hungry enough."

He was back at lunch time to tell me Maria was serving macaroni and cheese and there was plenty of pie left over.

"I told you I wasn't hungry!" It was easy to be cheeky when he couldn't reach me; the willows would never support him.

The next time it was to announce that he was about to have a spot of tea and a stack of biscuits. "You're welcome to join me."

I wouldn't be tempted; too distraught over what the next eight months might bring. It was thirst that finally got the best of me. I inched my way, branch by branch, with Cecil checking from the kitchen.

He acknowledged me into the house with a thin grin and said, "Good thing you came down. Cameron said he's noticed some bats flying around lately. You'd be out of those trees like a shot if one of them landed in your hair."

"Bats don't live in willow trees. Bats are blind! They can't fly through the leaves. I read about them in the National Geographic."

Maria said I was sassy and that Cecil should do something about it. He passed it off without comment.

"I wish I didn't have to go myself," he said. "It's going to be damned cold and miserable that far north."

"We'll have to live in a trailer," Maria added. "I'll probably be the only woman up there."

"We all have to make some sacrifices, Dorian. Eight months will fly by before you know it. The Harrisons are nice people. You'll be back at school with your old friends."

Later, Cecil chuckled to Maria that I was a stubborn little cuss. Now I knew why he withheld a scolding. I'd played right into their plans by not being welcome at St. Theresa's. As disappointed as I was for myself, I was truly as disappointed for him and Maria.

Disappointment shifted to alarm the day Cecil and Maria drove away and Peter swaggered into the house with his parents. He was well past the six foot mark which Edgar took as grounds for bragging. He was sure his son's size and athletic potential would be an advantage when he entered college the upcoming year. I tensed when Peter looked at me. He was repulsive. His mother, Rachel, left correction to Edgar. For the most part Peter did what Peter wanted. After Rachel warned me about his temper I was all the more certain of some dreadful experience in the offing, especially when I added it to the magazines he read when his parents were absent. Peter reeked with the same evil I'd been subjected to before by a man who hid his magazines from his wife.

Peter told his mother he would help me with my homework, making himself the hero, when he only wanted to rub his leg against me under the table, and with Rachel and Edgar out of range in the living room, he would have ample warning should either of them approach the kitchen. The first time he touched me I folded my books, retreated to the opposite side of the table and lowered my face over my lessons with a pounding heart. He lunged across the table and snatched my pencil.

"Don't you move away from me. You sit where I tell you – or else!"

Or else? His expression, tone, and blatant liberties confirmed my earlier suspicions of harm-on-the-way. It wasn't long before he started tormenting me with quick kisses and laughed when I spit and wiped my mouth.

"That's not very polite. When someone kisses you, you're supposed to kiss back."

"Never! Don't touch me! You make me sick."

His hands were all over me.

"If you don't stop, I'll tell your mother…"

"Go ahead. She'll never believe you. Maria told us you were quite a liar. She even said you'd probably tell some whoppers because you didn't like us being here."

Edgar and Cecil were best friends. Cecil owed his present job to Edgar. Could I write to Cecil? Report to Margaret Cameron? Or Mary? The answer was always the same. And didn't Cecil make it perfectly clear that I'd better mind my

P's and Q's while he was away? And that I had better not embarrass him? There was no place, and no one to run to, yet I chided myself because I was a coward for not finding a way out.

I wrestled with self-pity and self-disgust, both emotions contesting for a verdict that would somehow ease the burden of living with Peter. I'd heard it said that self-pity never did anybody any good; one had to pull oneself up by the boot-straps and get on with it, which left me at the mercy of self-disgust over allowing myself to be used for such purposes. I was outraged at Peter's advantage over me; that he felt he had a right to help himself to me the way he did. Alma McGregor once told me that our bodies were the temple of the Holy Spirit. My temple was in ruins; desecrated.

Rachel wasn't keen on living in a house that wasn't her own, and because all their friends were across town, I was forced to live on the verge of their next night out. I don't know where Peter kept his "girlie magazines," as he referred to them, or if they were actually his or Edgar's; they never surfaced in number until his parents were absent. Occasionally he was so bold as to hide one in his notebook while he attended to his studies at the kitchen table with me.

Peter was obsessed with pornography and the diaboli-cal demands they stimulated in him to make upon me. I was eleven and a half years old, passing from week to week, loath-ing what I had to do, closing my eyes when I touched him; holding my breath when he clamped his thick lips over my mouth – listening to him moan as he oozed into my hand – begging to be allowed out of the room to wash myself clean; pleading until he was no longer amused and let me go. No matter how long I washed, how hot the water, I was never clean of him.

Peter wasn't the only one abusing me. I had no protec-tion against the wheels that turned in the night; no way to garrison my mind against molesting shadow people. An attack of flashbacks made me all the more vulnerable through fear conditioning of an earlier time and an abuser, when I saw photographs of helpless women at the hands of brutal captors in similar magazines. I was Peter's captive. I had to be very careful or something worse might happen. It was also during this time that a frequent and confusing dream (having to do with several boys, a school yard, a box of kittens, and a man in a drug store), which from that time on became my mystery dream, imposed on me regularly. While I never made sense of this dream, it had the power to wake me, panting in fear. I was back to packing myself with pillows when I went to bed.

Midway into the time I was placed under her care, Rachel came into my bedroom saying Peter wanted to sleep with me. Without hesitation she lifted my bed covers, pulled me by the hand from the bed and led me to him. Shock held me obedient when she told me to lie down and cover up. She turned out the light, and as the door closed behind her, Peter pounced upon me. I thrashed on the bed, grappling with his hands, and gathered every ounce of strength to let out one long, powerful scream.

Rachel was at the door telling Peter that this wasn't such a good idea after all and I would have to back go to my own room. I huddled under the paisley comforter, rubbing my upper body where Peter had tried to pound me under control. Rachel was now as much a threat as Peter, as was the possibility that Edgar could be as dangerous as his wife and son. And if she could serve me up to Peter like a pot roast, she was capable of anything. I saw her as an accomplice; suspicious of just how much she knew about what went on when Peter and I were alone. Only her concern for reputation with the neighbors over my screaming intervened against Peter. This incident, compounded with the distress of continued nighttime invasions of the mystery dream, brought blinding headaches, a loss of appetite, weakness, and thoughts of the skull and crossbones on Cecil's blue bottle of Chinese medicine, and had it been in the bathroom cabinet I was sure I wouldn't botch it a second time.

Peter progressively whittled me down to where I performed like a robot – rigid, expressionless, and dutifully.

He began to demonstrate more of the characteristics of men who posed for pornography, enjoying his reign of terror with torturous holds, body punches, strangulations and vulgar expressions of how I was to perform for him.

Little girls.

Grown-up girls.

And in-between girls.

All put to the same humiliating use.

Chapter 7

*"...[he] was physically gone, but his presence
lurked in the shadows."*

Maria and Cecil piled out of the car rumpled and exhausted after driving through the night.

Cecil frowned at me. "You're a little on the thin side, aren't you?"

"She's a picky eater," Rachel said.

Cecil raised an eyebrow in my direction and said he wanted "A pot of good stiff tea, a long hot bath, and a nap, and in that order." He was never so glad to be home.

The Harrisons would be waiting out the last few weeks with Rachel's mother until their new home was ready. What was going through Peter's mind as he helped his father carry out their belongings? I wanted him tormented by doubt as to whether or not I would turn him in to Cecil; hoped he would spend the rest of his years wondering if anyone knew. But he was safe; as safe as if he were innocent. They would never learn of his ugly practice, or that I was so cowardly as to let him bully me into his service. I wept with relief when the Harrisons drove away.

Peter was physically gone, but his presence lurked in the shadows. If I could enjoy any justice it would be that I, too, would live in the shadows of his life; that as my life carried his defilement, his would be encumbered by guilt, and if he ever married and had his own daughter, that he would suffer all the more because of what he did to me.

❧

Maria grumbled over the state of the house. Rachel had taken too many liberties with her kitchen; nothing was in the right place.

"I don't think the Harrisons were contagious," Cecil said, when he found us cleaning the inside of the kitchen cupboards with disinfectant.

It certainly was good to be back in her own kitchen. Maria was looking forward to some "serious cooking" with Christmas on the horizon. Cecil reminded her to "go easy" on the groceries over the holidays; he was out of a job again. They were discussing the household budget when Cecil asked Maria how much business she was giving the milk man. They were both tired of pinching pennies, but until Cecil found another position, or Ben Whyte's estate was settled, they would have to do just that. I longed to do my part to make things easier for them.

"I know how we can cut down. I can do without milk."

"Nonsense!" said Cecil, "Every child needs a quart a day. It's good for the teeth and bones; best food for a growing child."

"But it didn't hurt me to go without it at St. Theresa's."

"What?"

"I didn't have milk at St. Theresa's."

"Dorian? You telling me stories again?"

"No! Honest! You didn't send the milk fee so Sister said I wasn't entitled to it. But my teeth are still good. See? So are my bones."

Cecil threw back his head and roared, "Maria! Did you send the money for Dorian's milk to the school last term?"

"Of course!"

Twenty-two caliber eyes shot through me.

"Somebody's lying! I'll get to the bottom of this! Even if I have to spend the money for a long distance call."

Cecil stormed out of the house, slamming the door with such force that the windows on either side of the entry vibrated. I fled up the stairs. The headlights of the Plymouth streaked across my bedroom wall as Cecil backed out of the driveway.

I waited; watching for two amber spots. Maria cried in the living room until Cecil's headlights flashed back on the wall. There was a nervous cough from Maria. Cecil was speaking.

"I have a hunch she's telling the truth this time. How about you?"

Maria's confession shocked me. She deliberately with-held the funds because Cecil accused her of not managing the household finances properly. Her only interest was to save money; she never for a moment believed the nuns would actually deny me milk.

Cecil continued to pry. "What did you do with the money?"

"I ran the house with it; and it took every penny!"

"I don't believe you!"

"Well… I never…"

"I've lived with you long enough to know when you're telling the truth!"

"How dare you – just because a person tells one lie is no reason to…"

Cecil interrupted. "Tell me what you spent the money on. You might as well come clean. We'll stay here until I get an answer. And it better be the truth this time!"

Dead silence. Cecil pressed her a second time; she might as well "come clean."

More silence; then a sudden flurry of steps; drawers opening and closing; cursing. I cracked my door; then moved to the head of the stairs. They were in the sunroom.

"Is it in here? In here?

"I don't have it, I tell you."

I crept downstairs and teetered on the bottom step, primed in case I heard them coming.

"Ah hah! What's this?"

Maria pleaded, "I can explain!"

"How clever of you. I would never have thought to look in here."

Cecil was counting.

Maria bought stocks with the money, taking it, plus whatever she could save from his "stingy" allowance and hid them in the bottom of her sewing basket under a pile of dress patterns. Now that she was found out, she wanted Cecil to realize what a good business head she had on her shoulders. He could turn around and sell the stock for many times what she paid for it, and with Ben Whyte's estate tied up, he could show a little appreciation.

"I know you'd like me to believe you did this for us, Maria, but first you'll have to explain why these are in your name only."

I recounted the day I asked Sister to make sure there was no mistake about the milk fee; relived the feelings of learning there was no mistake. Maria stole from me then lied about it. The stink of weekends imprisoned in my room jogged my anger. I bit into the pillow, outraged, my only compensation that of knowing she'd been found out.

Nothing more was ever said about the milk money, but Cecil assured me that the milkman would be the last place we would cut corners.

Chapter 8

"Everything could still turn out all right in the end..."

It turned into a most unpleasant winter, an unusually cold winter; one blizzard after another, and every bit as chilling as far as job opportunities. Every position Cecil pursued escaped him. When Maria walked into the company office and asked if she could get back on the payroll they snapped her up on the spot, but they didn't want him; not since Ben Whyte died. Cecil said it was a "sorry state of affairs when a woman can find work and a man can't." He didn't know what the world was coming to. Maria reminded him that a number of people were having trouble finding work, and while she did have her job, it was only part time. She expected him to keep looking.

Cecil spent long periods of time in his chair next to the three-tiered table that housed his smokes, current magazines, and photo albums. He was more and more into his albums now, and wanted them handy in case he "got an urge." The albums were pre-Maria; she avoided them altogether. I did my best to sustain an interest as he told, and retold, the events recorded in the albums, knowing how much he enjoyed talking about "back then."

The change must have started as soon as he finished up in Dawson Creek; possibly while he was still working on the

Alaskan Highway. I should have suspected something when he told Maria we were going to forgo any plans for Christmas Day. John Cameron came over to personally invite him in for a nip of holiday cheer, but Cecil turned him down and napped on the couch instead. He was losing interest in his radio programs: Fibber McGee and Molly; even Amos and Andy. It wasn't like him to miss his programs.

It was mid-February. We were dismissed early because another storm was due. The teachers urged us to hurry home before the streets drifted; the winds were already beginning to whip up when we filed out of the building.

The house was cold and uncomfortably quiet except for the spray of snow against the glass. I expected to see Cecil in his chair by the fireplace. There was no fire; no Cecil. I heard a noise in the sunroom.

He was sitting on the floor with albums strewn around him, appearing as a frightened child with a quivering mouth and tear-streaked face. I responded as I would to Mary's infant daughter, and knelt beside him, helpless to do much beyond offering him comfort.

"Let's look at some pictures, Daddy. How about the time you caught the fourteen-pounder at Gap Lake?"

A silent grief rolled down his cheeks. His eyes brimmed, spilled, and filled again. I thought of going for help next door, but knew he would never want to be seen in such a state. If I called Maria she couldn't get home any sooner that she was already scheduled. She was due at 3 o'clock unless the storm hindered her.

I rubbed his back, stroked his balding head, caressed his hands and read aloud from the newspaper. He stayed as still as the Centre Street lions.

I met Maria at the door. "Something terrible happened to Daddy. He's crying. He won't get off the floor."

She shook him; clapped her hands to startle him; got within half an inch of his ear and yelled at him. He wouldn't budge.

☙

Mary and Victor stayed in support of Maria after they took Cecil away.

"Didn't I tell you he was going strange on me, Mary? Didn't I warn you he was going off in his head?"

"Yes, you did, Maria, and I'm sorry we paid so little attention to you."

Nobody thought it would come to this; everybody maintained there was nothing any of them could have done to prevent the breakdown. Victor went on about how the doctors were going to bring him around, saying "Now Maria … if there's anything you need…anything we can do…"; the same expressions I heard at Beatrice's funeral. There was a lot we needed, a lot that needed doing. Whenever a situation reached hopeless, people always said things like that, but they never did anything; nothing ever got any less hopeless.

Mary and Victor stayed long after I was in bed, and as they chose to stay at the kitchen table, I was cut off from their conversation until they were at the foot of the stairs and on their way out. Victor repeated his offer to help and asked Maria to let them know immediately should Cecil take a turn for the worse.

Maria said, "Things couldn't get much worse," bolted the door, and went directly to her bedroom. Every noise, shadow and shape entering my bedroom was magnified. Winter willows at the mercy of a stern north wind moved in grotesque animation on the closet door. I lowered the shade; the moon filtered through the bare trees, casting the image of tapered fingers clawing through the blinds and sent me fleeing to Maria's room.

"Maria! Maria! Can I sleep with you? Please let me sleep with you!"

She flipped open the covers then turned toward the wall. No shapes threatened in her room, only the wind wailing about the house. As soon as she started to snore, I warmed my feet against her. I had to touch her. It didn't matter that she didn't love me; even that she withheld the milk money. She was far nicer to me than she used to be, and I was making an honest effort to go out of my way for her. Besides, she was all I had.

Maria gave me the particulars on Cecil the following day, holding nothing back. He was diagnosed a manic depressant with suicidal tendencies, and placed in a special ward where he could be watched 24 hours a day.

"He will get better though, won't he? They can do something about it, can't they?"

She was in the dark as to what to expect, with no idea what the effect of a series of shock treatments would have on him.

"I don't have much faith in this new treatment. It seems downright inhumane to jolt a person with electricity, but they tell me it's the best they have to offer."

"I'm scared, Maria."

"I'm very worried about these treatments. I hope those doctors know what they're doing."

Maria went to the hospital the day of Cecil's first treatment, displaying the identical courage I was reading about in history. I was taken with the stories of pioneer women who settled the provinces, and recognized a similar spirit in Maria in the way she handled the strain; her willingness to make the best of trying times when I would have expected her to complain. She gave no indication other than that of a wife concerned for the welfare of her husband, and for the first time I understood how much she loved him – in spite of their differences. It was also clear that Maria knew how to muster courage. She had little to say when she returned except that it was very unpleasant and she didn't want to discuss it.

Maria called a meeting of the McGregor clan and presided at the head of the dining room table, looking to the brothers for financial support. Cecil was running out of money, in need of lengthy medical attention. She was going to count on them for assistance.

Clarence ran the family store. "This comes at a bad time for us. The furnace just went out at the store. We won't have many customers if it's as cold inside as it is out."

He suggested that because Paul was a dentist, with a far greater income, he could commit to a larger share of the responsibility. Paul considered his older brother, Grant, more established, much better off, and tossed the greater burden to him. He then went on to share concerns for his own finances now that his wife, Rita, was due to present him with a second child in a matter of weeks.

They volleyed incomes around the table, each pointing to the other's financial strength. Grant shook his head. "You know this would never have happened if Beatrice hadn't passed away – he's never been the same since she died."

His wife clipped him in the leg with her shoe. "Oh, no offense intended, Maria."

From my position in the living room, it was apparent that she was; nonetheless, the offense did not dampen her insistence that the brothers help out.

"And, we have to decide what we're going to do about Dorian."

"What about her? Surely you don't expect one of us to take her!"

"I'm not suggesting anything of the sort."

Grant was shaking his head. "Why they adopted a child so late in life is beyond me. She certainly complicates matters. Mother arranged it – maybe she'll have some ideas."

Clarence was quick to silence him. "We'll settle it among ourselves. By the way Maria, you have been keeping mother up to date on Cecil's progress?"

"I assumed one of you would have taken care of that! I've been running my legs off going back and forth to the sanitarium every day. I thought that was the least one of you could have done!" She looked from brother to brother.

"You mean to tell me she doesn't know a thing about this?"

Everyone was buzzing; everyone blamed everyone else because everyone forgot to tell Mother McGregor. Paul was voted the best one to make the call. He encouraged her to stay in Vancouver. He would keep her posted and planned to speak to the doctors himself.

Paul was good for "Fifty a month, no more than that, and there may be months when I can't even scrape that together. It depends on collections." His offer sparked the others to ante up.

Clarence was shaking his head again. "This never would have happened if they'd settled Ben Whyte's estate. Any idea when he'll get his share?"

"I've all but given up ever seeing any of that money. If he gets a cent, I'll be surprised!"

"Guess that about does it, then." Clarence eased away from the table.

"Hold on there," Maria said, "we still have to agree on what to do with Dorian. I've found a school here in Calgary…"

Paul moved they settle on St. Mary's. "It's the only sensible thing to do!"

"You do understand there is a monthly fee for the school."

They understood.

"I'll have to sell off some of the furnishings; I have my eye on a small place near the sanitarium. There won't be much room."

The two visiting wives took immediate interest in the pieces Maria would be "letting go," and arrangements were made for Cecil's highboy and matching bedside tables; Clarence bid for the piano and two Queen Anne chairs.

Grant and his wife were eager to make off with Beatrice's dining room chairs, cramming two into the back seat of their car with the promise to send for the remaining six. I consoled myself with thoughts of getting them back someday; and the piano; everything that belonged to the house.

Preparing for another school was distressing, but I could get through it. At least I didn't have to live with Peter. Maria was taking everything in stride; so could I. This would all be over some day. Everything could still turn out all right in the end. I had to hang on to that.

Chapter 9

"The prospect of a new batch of caretakers was unsettling..."

St. Mary's School capped off the end of a comfortable residential street, her grounds studded with tall tree skeletons and spindly-boned shrubs. Old snow tinged with coal soot skirted a network of pathways between the school and auxiliary buildings. A grounds keeper, fussing over the brass handles at the front door as we approached, stuffed his cloth into a back pocket, opened the door with a cordial "good afternoon, mum," and pointed us toward the office.

The Reverend Mother sat behind an enormous desk. She took my vital statistics with an arthritic hand, wedging the pencil between her thumb and middle finger. She gave me a cursory going over, then honed in on Maria.

"The girl is not a Catholic. We usually give preference to those of the faith."

"You made no mention of any religious requirements! But I'm a Catholic – the girl's adopted mother was Catholic. Won't that do?" Maria folded her gloves and placed them confidently on top of her purse.

"You are Catholic, Mrs. McGregor?

"Yes. My maiden name was Vincente."

"Of course – and the name of your parish?"

Maria blushed, admitting she stopped attending church after her marriage.

"Then you married outside the church? I see. But you are sure the girl's mother was a Catholic?"

"She was!"

"Then there would be no objection to instruction in the faith?"

"None whatsoever! A child needs religious training."

I was dismissed while Maria made financial arrangements. It wouldn't be so bad living here. It was much fancier than St. Theresa's. I would still be in Calgary; close enough to keep up with what was happening to Cecil; perhaps visit him in the sanitarium. We stopped at the sewing room on our on our way out. The traditional navy uniform was marked and promised for Saturday.

Maria had three comments on the way home. First, to express her need of a "good stiff drink," and upon stepping off the street car, "I hate winter." We scrunched our way through four blocks of crusting snow, deep in our own predicaments. Maria never learned to drive, and gas rationing gave her a perfect excuse to turn down Mary's offer to teach her. Her last comment was that come summer, she was bound and determined to take the plunge; she just wasn't sure Mary was the best one to show her how.

The house was biting cold; Maria was conserving coal. I went immediately to my room to warm up under the comforter; Maria went for the phone.

"We did it, Mary, she's to check in on Saturday." Maria paused to listen a few moments.

"I know, I know. No, she hasn't, not once. I'll say this much for her, the kid's got spunk."

A compliment from Maria! What a pleasant experience to have her credit me with spunk. Surely that was as good as courage.

I buried myself under the comforter.

In 62 hours I'd be gone.

In 84 hours we'd all be gone.

Maria started packing up the house the day of the family conference. As there was no reason to attend school now that I was due to report to St. Mary's, I turned to packing dishes, wrapping each piece individually, taking special care of Beatrice's Blue Willow china service for twelve. Cecil was planning to give it to Bill when he found "the right girl."

We sorted through Cecil's magazines. Maria debated bundling his National Geographics because he'd already plowed through them time and time again. "Your father is always having to look something up. You'd think once he read it, he'd know what he needed to know. Still, we'd better save them. We can stash them at Mary's."

The house was readied a room at a time, essentials marked for Maria's efficiency apartment, the rest for Mary's basement. The grand house on the hill was reduced to a pitiful state; nail-poxed walls and patches of original colour once covered by pictures revealed a place in dire need of paint. Without the accessories of gracious living, it was quite an ordinary house. Maria tackled the work with her hair tucked underneath a scarf, moving one of her "good stiff drinks" from station to station. I watched her, wondering if she was thinking what I was thinking: about the first time I ever saw the place. She must have been impressed when she saw it for the first time, too. It was beautiful then.

The prospect of a new batch of caretakers was unsettling, but time would dilute those concerns. I saw Maria at her own disadvantage, and in the sense that she had vowed for better or for worse, she was surely tired of the worse.

Chapter 10

"Somebody had the right answers; the rest were wrong...."

Helga was in the midst of a group of students who were chanting "Kraut! Kraut! Sauerkraut!" and in obvious distress when we first met.

"Why were they teasing you?"

"You don't know?"

"You're German?"

"Yes."

Moments into our first conversation I knew we were destined to be friends. She had quite a story. Her Poppa went to Germany for one last visit with his parents and got caught up in the war. After her mother died of a ruptured appendix, Helga made the rounds of relatives until she was put in St. Mary's to be properly brought up.

"Does it matter to you if I'm German?"

"Of course not. Beethoven was a German; everyone loves Beethoven. And what about Bach? Didn't he come from Germany?"

"You must know a lot about composers!"

"Nah, just what I picked up from my cousin, Bill. He's the one who knows a lot."

My reason for being at St. Mary's was valid; through no fault of mine. There was no cause to hide anything this time so I shared Cecil's illness and why I was enrolled.

Three types of students attended the school: day students kept public school hours; weekly boarders left Friday afternoon and were expected inside the front door no later than eight o'clock Sunday evening. The rest of us received visitors in the parlor on Sundays. Full time students were granted afternoons and over-nights off the grounds at the discretion of the Reverend Mother. The place ran by the same set of rules as St. Theresa's, including black books and demerits. All permanent boarders rotated duties.

Helga had been sitting on a secret since she arrived at the school.

"Dorian, do you promise, if I tell you something, you'll never tell anyone else?"

"Sure."

"This is very serious business. I've never told anyone, not even the nuns. Especially not the nuns. Nobody in the entire school knows about it."

"It must be serious," I said.

"Very serious. Do you swear?"

"If you want me to."

I raised my hand, crossed my heart, and hoped to die if I ever told a single soul. Then Helga confessed her Jewish heritage. She was enrolled as a Lutheran, because being both Jewish and German had cost her admission into other schools. Warned by her relatives to keep her secret or "be out on the street," Helga played the Lutheran, prayed to her Jewish God in secret, and hoped He understood.

"Does it matter to you that I'm Jewish?"

"Why should I mind? Jesus was a Jew! He was King of the Jews! I don't see why you have to keep it a secret."

"You aren't going to give me away are you?"

"I swore, Helga. I wouldn't want to see you out on the street. I wouldn't dare give you away. Besides, you're my friend. You're my only friend."

"Just think – you're the only Presbyterian in the entire school! And I'm the only Jew! Everyone else is Catholic."

"Then we'd better stick together!"

Catechism was disturbing; being Catholic was a good deal more complicated than being Presbyterian. As a non-Catholic I was not required to study Catechism at St. Theresa's. Most of my information came from Gabriel and what I picked up from the example set by the nuns. As a result of seriously studying church doctrine, I became tormented over the whereabouts of Mummie and Beatrice; where Maria might ultimately end up. And what if Cecil did commit suicide?

If I were to take what Sister Agatha said to heart as to the position of the Catholic Church with regard to people who committed suicide or married outside the church, I would have to live with the certainty of both of my mothers resigned to hell for eternity. And wasn't Maria headed in the same direction? I now had three positions to consider: Alma's, Cecil's, and the Catholic Church. Somebody had the right answers; the rest were wrong. I was extremely burdened by it all; extremely fearful for my own soul as well.

I decided to pass my fears on to Alma, seeing her as my only available and trustworthy source on spiritual matters. She spared no time in letting me know that the McGregors were Presbyterian, therefore I was Presbyterian, and not to put any stock in Catholic doctrine. The Catholics and Protestants had been at each other ever since Elizabeth put the ax to Mary, Queen of Scots. Further, there was more bloodshed, more cruelty over religious differences than all the wars in history. She was sick and tired of it – and so was God! I could rest assured neither Beatrice or Mummie were in hell, but safe in Heaven with the Lord. I was not to be disrespectful of the Catholic faith, but never to believe a word of it. I shared the letter with Helga. We both felt better. One area where Alma sided with the Catholic Church had to do with the roaring lion that went about seeking to kill and destroy. If the Catholics and the Presbyterians were in agreement over the devil, it gave me all the more cause to take what I knew of him seriously.

ॐ

Mary and Victor paid a surprise visit to the parlor to tell me Cecil was out of the sanitarium and they were taking me for a visit. Victor prepared me on the way. "You may be in for a bit of a shock, Dorian." "What he means," Mary added, "is that after a person's been through a mental illness they're bound to look a little worn."

We pulled up to a building in the down-town section and shimmied up to the third floor in a wire cage elevator. My first glimpse of Cecil came between Mary and Victor juggling themselves through the door, with Maria plastered against the wall to allow the entrance to a crowded one room effi- ciency apartment. He was propped on the sofa, a cigarette pasted to his mouth. Two loaves of swollen flesh half-mooned under his eyes; scrawny arms and legs poked out from under a pair of maroon striped pajamas and matching robe.

He patted the sofa, inviting me to sit down. "Have you been behaving yourself?"

"Yes, Daddy."

"Atta' girl!"

Maria managed the conversation, avoiding the trials of the past months, and we chatted, like people getting together after a brief separation, everyone silently summing him up. Cecil was a diminished man, sapped and spiritless, with a voice gone flat and tremors of the hand. He didn't object when Maria called a halt to the visit.

Victor felt it was a crying shame what life could do to a man.

Mary thought they let him out too soon.

"He was in worse shape than any of us realized," Victor said. "It stands to reason it's going to take longer than any of us thought before he's right again. But he'll come around, in time."

I'd been living on expectation; looking to each day as the day the call would come; Cecil would be released and we could move back to Crescent Drive. Seeing him in such a condition leeched all promise of a happy ending. He was not going to "come around," no matter how ardently Victor professed it. And Maria was looking sickly as well. It wasn't like her to be so unprepared; she always took time to "put on her face" for as long as I'd known her. She was looking haggard; her skin was creped. That Sunday afternoon I loved her every bit as much as I loved Cecil; I didn't want to lose either of them. All previously held spunk was unraveling; my faith failing. I couldn't remember the last time I'd had an answer to prayer.

"Victor, what if Daddy never gets any better?"

"Oh, he'll get better; eventually."

"But just suppose he didn't. Then what?"

"He'd just have to make the best of it."

"What would Maria do if he doesn't get better?"

"She'd have to make the best of it too. That's what people do. They just make the best of it."

"Oh." I sunk deeper into the car seat.

When Helga asked me how my father was feeling, I told her I thought he was coming around.

Chapter 11

"…It was the first time Maria ever…expressed an understanding."

Cecil was walking about the room on our second visit, and the signs overlooked in the excitement of the first reunion were now glaring evidence of the toll of his condition. A progression of extra holes in his belt cinched up an excess of trousers; his shirt, once a perfect fit, stood well away from his neck; the scar behind his right ear more prominent now that there was less of him underneath it. Maria invited us to get comfortable. Cecil had something to say.

Now that Ben Whyte's estate was settled, he would have some real money coming in. He was looking forward to starting over, and on the verge of tears by the time he finished.

Maria made one of her apple pies for the occasion, and showed me a knowing smile when I "Oh'd" and "Ah'd" my appreciation. Cecil was embarrassed over needing a napkin under his chin. We were careful not to watch while he was eating.

Mary was of the opinion there was a definite improvement over our first visit. Victor kept his opinion to himself. My worst fears were proved later that very month. Cecil was back in the sanitarium. Maria left word that she would be in touch when she had anything significant to report.

One week Mary called to say Cecil was coming around, then another setback. Then she stopped calling all together. The months ripened on the calendar. I was trapped – like Helga – destined to live out my schooling at St. Mary's. Anxiety gave rise to the same belligerence for breaking the rules that barred me from St. Theresa's, driving me to strike a nun after I was caught stealing sweets from the nuns' pantry.

"Wicked girl! Thief!" She was snorting with rage, ridiculing me before several students assigned to kitchen duty. When she slapped me across the face, I doubled my fist and sent her reeling into the wall.

She sputtered, "How dare you," took a vindictive hold of my ear and led me through the hall. "We'll see what Reverend Mother has to say about this!"

What the Reverend Mother had to say about it was "Out!"

I tried to explain. "But Reverend Mother – she hit me first."

❧

Instead of delivering a well-deserved tongue lashing when she was summoned to the school, Maria offered me her open arms. I ran to her sobbing into her neck, "I'm sorry, I'm sorry. It's just so terrible living here – not knowing what's happening with Daddy. Isn't he any better? He isn't REALLY going to commit suicide – is he?"

"You poor kid," was all she said. It was the first time Maria ever touched me, ever expressed an understanding. I tightened my hold on her, then as if we were simultaneously made aware of the affection flowing between us and the improbability of what we were doing, we both stepped back, embarrassed.

Maria needed some time to work out a solution; she got five days. The transom must have been open; somebody must have been listening, because somebody knew every last word exchanged between Maria and the Reverend Mother and passed it on to everybody else.

Helga cried, "How could you do this to me? How could you get yourself expelled? Do you have any idea how rotten my life is going to be from now on?"

"I am sorry Helga, truly I am, and I'm not going to forget you. I'll come by and visit you."

"You don't even know where you're going to be; for all you know, you'll end up just where Sister said you would – in a reformatory!"

"No I won't! I'll probably just have to move in with Maria. I'll ask Sister if you can come to see us every now and then."

"What good will that do? They aren't going to let me visit a common thief!"

"Well, if that's the way you feel!"

"I'm sorry. I didn't mean it. You know I didn't mean it."

"Okay."

ॐ

I wanted to slip away unnoticed, and as long as everyone was in the dining room when Victor came for me, I thought I would get away with it, but when he drove off the entire student body (with the exception of Helga) was jammed at the windows. Victor turned the car toward his end of the city and a neighborhood of comfortable, tightly packed copy-cat houses. He was quiet. I followed his lead, sensing his mood, suspecting he was not pleased to have his day interrupted with driving chores.

Maria and Mary were waiting at the house. I expected Maria would have a few words for me by way of the reprimand she spared me earlier. All she had for me was a "Hi ya' kid" and a salute from an empty wine glass.

The entire contents of my bedroom were in Mary's spare room. She wasn't sure how long I'd be staying, but for the time being I'd go to school with Leona and my old pals. All she expected of me was to help out with two-year-old Angela.

"Mary, what's going on with Daddy? Is he still in the sanitarium?"

"Your father's visiting in Lethbridge. And he's just fine. We'll talk about him after supper. But you'd better not bring up his name to Maria. I'll explain later."

While we were doing the supper dishes I learned that Maria and Cecil were in another phase of working things out. Cecil was "cooling off" at his brother's, and had no idea I was expelled. Maria refused to tell him because they were not on speaking terms. Victor had already warned her that if she didn't snap out of it, he'd place a call to Cecil himself.

Evidently a lot was going on while I was in St. Mary's, and Mary felt like talking. Bill joined up with the United States Army and was in the thick of things in Europe. Bill's motives were not entirely patriotic; he could qualify for student aid to finish dental school, and enlisting with a rank of 2nd Lieutenant was certainly an incentive, especially when his commission included automatic U.S. citizenship, if he wanted it – and he did, which sent Cecil into a tailspin. Bill had found the right girl and was planning to marry as soon as his tour of duty was up. With Ben Whyte's estate settled, Cecil was enjoying a nice interest in the company, which was doing quite well; expected to do even better. He was taking a squirrelish attitude with his inheritance, opposed to converting the stock to cash to meet his expenses. It was bound to go up, and he was throwing good money away. He found it hard to believe that none of his brothers would make him a short term loan with the stock as collateral, standing on the argument that in light of world affairs, no stock was a good as gold.

Leona greeted me at my old school with a sarcastic, "What are you doing back here? How long will you be staying this time?" Something had happened to Leona since I last saw her, but two hours commuting would never allow the time to uncover what it was: out the door at 6:50 a.m. for a two block dash to the 7 o'clock bus, back again at 4:45 p.m. in time to keep Angela out of Mary's hair until supper, do the dishes, pack my lunch and delve into homework. I studied in earnest now; unless I passed my qualifying examinations I would not advance to high school, and there were only four months to prepare.

Continued silence from Lethbridge prompted Victor to take matters into his own hands. He put my dismissal to Cecil very diplomatically. Apparently the two men had established a solid friendship; Victor made several comments which led me to believe he was siding with Cecil against Maria. I was hanging around the kitchen, nervous, waiting for my turn. It would be too much to expect Cecil to let the incident slide the way Maria did.

Victor said, "So long."

"Didn't he want to talk to me?"

"Not tonight. He'll be back in a few days. He'll have plenty of time to visit with you then."

"Was he angry about St. Mary's?"

"He didn't say one way or another."

"When will he be here?"

"He didn't tell me that either, but he'll be along sometime next week."

"I hope he isn't too upset."

"You'll find out soon enough."

From the first day I sensed I was an irritant to Victor. When I asked Mary, she attributed his coolness to his being dead set against meddling in other people's affairs. And, sister-in-law or not, Maria was wrong to bring her troubles into his home.

"Besides, he likes your father. Now he's forced to take sides. He wouldn't hear of me calling you after they started having their difficulties this last time."

"Do you think they'll ever learn to get along with each other?"

"The Lord only knows."

"It's been over a week since Victor talked to him. Shouldn't he be here by now?"

"You'd think so. But Victor seems to think he may be headed for Edmonton."

"Edmonton?"

Chapter 12

"Why do I always end up where I don't want to be?"

Cecil was doing much more than just heading for Edmonton. There was another woman! Maria was sure of it. Mary's advice was, "If I were you, I'd stop grousing about what you think he's up to and confront him."

Maria reported back to Mary. "Well, I took your advice. I confronted him."

"And?"

"He wants a divorce! After all I've been through, he wants a divorce!"

"On what grounds?"

"Adultery!"

"Adultery? Who's adultery? Not yours!"

"Of course not! He's the one who did it. Says he isn't ashamed of it either! Says any woman with an ounce of pride would be glad to get rid of him. Says I should divorce him. And the sooner the better! If I ever get my hands on that woman... If she thinks I'm going to hand him over without a fight...."

After listening to what Cecil was up to in Edmonton I was torn between love for him and disgust over his treatment of Maria. My feelings for Maria continued to grow, further nudged by the imprint of her embrace the afternoon I was expelled. Mary said if he didn't mend his ways he was on his way to hell. Maria thought it was a good place for him.

"You don't have to turn him loose if you don't want to, Maria. Canadian law being what it is, you can hang on 'til your dying day. The only way he could turn the tables on you is if you commit adultery, and even at that he'll need a witness to prove it."

"I'll never have anything to do with that man as long as I live!"

Maria wasn't fooling Mary. "If he showed up on our doorstep tonight and asked your forgiveness, you'd take him back in a minute."

"It seems to me," Mary continued, "it all boils down to who can hold out the longest. He'll have to support you even if you aren't living under the same roof. And when he finds out how much another woman can cost him he may have second thoughts. Take my advice – lay low – bide your time. He'll come to his senses, eventually!"

Mary was a little too free with her advice, according to Victor. He cautioned Maria to make up her own mind. "And while you're at it, you'd better decide what we're going to do with Dorian. She can't stay here – not now."

"I told Cecil you didn't want her here."

"And what did he have to say about that?"

"He promised to settle up with you when he gets back into town."

Victor wanted Maria to take me back to her place.

"I'm not responsible for her."

"Neither are we!"

Mary told them to shut up. "The two of you make me sick. Keep you voices down, she'll hear you."

April 11, 1945, an announcement came through the loud speaker that we would join with our American allies in a day of mourning: Franklin Delano Roosevelt was due the respect of the nation. Mary sniffled over her cooking pots. "It couldn't have happened at a worse time." Victor said there was never a good time for a head of state to die, and Truman could probably run the country as well as Roosevelt. Germany surrendered May 7; Cecil showed up on the eighth, ready to declare his own war on Maria; but not until he celebrated with champagne and "the best cigars money could buy."

Mary muttered how Cecil had some nerve walking in on them as if he were family. Victor reminded her he was, by marriage, and wasn't that why I was there? Cecil and Victor toasted the Canadians, the English, the Americans, all who fought against Hitler. "And here's to the poor chaps that didn't make it back."

Mary didn't allow cigars in her home so Victor and Cecil were forced into the backyard shortly after I retired. They were under my window. I sat directly under the sill so as not to miss a word.

"Of course I intend to reimburse you for keeping her. If you could just see your way clear to let her stay through the end of the school term, I'll make it worth your while."

"What will you do with her if you and Maria don't patch things up? Send her to another school? She's apt to get thrown out again."

"Oh, I have no intentions of patching things up with Maria. It may sound hard on my part, but if you could just meet my Barbara. She has such a sweet way about her; she reminds me of Beatrice, even looks a little like her, only taller."

"Spend a lot on her do you?"

Cecil chuckled, "Do you have any idea how much six youngsters can eat?"

"Six? You've taken on a woman with six youngsters? You're a damned fool, McGregor."

"That seems to be the opinion of just about everyone I run into these days. You wouldn't say that if you could meet her. This woman is a treasure – a real treasure."

"What happened to her husband?"

"He's retired Army. Hard as nails, too. He beats her. That's why she left him. She's had it pretty tough, but now that she's got me, things are going to be a lot different…"

I kept my position under the window, stunned. How could Cecil dispose of Maria after she stood by him when he was sick? Why didn't Victor stick up for Maria? What was going to happen to me?

Mary's reaction when Victor relayed Cecil's description of his treasure was, "And I'll bet he's spending one on her, too. She'll clean him out before he knows it. Then we'll see how long she hangs around."

Victor said, "He isn't the first fool – he won't be the last."

"Maria's going straight through the roof when she gets wind of this!"

"Then don't tell her, Mary. You keep your trap shut! Let Cecil tell her what he wants her to know. Don't you go stirring things up. Don't go giving advice and trying to get them back together. It won't work. He's made up his mind."

"I can't keep out of it! She's my sister!"

I never knew if Mary told Maria everything she knew about Cecil's treasure, but common sense says she did, because it wasn't long before Maria announced her final decision. She would bide her time!

"I'll sit this out, come hell or high water. If he wants a divorce, he'll have to get something on me! If that hussy thinks she's getting my husband…."

Cecil returned to Edmonton. Maria hired on again at her old job in the Lethbridge office and moved, where, she said, she should have stayed in the first place. Cecil had been nothing but a heartache for her. Mary broke the news to me.

"I want you to know this is none of my doing. As far as I'm concerned, you are perfectly welcome to stay with us. You've been a big help, and Angela has certainly taken to you, but your father has made arrangements…."

"Where's he sending me now?"

"To live with his brother, Paul."

"I don't even know them."

"From what your father says, Paul was always his favorite brother. They have two small children – and you're so good with children. They'll be lucky to have you."

"Why do I always end up where I don't want to be?"

"I know you've been shuffled around a lot, but one of these days life will take a turn for the better."

"When?"

"One of these days – maybe in Montana. I think it would be very exciting to live in the States."

"Is it any different than Canada?"

"Oh, my yes! People have a great deal more to spend down there. And your uncle Paul is a dentist. You know how much money they make. And Cecil told Victor that Paul is well respected. Anyone with Dr. in front of their name is always respected, especially in a smaller town."

"How small?"

"I can't say for sure. You'll have a lot to look forward to – starting into high school, making new friends. It could turn into quite an adventure."

"I am SO sick and tired of adventures! They're always sending me off on an adventure; always telling me how wonderful it's going to be when I get there, and it never is!"

Mary encouraged me to do the best I could with my final examinations when I told her I didn't know how I was going to get through them. She understood the upcoming move was affecting me, but as one who never finished high school, she wanted to encourage me.

"Mary, I never would have guessed it. You never finished school? What happened?"

"None of us got through high school. Maria was the smart one. She went to night school for her certificate. I always regretted not doing what she did. After Dad got hurt in the explosion, we all had to work at the cannery, and even at that, we still had to farm out our little brother Roberto to a cousin for awhile."

"Tell me more."

Mary was proud of her mother who brought four daughters from a small village in Italy after waiting two years while her husband worked in the mines for their passage. Mary was barely three. None of them knew a word of English.

"What about the explosion?"

"Everyone knew it was the company's fault." Her back stiffened. "He broke both legs – took a terrible blow to his head, too. It cost him his hearing on one side. It was terrible! Terrible! He was never the same. That's when we started working at the cannery. Dad swore they'd never get Roberto, but Roberto hired on as soon as he was old enough to work. Dad found out and threatened to pay some thugs to beat him up if he ever went back. So Roberto learned to lay brick."

"How tragic! Oh, Mary, I had no idea. You haven't had it so easy either, have you? Or Maria?"

"Makes it a little easier to understand Maria, doesn't it?"

"Poor Maria!"

It was exhilarating to be able to proclaim my full support to Maria. "I've been doing a lot of thinking about what Daddy did, and how he's hurt you. It's downright wicked of him to break your heart this way. I think you've made the right decision. You just bide your time. He'll come around, eventually. And I'm going to pray for that to happen. You have my word."

If Maria could wait for Cecil to come around, I could too. And I wasn't going to give up hope of us all becoming a regular family someday. As the date of my departure to Montana approached I chewed my nails, suffered with insomnia, and gobbled aspirin.

"A lot of women suffer from sick headaches," said Mary.

"The school nurse said they were migraines – and that there isn't much I can do about them."

Chapter 13

*"...I remained the least in a line of
beggars for his affection."*

We were nearing the border town of Sweet Grass, Montana
before Cecil brought up my hasty removal from St. Mary's.

"You bet I was upset! But I've had some time to think
about it. You've been punished enough over the years, so I'm
letting you off easy this time. You've been wondering when I
was going to call you on it, haven't you?"

"Yes."

"I will not have you embarrassing me like that again!
You're too old for such antics. Understood?"

"Understood!"

"Then we'll consider it done with."

The border guard recognized Cecil. "McGregor isn't it?"

Cecil thrust his hand out the window. "Right you are."

"Anything to declare this trip?"

Cecil offered him a cigarette. "Nothing this time. I'll be
back through day after tomorrow – just running down for a
quick visit with my brother."

He checked our passports and waved us through. Cecil
snickered, "Good thing he was on duty. I'd have been hard
pressed to explain two cartons of Parliament cigarettes

under the seat and three tins of Empress preserves in the trunk."

"What would they do if they caught you lying?"

"Fine me. Confiscate the goods. I've gotten to know that guard over the years. He's a nice chap. They don't check the cars like they did during the war. I was pretty sure I could get away with it."

"Surely they have preserves in the States."

"Paul can't buy Empress brand down here, and he says nothing they have compares with Empress strawberry preserves."

"He doesn't like their cigarettes either?"

"Paul may be an American now, but he prefers to smoke and eat Canadian whenever he can."

Montana mirrored Alberta in a marriage of prairie and Rocky Mountains. The wind blasted us, leaving our nostrils parched and stinging with dust. Cecil drove with one hand, mopped his face and neck with the other. An hour after our entry into the United States of America we were driving down the main street of Cut Bank.

"It isn't very big, is it?"

"Close to five thousand right now, but it's growing. It's turning into a real boom town with the oil fields close by. Some mighty big cattle ranches around here as well. Paul settled here on my advice. If he'll just give the town a chance, he'll do well. There wasn't a dentist within 30 miles until he set up shop. This way he can grow and prosper with the community. It's always best to be a big fish in a little pond instead of the other way around."

Mary was right. Montana was different, but not much more advanced and up to date as she led me to believe.

Two quick blasts of the horn brought a collie mix trotting down the driveway. Paul followed with his four-year-old son in tow. Rita, a stunning brunette sporting a Betty Grable figure in red halter and shorts, clomped down the stairs on a pair of striped wedgies in pursuit of a chubby toddler intent on escaping into the next yard. Paul was about two inches shorter than Cecil, stockier, bearing a strong resemblance to his mother.

110

"You made good time," Paul said.

"We barreled right straight through. Hotter than blazes, too! You people are as hard up for rain down here as we are."

Rita and Paul lived in a modern ranch-style home in a new tract of houses. The living room was a blinding contrast to the traditional setting I was familiar with. Blonde-toned tables set with heavy ashtrays in pale pinks and turquoise picked up slubs in the fabric covering an obese sofa and two stout side chairs. A mantleless fireplace yawned low in the center of one turquoise wall.

"Well, Dorian, what do you think of it?" Rita asked.

What I thought of it was, it would take some getting used to, but I rallied with a lively, "It's very nice."

"We like it! I wanted the very latest thing."

Jimmy was tugging at his mother's shorts. "Jimmy has something he wants to say."

After a few false starts, Jimmy gave me his well-rehearsed, "Welcome to Montana."

I thanked him, then turned to acknowledge Melissah, an 18 month-old tow-head who screwed up her face and protested when I walked toward her. Paul apologized. "She's not good with strangers right off the bat, but give her a few days and she'll be all over you."

"Dorian's very good with children," Cecil said. "She looked after Mary's little girl. I thing Mary really hated to see her go."

Cecil hawked my talents, sounding more like an auctioneer in a slave market than a father: "Strong as an ox, used to doing her share, can keep a house and iron as good as any woman. She's even up to doing a little cooking if need be."

"How are you at fixing breakfast?" Paul shot a daggered look at Rita.

"I can manage."

"Good!"

When Rita went to secure her children for the night, the rest of us settled down in the living room. Cecil and Paul shared investment tips. I added the number of pink and turquoise tufts in the upholstery, deciding on turquoise as the predominate colour; no doubt the reason Rita chose twice as many turquoise accents. Rita was an exacting woman. Everything would have to be just so in this house. The furniture was comfortable; I wasn't.

Rita entered the room and flopped into a chair, draped her red-tipped fingers over the fat arms of the upholstery and sighed, "If I had any idea the second one was going to be such a handful... I should have waited until Jimmy was in school."

She crossed one shapely leg over the other, letting her shoe slip from her foot, bouncing the top leg so that the shoe slapped against her bare foot. She spoke toward Cecil's side of the sofa.

"She'll need some school clothes. How she looks is going to reflect on us! The first thing Monday we'll get her some decent shoes. Aren't you embarrassed to have her seen in those horrid black oxfords? It's summer; she should at least have some loafers."

"She's been spending most of her time at private schools; they're required to wear oxfords."

Rita said, "She's been out of those places a good six months. Dorian are those your only pair of shoes?"

I nodded.

Rita's face flushed. Cecil's face flushed. Paul suggested another round of drinks and didn't I think I should go to bed now? The clapping shoe was doing double time when I left the room. Rita's instructions trailed after me. "Remember to take the roll-away so your father can have the bed."

The spare room in the basement was paneled, pleasant, and crowded with traditional furniture exiled by the recent renovation. Their dog, Smokey, was whining at the window. One blue eye gave him a wild look, but his antics proved him friendly. The dog's company raised my spirits; one never had to qualify for the affection of animals. I remembered the consolation I'd found in O'Brien, and was inspired by what this new friend could mean. Adept as I was to adjusting to new living situations, I felt the fatigue indigenous to settling into a new place; the concern of not knowing how I would fare with the new caretakers. Rita's distaste over my paltry wardrobe was further encouragement; there could be an advantage to being placed under her thumb. She was more than pretty. She was classy; what Cecil would refer to as "an uptown woman." Perhaps some of her would rub off on me, and I could finish growing up more like her, less like myself. Montana might not be altogether dismal after all.

It would have been so much better had I fallen asleep; if the bedroom was anywhere but under the living room; if their voices hadn't come through the ceiling. But as was so often the case, I was privy to the very conversation I was dismissed from by the nature of the layout of the house and the open-windowed time of year.

Cecil laid out his plan to bribe Maria into a divorce. Then he and Barbara would use the same tactic on her estranged husband. He could be bought for very little. Maria would need more coaxing. Cecil was back in the money now; convinced he could "strike a bargain" with Maria.

Paul cautioned him. "Don't you think it's a little too early to be jumping to conclusions? Have you considered the yoke you're putting on? I think a woman with six children deserves a second thought!"

"But you should see her children; especially the youngest, little Dorothy. That youngster has me wrapped 'round her little finger. I'm as crazy about her as if she were my very own."

"And the others?"

"Oh, there's one bad apple in the bunch, but for the most part they're a pretty fine lot."

There is a feeling that bites into your gut when the very thing you always suspected presents itself as the truth. And you have no choice but to submit; and suffer. Cecil never blessed me with words of love; never offered any declaration of how he felt about me. And he had almost convinced me of the practicality of sending me to the States until he settled his life. His life was not so unsettled he couldn't share it with Barbara and her brood. He was head over heels in love with her, and her children, while I remained the least in a line of beggars for his affection.

The conditions under which I was to live out my remaining school years came as a grievous affront. A five-thousand dollar loan given to Paul when he set up his practice was six years in arrears; keeping me would be Cecil's way of collecting what was due him. Rita's plea for credit during the time they contributed to Cecil's expenses while he was ill were of little consequence after the interest was tallied and the full debt laid on the bargaining table. Cecil was prepared to tear up the note as long as Paul agreed to keep and support me until I graduated high school; if he would take me "off his hands."

"Think of it, Rita, from now on you can get away from the house whenever you want without giving it a second thought! You and Paul can even get away on a holiday every now and then."

When Cecil came to bed, as far as he was concerned, I fell asleep as soon as my head hit the pillow. Again I wondered why nobody was standing up for Maria; not even Rita. We were in the same camp. Cecil was as anxious to be rid of me as he was of her; lessening his inconvenience by claiming payment from his brother; making it sound as if they were getting the better of the bargain.

Smokey was at the window early in the morning. I went out into the yard and sat down on the grass to get acquainted. In the way a dog can become instantly faithful, he curled up beside me with his head across my knee.

"He's a nice dog, isn't he?"

Paul was at the gate in pajamas and slippers.

"He's super!"

"He's half coyote, you know."

"Really?"

"A rancher just outside of town has an Australian Shepherd. She mated with a coyote; we have plenty of them around here. Just wait until you hear him baying at the moon. One of his littermates lives across the alley. He usually starts it, then Smokey picks it up. I think five of the eight pups live within a 6 block radius. They drive Rita crazy when they get going."

Cecil and Rita were sleeping in so Paul and I did up a batch of French toast. Jimmy sidled up to me at the table; Melissah kept to her father, screaming when I as much looked her way. What she really wanted was to get into her mother's bedroom. Paul hiked her under his arm around noon, and shuffled down the hall with Rita's coffee. When Rita finally made her entrance she came looking much less like an uptown woman than the night before.

Tomorrow Cecil would be on his way to Calgary, and it would be good riddance. Maybe there would be a new border guard on duty by the time he passed through customs; maybe he'd get fined for the four bottles of scotch he was going to try to sneak across the border. And the day after tomorrow I was getting my first pair of loafers; and a regular wardrobe. No more navy blue uniforms and black stockings and oxfords for me!

Cut Bank just might prove out after all. There was always the chance that Paul and Rita would look on me as more of a cousin and less of a hired girl.

Chapter 14

"How exciting to be wearing normal clothes again…"

True to her word, Rita got us to Miller's Department Store as it was opening. She made a beeline for the shoe department and ordered the clerk to fit me with a pair of loafers.

"And we might as well look at your saddle shoes while we're at it."

What great good fortune to be living in the States with a woman who recognized the importance of shoes. She insisted I wear the loafers and instructed the clerk to dispose of my oxfords. We searched the store for the "very latest." Rita picked clothes from the racks, taking six of everything: skirts, blouses, sweaters, explaining a mixing and matching technique that would have people thinking I never wore the same thing twice.

My first pair of blue jeans were a curiosity.

"These are awfully stiff!"

"Only until you break them in. You'll be chaffed the first few times you wear them. But you can't wear them out. One pair will last forever unless your figure changes."

The prospects of Rita's dressing technique eased some of the worry over being accepted in the new school. I wanted to make a good first impression. How exciting to be wearing normal clothes again.

Paul arranged a meeting with the high school principal, Tom Mumford, a close friend and neighbor of four doors down. Mumford said I was well ahead of my peers, as was often the case for those from institutional learning, but as a Canadian I lacked American History. The only way to keep me busy was to have me repeat some subjects and fill in with electives and free study periods in the library. Paul was going to hold me to top grades with so much free time on my hands.

Rita wanted me to make the right friends and sent me to call on Betsy Dyer after describing her parents, Maude and Jake, as one of the wealthiest ranching couples in the state.

"I've come to meet Betsy."

"We've been expecting you," said Maude. "Betsy! The McGregor girl is here to see you!"

My first thought on meeting Maude Dyer was that it was a good thing she was wealthy. A woman with protruding eyes and a face peppered with moles deserved some compensation.

"Hello."

One would never mistake Betsy for someone else's daughter.

"Hi."

"Wanta come with us while we take lunch out to the hired hands?"

"Sure."

We traveled through miles of ripe wheat to where Mr. Dyer, his son Frank, and four hired hands were threshing. Frank spotted us first, threw his hat into the air and came running. I sat sideways in the front seat with my feet on the running board while Maude and Betsy served from the back of the truck.

After polishing off three baskets of food the men relaxed against the truck, picking their teeth, eyeing me and Betsy while Jack Dyer, a surprisingly handsome man, escorted his wife a few yards away for a private talk.

Frank Dyer strolled over to my side of the truck.

"You're Dr. McGregor's niece!"

"That's right!"

"How about you an' me taking in a movie this Saturday night?"

Frank favored his father, but covered in Montana dust and sweat, he was far from appealing. This was the first time a boy had ever approached me in this manner; his boldness frightened me.

"I don't think I'm allowed to go out much."

"I bet your aunt and uncle will let you see a movie. They know me. You ask them. I bet they'll say yes."

Mr. Dyer gave Maude a peck on the cheek and motioned to his son to get back to work.

"Frank! That's enough loafing."

"Gotta go. Now don't forget to ask your uncle about Saturday night." Frank looked back over his shoulder several times on his way to the combine.

"Did my brother ask you out?"

I nodded, hoping Betsy would fail to notice the heat rising to my face.

"Did you say you would?"

"No."

"Would you like to? He's not bad looking when he's cleaned up."

"I can't. I have to take care of Jimmy and Melissah. Paul and Rita always go out Saturday nights."

Pride in her father's holdings kept Betsy's tongue wagging; by the end of our first visit she had listed every asset in the Dyer family. Before school started she wanted to show me her father's prized Black Angus.

Rita wanted my opinion of the Dyers. "They must own half of the State of Montana."

It was reassuring to have Betsy stop by the first day of school; Maureen Flagg and Isabel Turner caught up with us midway.

119

Betsy introduced them as her best friends. Maureen was twittering about her boyfriend, and wanted to know if I had one.

"Not yet."

They praised certain boys, plotting for a seat next to them in class. When Maureen's hand went to her waist, indicating a six pound loss, I told her I'd never yet lost my appetite over a boy.

"Then you've just never been in love, because that's a sure sign."

Boys were lined up on either side of the steps, voting with whistles and groans as the girls paraded in their back-to-school garb.

"That must be Dr. McGregor's niece."

"I bet she thinks she's really something."

"Yah! She's probably stuck up, just like her aunt."

Betsy was taking American History with me; the rest of the day I was on my own, conspicuous in a school where everyone knew everyone else.

On the way home I asked Betsy, "Is Rita stuck up?"

"Some people think so."

"Do you?"

She shrugged. "You're coming to the drug store aren't you? Everyone does."

"I'm supposed to come straight home. Rita has things for me to do."

"Well, I'm going so guess I'll see you tomorrow morning."

"Sure."

To my thinking, a snob enjoyed a position of envy, and for that reason I was willing to be labeled one. Maureen and Isabel were solicitous: their mothers knew Rita, their fathers did business with Paul. Any social position enjoyed by Paul and Rita would reflect on me, and respect, even second-hand respect, was a new experience. I liked it!

❧

During the first weeks with Rita and Paul I sized them up, learning what pleased or displeased them. I wanted to avoid trouble. And there was trouble to avoid. It wasn't anything I could put my finger on, but knew it was related to Paul's being a big fish in a little pond when Rita would rather live in a bigger pond. They usually squared off at the dinner table.

"Collections are off again. Where do people get the idea I'm well off?"

"If you'd listened to me, and stayed in Chicago instead of coming to this rinky-dink town…."

Breakfast was peaceful. Paul and I rubbed elbows, feeding the children, packing lunches. Paul fussed over his sandwiches, wrapping them in a double layer of wax paper before slipping them, along with a stack of sweet pickles, into a lunch sack. The same lunch, day after day. He left for the office round shouldered, down in the mouth, returned more stooped, more down in the mouth. I pitied him, and found myself taking sides; his side. Rita missed it all, sleeping until Smokey alerted me that Betsy was at the back door and I sent Melissah and Jimmy down the hall.

If Rita was in a good mood when I returned, I felt fortunate to have her company. Fourteen years separated us. She enjoyed showing me how to make the most of my wardrobe, giving advice on skin care. Just because I'd been blessed with a good complexion I should never take it for granted. A dirty face invited pimples; a dry one invited wrinkles. It was never too soon to start applying moisturizer under the eyes and to the neck. If her regime could benefit me to the extent it did her it was worth taking to heart. We were exactly the same height at 5 feet 3 and one-half inches. I was 15 pounds heavier. She suggested I try one of her diets.

Her irritable spells were always preempted by an exaggerated crossing of legs and the slap of the shoe against her foot; a cue for Melissah's fussy nature, and a signal to send Jimmy retreating to his room with Smokey. The kiss of the shoe against her heel was inevitable after a stormy dinner discussion.

All Paul ever wanted to do was provide for his family; to give them everything he never had as a boy. Rita's definition of everything in no way paralleled Paul's yardstick of what their standard of living ought to be. Rita wanted him to concede that being a woman was not a bed of roses, insisting that if he traded places with her for one week he would soon learn who had the most to complain about. He failed to see how she could feel put upon now that I was there to relieve her of the children. I began to suspect that Rita was troubled over something that extended far beyond beds of roses.

Frank Dyer was persistent in spite of my continued excuse that I had to stay home to watch Melissah and Jimmy. Maureen bemoaned the fact that the wrong boys always took notice of her, the right ones never did, and admitted her crush on Frank.

"I'd love to date a senior! I wish he'd ask me!"

"I wish he would too, because I'm never going out with him."

"Why not?"

"I just don't want to, that's all!"

It was the way he looked at me, reminding me of Peter and those before him. I was exchanging books at my locker when Frank put his hands on my shoulders and pressed his face against my cheek. I screamed. He jumped back, red-faced, startled. I buried my head in the locker to avoid a gathering crowd of students and teachers.

"What's the matter with you? I just want to talk to you."

"Why don't you just stay away from me?" I kept my voice low to spare him any further embarrassment, but he flared, giving himself away.

"You bet I will, Miss Priss. And why don't you go back to Canada where you belong?"

Someone said, "That's what you get for trying to rob the cradle."

The gossip died down, but from then on if I called on Betsy and ended up in the same room with Frank, he found reason to leave. Now that he was having nothing to do with me, I looked forward to being in the Dyer home. Rita never challenged me when I asked for time off to study with Betsy, but then I was careful not to overdo it so she wouldn't discover my real reason for going.

I envied Betsy for her parents; especially a father who treated her as though she were the fairest of the fair. Maude and Jake were affectionate with each other; I liked being with them because of the way they treated each other. The Dyer's oval kitchen table was covered in blue and white oil cloth, ringed with odds and ends of carved oak chairs from various family members "long gone from this world." Maude always just happened to have something left over from the previous meal, and nothing pleased her more than to see folks filling up the chairs, enjoying her cooking. I came to love Maude's homely face.

Paul resented the cost of extra food and school supplies. When I complained of a toothache he swore over the condition of my mouth; the time and materials needed to prevent the loss of "every tooth" in my head.

"On top of everything else, now I have to give up my leisure time to save your teeth. And your father won't pay me for it, either! He'll expect me to do it gratis!"

"You don't want her to lose her teeth," Rita said.

"Of course not, but we'll see how you feel about it after a few Saturdays at the office when you want her here helping out at the house. The girl's got enough work to keep me busy for months!"

Three to five hours at a stretch, drilling, picking, pounding. As fast as Paul caught up with the decay, new cavities appeared, seemingly overnight.

"I'm sorry, Paul. I don't like them either. You can let them go, if you'd rather. I can always get them fixed when I'm older."

"If I do that, you'll be wearing dentures before you're 18. And I won't have that on my conscience!"

Once I grasped the potency of his resentment, I was overtaken with guilt: guilt over cavities – guilt because I was eating too much – guilt when I needed money for school supplies. In order to pay for my own school supplies, I started hiring myself out to Rita's friends for housework and babysitting when she didn't need me, but it didn't soften his resentment.

"We made a serious mistake, Rita – going along with this setup. We'd be far better off paying someone to look after the children and hire a woman to clean once a week. It's going to be costly keeping her for the next two-and-a-half years. We'll have to come up with an alternative."

What possible alternative? Cecil wouldn't stand for any interference in his plans with Barbara. I wasn't in touch with Mary or Maria. Perhaps if I ate less, stayed awake from now on so Paul couldn't argue how pointless it was to leave me in charge when they went out. No matter how good my intentions to be on guard, "in case the house catches fire," I was asleep on the couch when they got home. I relied on Smokey to rouse me in case of an emergency.

Rita noticed I was eating less. "On a diet, Dorian?"

I lied and said I wanted to lose five pounds. "It's sort of a contest. Maureen and Isabel against Betsy and me to see who does it first."

I took less at the table, then gave into a grumbling stomach at night. A horde of crackers and cheese, and boxes of Jell-O sneaked out of the kitchen made up for what I declined at the table. A packet of Jell-O eaten with a moistened finger made a good dessert. I chose a cubby hole behind a loose board in back of the toilet in my room as a hiding place. Rita must have been doing some serious snooping to find it, and when I was seated at the table with her and Paul at opposite ends, arms folded, I knew they would never understand if I told them I was trying to make it look like it didn't cost as much as Paul thought to have me there; that I couldn't risk getting tossed out again. Cecil would never forgive me. I had to make a go of it this time. They would never believe me if I told them I was always hungry; that I was trying to control my appetite.

"What else have you stolen from us? Money? Why would you want to steal food and hide it?"

When cornered into an explanation I had none.

"If you were hungry why didn't you eat at the table like the rest of us?"

"I don't know. I'm sorry. I'll never do it again."

"That story about a diet – it was a lie wasn't it? A bold-faced lie?"

"Yes sir."

Rita pointed at me. "If there's anything I despise, it's a liar. Out of my sight!"

I stumbled down the stairs in disgrace. Paul and Rita were embroiled in what was to be done with me. "I'm calling Cecil," Paul said, "first thing in the morning. He'll have to come and get her. I'll not have a liar and a thief in my house."

"Isn't that why she was kicked out of St. Mary's? For stealing food? What in the world is wrong with her? Do you suppose she really was brain damaged by the gas? Don't you remember how worried Cecil was about that?"

A call to Cecil left Paul resigned to seeing me through to the end of the school year. Cecil was going to write and straighten me out. They would have no further trouble with me.

"One more episode, Rita, just one more and she's out, end of the school year or not!"

"I told Maxine Mumford about it. And do you know what she said? "If the girl's disturbed, maybe she shouldn't be taking care of the children."

Cecil was fed up with me and the same bizarre behavior that expelled me from St. Mary's. My only protection against the wrath in his letter was to stop reading, tear it up and take it to the trash can in the alley. Then I came down with a migraine. What would Mr. Mumford think of me? Would he say anything to the rest of the teachers?

The more I tried to control my appetite the more it escalated. I was stopping by Betsy's in the morning rather than wait for her to call for me, arriving five minutes earlier than necessary, knowing that Maude would offer me something to eat while Betsy finished her breakfast; I asked Betsy for whatever was left of her lunches.

"You never get filled up, do you?"

"I can't help it, Betsy, I'm always hungry."

"How can you eat so much and keep losing weight?"

"Beats me. But it's awful. And if I eat too much at home, Paul says I'm a glutton."

"There must be something wrong with you."

It was more than a question of appetite now: night sweats, hand tremors, one migraine after another. I stumbled from day to day, popping aspirin until my stomach burned.

I was stuffing a sandwich into my mouth during biology class when our instructor, Mr. Costello, sat down beside me on the lab bench. "You must be pretty hungry to eat during this class."

"I can't help it, Mr. Costello. I get the shakes if I wait 'til lunch time."

He approached me a second time after the bell rang.

"Let me see your hands. How long have you had these tremors?"

"For a while."

"Do your hands perspire?"

"How did you know?"

"I'm going to give you a note to take home. If I'm not mistaken, you've got an adolescent goiter. It's fairly common in this area. We're located in a goiter belt. It extends into Alberta, too. Your eyes are a little prominent – that's another symptom. And I bet you're always hungry!"

"Always!"

Paul was insulted. "If she had a goiter, don't you think I'd know it? This is none of his business, and I'm going to tell him so!"

Evidently Costello got the better of Paul because immediately after their conversation Rita took me for a check-up. Costello was right: I had an adolescent goiter and an excuse for my run-away appetite. Lugois solution, twice a day, and if that failed the doctor had other remedies.

"What about my eyes? Will they go back to normal?

"Sometimes they do. Sometimes they don't. In your case, I think they will."

Paul assured me I wasn't going to end up like Maude Dyer. The more he stressed the "unlikelihood of any long-lasting effects" the more I was convinced the outcome would be in keeping with my affinity for unfortunate acts of fate. I took stock of other students who might have contracted this "common disorder," but found myself to be the only swelled necked, bug-eyed student in the entire school. I begged Rita to do something. "Can't we get another opinion? Maybe another doctor will have better treatment. Look at me! I'm a freak!"

Consultation with a second physician left us with two opposing opinions. The first doctor said, "Up the dosage." The second doctor said, "Remove the thyroid." Paul said, "Wait and see."

My appetite continued to amaze and disgust Paul. References to the high cost of having me around, and something had to be done about the situation, led Paul to make another attempt to wiggle out of a bad bargain. He told Cecil I was no use to them in my condition. I was too much of a responsibility. They no longer trusted me. Anyone who would steal food and hide it away like a rodent was disturbed.

Paul admitted to some understanding. "Of course her appetite would increase. But goiter or not, any normal girl would eat all she needed at the table. We don't think she's suitable to have around the children."

I could have understood it if he had taken this approach immediately upon discovering the stolen food, but coming after the discovery of the goiter was another thing entirely. Cecil wanted to know why I persisted in making life so difficult for everyone. As soon as he could locate a school that would take me, preferably in the States, I'd be on my way.

It was certain to be all over town by Monday. Rita and Paul spent every Saturday night at the Elks Club, as did Maude and Jake Dyer. I wasn't surprised to hear from Betsy.

"I understand Rita and Paul are getting rid of you."

"Who told you that?"

"My folks were at the dance at the Elks Club last night."

"Did you ever think I might have planned it that way?"

"Whadda ya mean?"

"I'm glad I'm leaving. All I do is work; look after Jimmy and Melissah. I'm glad my Dad's taking me out of here. I never wanted to come here in the first place."

"You know where they're sending you, don't you?"

"My Dad is sending me to a private school."

"St. Thomas Orphanage is not a private school. It's where they send orphans and problem girls."

"They'd never send me to an orphanage!"

"Oh but they are – and I don't think you're going to like it there."

There was one bright prospect about leaving town. Nobody at St. Thomas would be able to refer to me as "froggy" as Frank and some of his buddies had. My eyes were almost back to normal.

Chapter 15

*"Why would God, all powerful as He was, choose to enter
into our suffering rather than do away with it altogether?
What good could come from suffering?"*

St. Thomas Orphanage was built on the fringe of the city of
Great Falls at a time when the population was never expected
to catch up with it. The rear grounds bordered the highway,
but across the street, residential bungalows and young trees
were making a stand. Two fir trees on either side of the entry
to the school were a hand's reach from the fourth floor.

The first wave of nausea hit me at the staircase. Saliva
flowed at the second floor landing; my stomach cramped on
the third. Sister's wide feet were visible under the abbrevi-
ated door of the lavatory when I knelt at the commode on the
fourth floor retching with a migraine and the humiliation of
my exile to St. Thomas.

The dormitory was twice the size of St. Mary's. I took the
bedroll from the foot of the cot and began to prepare my sleeping space. An elderly nun was laid back, dozing in a rocker,
oblivious to the chatter around her. It was only after several girls began to argue in full voice that her body twitched
and she opened her eyes. She was still stiff from sleep and
glared at the group of girls who were now shoving each other

around. The old woman hunched under her black robes and descended upon the bickering bunch like a witch from the pages of Macbeth.

Belligerent, provoking students frightened me; an acquired stance; a menacing look. It would be wise to keep to myself, a role that would manifest itself naturally due to my being the only non-Catholic student among the upper grades. One of the nuns said I was an answer to prayer. They were in need of someone to free them of the care of the preschool dormitory: sixteen children in all.

"Most of them can manage quite well on their own, but I must warn you, they will try to get away without brushing their teeth. As you already know, they don't come to the dining hall, so you'll be having your meals with them upstairs. You'll get the food from the dumb waiter."

It was more than a fair exchange: added responsibility for the company of sixteen sprouts in dire need of mothering. I took it as a near miraculous happening: to be the only non-Catholic in my age group in a school of this sort, thereby opening the door to such a position. There was no need to inflict 6:15 Mass on me for the well-being of my soul, because as one nun put it, "Going to daily Mass was not going to influence God one way or another because you are not one of us."

I pried the tots from their beds at 6:30. They went to their knees, made the sign of the cross and mumbled their prayers. Some rested their heads on the mattress; I never insisted otherwise. The smallest one, "baby Alice", was almost three. She made a valiant effort to imitate the others. Those who couldn't button or tie lined up in front of me.

Their lives, and the formidable years ahead of them, tugged at my heart. Perhaps when they reached my age they would see it differently; if they were never in the world, they might never miss the world. But the world wasn't that far away. Across the street privileged children romped behind picket fences and manicured shrubs. Life was entirely different across the street. What explanation would the nuns have when asked about the children living on the other side of the fence?

In two years I could walk away from the place. Looking ahead to the day I would be on my own raised questions about my own future. Where was I going to go? I couldn't just walk across the street without a destination or somebody to see when I got there.

If anyone cared about what happened to me after I graduated it would be Mary, so I wrote, enclosing a second letter to Maria asking that Mary forward it as a ploy for information as to Cecil's whereabouts, if Maria answered, which she did.

Cecil was coming to Lethbridge for Christmas, and I was invited. Maria was fairly sure that he was finally coming to his senses. I sat on my cot, dressed in goose-flesh, fingering the bus ticket. An invitation to spend Christmas in Lethbridge with Cecil and Maria! What could it mean? A week later I boarded a bus bulging with passengers and Christmas hope.

Maria's conviction that Cecil was about to come to his senses was a far cry from what I discerned. Cecil was in the guest bedroom; there was no mistaking the small suitcase he carried into Maria's blue and white storybook house. Maria and I visited between twin beds at night, and, in keeping with what was now a persistent spirit of optimism, she spoke of what she thought was taking place in Edmonton.

"I think his lady friend's just about had enough of him. She's gotten all the money she's going to get – now she doesn't want him anymore. He all but told me as much. She's gone back to her husband. If you ask me, I think the two of them set your Dad up to get him to pay their bills. But he's got the picture now. He still talks to Victor you know, and Mary passes it all on to me. Of course it's all second hand, but Mary tells me...."

It certainly seemed to be the way Maria presented it. That would explain his sour expression. He had been made the fool, a first class fool, and when Maria told him as much he turned on her, packed his grip and left. Maria apologized. She wanted it to be a nice Christmas; she was so sure everything was going to work out this time. She was as wrong as she was the year before, and the year before that. My last glimpse of Maria left me with the impression of a woman determined to win, and strengthened my conviction as to whose side I was still on.

It was safer in St. Thomas; one knew what to expect. I was surprisingly happy to be back. The young children rushed me, fighting for a lift up. Nobody ever missed me that I could remember! This wasn't the worst place to be after all; in fact some of the nuns were quite personable. I could lay aside my former resentments now, and see that they had our best interests at heart, and wanted only to prepare us for life after St. Thomas.

In keeping with that preparation, we were forced to reach beyond the chain link fence; to participate in state competitions. I received a fancy certificate and a check for an essay on "What It Means to be an American." It was of no consequence that I wasn't a citizen because, as far as Sister Claire was concerned, I'd been here long enough to know the value of living in this great country, and in all probability would take the oath when I came of age. The American Legion sponsored an art contest. I was presented at a tea, stood on the stage in front of a reproduction of my poster displayed on an easel and accepted another check from a veteran of the first world war. They planned to use my entry as the official State poster for the upcoming annual State Veterans' Poppy Day Drive.

I talked all the way back to the school, telling Sister Claire how my natural father was an artist.

"I'm not surprised. He was probably a pretty fair talker, too."

Sister said I had just as good a chance as any in the school system, and she was not going to let me wheedle out of a play-writing contest.

"I've never done anything like that before!"

"And just how many art contests have you entered?"

Weeks later the student body gathered around the radio to listen as a group of local actors performed my play.

Sister doled out my winnings and set me up with painting materials in the corner of a room she used to store school supplies. I was content with my first real accomplishments, and had not the slightest interest in debating the Taft Hartley

Act versus compulsory arbitration when she suggested I represent the school on the debate team.

"It is a shame when a young lady fails to utilize ALL her talents."

If persuasion was a talent, it couldn't be one of mine. I'd never been able to persuade anyone; nobody ever listened to me before. If I had such a gift would I have ended up at St. Thomas?

"You'll make a fine debater."

"This calls for a great deal of preparation, Sister. I really don't have the time, what with the preschool dormitory to watch over. I won't have time for painting!"

"Someday you'll thank me. I've matched you up with Patricia Leeds. The two of you are well suited to each other."

By the time we won our way to the University at Missoula to compete for the State championships against four teams of male opponents, I'd accepted the bait of competition. Pat was thrilled over second place. I took the defeat poorly.

"You didn't really think the judges were going to give it to US, did you?"

"Why not? We were the best!"

An invitation from the local Bar Association awaited us in Great Falls. We presented our debate on the radio. Sister was proud of our delivery, and gave us each a plastic record; something for posterity; a reminder of what one could do when one put one's mind to it. I began an intensive campaign to speak an octave lower. Pat and I were well on our way with a plan to take first place next year.

Everyone was discussing summer plans. Pat would be spending her time with relatives in Idaho. I was not prepared for the emptying of the school, and found it remarkable how many problem girls were able to find a summer alternative to St. Thomas.

"When are you leaving, Dorian?"

"I'm not sure."

"Are you going back to Canada?"

"I don't know."

The last student was packed off, leaving me to share the dormitory with the old Sister of the boards. Rumor had it that she had condemned herself to sleeping without a mattress when she took her final vows. We all took a turn at lifting the sheet to examine the three rough planks. There was no padding; no pillow. The story was that she imposed penance on herself in order to bypass purgatory. Small wonder she was short tempered; that she groaned in the night every time she turned her old bones.

Now it was just the tortured old woman and me. I was the only student in the entire school with the exception of six of the youngest, now under the tutelage of a new class of postulants who passed them around like Christmas dolls. The youngsters were so indulged by the nuns-in-training they spurned my attentions altogether.

The Reverend Mother's young assistant, Sister Rose, moved me from the main dormitory into the visitors' dormitory until word came from my family as to where I was to spend the summer. The visitors' dormitory held eight beds, a less intimidating number of reminders of my position. One messed up bed out of eight; seven others, haughty in their neatness; each with a single pillow to remind me I was the only one left behind.

I was assigned to Sister Rose in the morning; free to do whatever I wanted with my afternoons. Sister Claire was visiting an affiliate school and left instructions with Sister Rose to encourage me to take advantage of so much free time; there were plenty of painting materials in the storage room.

It was of some consolation, that as long as I was detained at St. Thomas, I could share my time with one as likeable as Sister Rose. She admitted to 26 years, but still in need of some silliness. Two large protruding central incisors gave her a chipmunk expression. She had a way of crinkling her nose, of raising the wattage in her eyes whenever we raced the stairs; no qualms over hiking her skirts to mid-calf, or taking the stairs two at a time. Her final vows were still ahead of her. I doubted she would ever submit to the full rigors of Sisterhood.

ॐ

A truck from Swenson's chicken farm arrived the first of the week. The old hens were no longer fit for anything other than Mason jars, so Mr. Swenson was making a donation to the school. The driver explained how they started wringing necks at daybreak; if we hurried we could get them canned that very day. The postulants stepped forward in pairs to collect the crates. Sister Rose and I waited in a small adjacent work room where two open windows above a double sink begged for air. One of the nuns in the main kitchen picked up a hen and plunged it into boiling water for a few moments before passing it on to the nun next in line. A sickening snap and feathers popped loose. Minutes later the bird, naked but for a collar of matted feathers, was tossed into a wash tub. I watched the tub fill, and shuddered when it was brought into the workroom and placed at my feet.

Sister George entered the room and rolled up her sleeves, exposing thick, powerful arms. With legs apart for balance, she swooped down, snatched a bird by the neck, flopped it onto the chopping block, brought down the cleaver, pitched the decapitated bird onto the counter and sent the head sailing into the sink. Without missing a beat she swooped, snatched, flopped and chopped. Sister George taught English literature. I held her in high esteem, awed by her culture and insight into the classics. Her conduct in the classroom gave no indication of this disappointing aspect of her character. She was a butcher, executing with precision and extraordinary coordination what was obviously her true vocation.

She motioned me to her side, placed the knife against the bird, separated the breast from the lower portion of the body, plunged her hand into the cavity, and emptied a fistful of entrails into the strainer in the sink before holding out the knife to me. The room took on a sensation of a ship's galley. I put the knife to the bird but could not bring myself to make a cut. With a disgusted cluck of the tongue, she placed a firm hand over mine; intestines bubbled through the incision. I was to empty the bird, place the edible organs in the strainer and pick through them, separating livers, gizzards and hearts. We could waste nothing.

The workroom was stifling; a mean summer temperature attacked the carcasses and organs heaped in the strainer until my nose burned with the stench. Flies caught the scent of the rotting room and clambered over the sink, bothering about our faces. Sister Rose worked beside me, silent and serious.

The truck came again on Tuesday; and Wednesday. It came the next day; and the next. Five days of slaughter: bird upon bird, pale mauves, grays and greens, mounds of soft shapes, glistening pieces of them. What if I turned the blade toward my own body? How would my insides look? Then I would be limp, pale, like the hens. Sister would whack off my head, put me snug into little jars, and when the girls came back to school, they would ask, "Whatever happened to Dorian?"

Chicken death lingered on my fingers; the smell of chicken flesh haunted me. Alone, in my summer dormitory, I feared for my sanity, fantasizing chickens the size of horses stalking me at night in the dark, demanding I return their vital organs. I told them I was ashamed to have been a part of it, and promised never to eat chicken as long as I lived.

A suite of rooms located next to the Chapel was occupied by the priest who held mass and evening benedictions. He also heard confession, and worked in the surrounding parish. Sister Rose was in charge of his meal trays, and assigned me the duty of arranging the tableware on a fine heavy silver-footed piece, seeing that there were no spots on the silverware.

He ate promptly at six o'clock, and with the last chime of the hall clock, I knocked, and counted to ten to allow him to escape his study before I opened the door and placed the tray on his desk. It would be improper for me to see him without his collar. The rooms were as lavish as the Sisters could make them; his tray laden with more food than one person could eat at a sitting. The temptation to glean off a portion of what he would never miss was put aside. Too many nuns traveled the hall at that hour, but at 7 o'clock, when I retrieved the tray, I could safely help myself to the leftovers. He liked pie fillings but never ever touched the crust, and with or without filling, pie was a rarity at St. Thomas. He wasn't fond of cake, but never reported it because Sister served it to him every other day. There was an occasional creamy pudding, but he polished off every bite. Sometimes Sister would give him a choice of desserts; I was the scavenger beast of St. Thomas; reduced to cleaning the father's plates, disgusted at the practice; yet taking a neurotic satisfaction in what I did. Everyone needs some satisfaction.

The weeks piled up. Mother Superior was sure there would be word any day; then I could leave for my vacation. I missed the attention of the younger children. I was lonely, depressed, fatigued. Sister found me curled up in bed one afternoon and went for a radio to keep me company. She also suggested a "heart to heart" which opened the door to an old question.

"I've always wondered why God plays favorites, Sister. Why is it that some people get by scot-free – and some catch it every time they turn around?"

"You're speaking of yourself, of course."

"Well, how do you think I feel? Being the only one left over? Why me? What did I ever do to deserve this? Why is it that everyone always forgets about me?"

"Seems to me you're feeling very sorry for yourself."

"Wouldn't you, if you were me?"

"Yes, I suppose I would."

"I've always suspected that God had it in for me because of something I did, and that's why these things always happen to me."

"These things?"

I told of the loss of significant family members and the inability to stay put in one place for more than one year at a time.

"Are you spending time in prayer?"

"I used to. But I've given up. God hasn't answered my prayers in a long time!"

"God always answers; one way or another."

"Well, then, He's always said no to me."

"I think we need to spend a little time in the Chapel."

We knelt at the altar railing. She crossed herself and elbowed me to do the same. I fought off any serious thoughts of God; as if in rejecting Him I might avenge myself. My knees were smarting by the time she crossed herself again, calling an end to our visitation.

Outside the Chapel doors she said, "Every afternoon we'll take thirty minutes for Chapel. As soon as you start praying, I'll shorten the time."

"How do you know I wasn't praying?"

"Were you?"

"So what if I wasn't?"

She winced.

"Oh, Sister, forgive me. I'm sorry. I'm not angry with you. I'm angry with God! And now I suppose He'll strike me dead for blasphemy."

"He'll do no such thing. Besides He knows exactly how you feel before you speak it. He loves you – no matter how you feel about Him."

How could I be rude to such a sweet lady a second time by rejecting her opinion? Better to hold my tongue.

"He loves all His children, including you, and so do I."

She swirled around the corner into her office, leaving me at the Chapel doors. Any mention of love would be offered out of a sense of duty, of pity, after all, she was a Sister of Charity; her conviction that God loved me more than likely came from the same charity. Still, God was God, and it wasn't wise to disregard Him no matter what favour I might or might not have with Him. I went back into the Chapel and knelt before a facsimile of a smiling Jesus with outstretched arms. Tears blurred my vision; imagination transformed the plaster into flesh until I saw a living Christ. Encouragement radiated from His face. I was like one in a trance; my eyes fixed on a statue come to life out of so great a need.

The movie of the life of Christ portrayed in the Lenten movie at St. Theresa's came to mind, and for a second time I pondered the mystery of God. If we were truly His children, He would suffer all that His children suffered in the same way that I was discomforted when one of my young charges was crying. And in that case, God must endure an eternal state of heartbreak. Why would God, all powerful as He was, choose to enter into our suffering, rather than do away with it altogether? What good could come out of suffering?

We went to the Chapel daily, and I was stopping in on my own. Sister Rose answered my questions, reviving a faith that held to the love of God and His perpetual concern for all. Faith was in full bloom again; I could stop trying to prove His love by my circumstances. Jesus was perfect, but Jesus suffered. Father God didn't wave a sovereign arm and stop His plan of salvation. Jesus had to do what He came to do. What if I was created for a purpose? What if there was something God sent me to do? If that were really the case, everything that happened to me was wrapped up in that purpose, and what did it matter that I wasn't going anywhere for the summer? The comfort of the Chapel was all I wanted. This was my home. I would become a Catholic, then a nun; live out my life at St. Thomas fulfilling my purpose by taking care of the preschool children. What a marvelous solution to life!

As pleased as Reverend Mother was over my decision to convert, she had to have permission from my family. Cecil answered her letter with a phone call and asked to speak to me.

"Why aren't you in Cut Bank?

"I wasn't invited!"

"You mean to tell me you've been there all summer?"

"All summer."

"But I thought you were in Cut Bank. Paul said they would have you down for the summer."

"Well they didn't. I've been here all along."

"You stay right where you are. I'll get back to you within the next few minutes. Let me talk to the Sister again."

Reverend Mother motioned me out of her office and told me to shut the door. When she called me back I had already fantasized myself into her position behind her big desk.

"Your father will not give his consent. You cannot become a Catholic. Not yet!"

"Why not? Why should he care?"

"He simply will not permit it."

"What difference is it to him?"

"Let him have his way for now. When you are of age you can come back to us and we will help you convert."

"Come back? What do you mean come back?"

"Your father is returning you to Cut Bank."

"But they don't want me. That's why they sent me here in the first place."

"It seems there's been a change of heart."

"I won't go! They can't make me. I won't! I won't!"

She knew why I couldn't convert, why I had to go back, but rather than discuss Cecil's religious prejudices, she emphasized that I must abide by his wishes and wait until I was free to make up my own mind without interference.

"Remember. When you come of age you'll be free to make your own decisions."

I was eating my supper that same evening, sitting at the end of the work table in the kitchen, listening to the nuns chattering over their meal in the next room. Someday I would return and put on the habit of the Sisters of Charity. I wrapped a towel around my head to see how I'd look in the headdress: more like a man than a woman, I thought. But then there was no place for vanity among the brides of Christ. It didn't matter how I looked in my habit, only that I wore one.

Chapter 16

*"...I could tolerate insult; it was only temporary...
There was so much more than this life to anticipate."*

Main Street looked pretty much the same except for the new store front on Miller's Department Store. I was dreading my senior year; living with those who, only the year before, saw fit to banish me. School was due to open in a matter of days; evidence of further resistance to what must have been a verbal strong arming on Cecil's part to persuade Paul one more time.

Knowing freedom was only nine months out of reach, I found the confidence to declare my intentions. "I'm going to turn Catholic as soon as I'm of age. I don't care what Cecil says. And don't expect me to eat meat on Friday because I'm not going to. And I want to be baptized! It's very important to be baptized!"

"Your mother probably saw to that when you were born," said Paul.

"But I can't be sure. I have to be sure!"

I was baptized in the Presbyterian Church where Paul served as an elder. No one objected because I refused meat on Friday. Paul went so far as to ask Rita to serve macaroni and cheese and tuna casseroles; it wasn't such a bad idea to have a meatless meal once a week in the interest of saving a little.

Paul brought up Cecil's vendetta against the Catholic Church for not honoring his marriage to Beatrice.

"I'm warning you – Cecil won't take it very well if you convert – and he will certainly never stand for you becoming a nun!"

Rita thought I'd been brainwashed. "Now that she's out from under the influence of the nuns she'll soon lose interest in becoming one."

Letters from St. Thomas arrived in flattering numbers. Pat was looking for a new partner; Sisters Rose and Claire urged me to keep painting. Paul felt the letters were nothing more than a campaign to keep me tied into the Catholic faith. I shared my awards of the previous year in an attempt to prove the letters sincere.

"I wouldn't let that go to my head if I were you. Don't you think coming from St. Thomas might have swayed the judges?"

"Are you insinuating I didn't deserve them?"

"It seems more likely that there may have been a little charity thrown in. They probably thought you were a real orphan and judged you by a different standard."

It was just like him to say something like that. He was downright stingy with compliments. Even Rita, after preparing herself for a night out was forced to beg for approval with a straight out "How do I look?" How one looked was as important to Rita as it ever was, so we made a run on the local stores to fill in with what we could salvage from the wardrobe of my sophomore year. This time the emphasis was on how little we could get by on rather than "the very latest."

Betsy was at the back door, right on time the day school started.

"What was it like living in a place like that?"

I spoke fondly of St. Thomas, and shared my plans to become a nun.

"You better be sure. Once you get into that sort of thing I hear you can never get out of it."

☙

The boys still lined up on the steps to judge the girls the first day of school. I couldn't help but notice that some of them had grown up in my absence.

"Hi, Dorian. Welcome back!" Bobby Clark was walking toward me, looking like a studious Clark Kent in his letter sweater. He stepped along side of me and escorted me into the school.

Betsy caught up with me at my locker. "What did he say? What did he say?"

"I don't remember. I wasn't paying attention."

"He's the captain of the basketball team! He's just about the most popular boy in the entire school! He walked you all the way to your locker!"

"So?"

"What did he say to you – what did you say to him?"

"I don't remember." What I did remember was feeling conspicuous; staring at my feet because I couldn't look him in the face, knowing that others were staring; that I was blushing.

The girls crowded Bobby in the hall between classes. I stole looks only if I was sure he couldn't catch me at it. Bobby Clark was different; I wasn't afraid of him. It wasn't long before I was thoroughly taken with him, and a good thing it was too, because when Rita told me she was renting my room out to two school teachers for fifty dollars a month, I needed a diversion.

"You'll probably enjoy their company. They seem like very nice girls."

"Where am I going to sleep?"

"You can bed down in the laundry room. Paul is going to run a pipe for your clothes in the space under the stairs."

Every ounce of self-esteem gained from St. Thomas drained off in a single afternoon. My self-respect wasn't worth fifty dollars a month; it warranted no more than a corner of a gray concrete blocked room crawling with water pipes. I hosed down the box springs Paul brought in from the garage and crammed my clothes under the stairs. Rita gave me a discarded bath mat and some retired cut-off kitchen curtains for the window above the washing machine. A drain in the center of the concrete floor took on the role of a large, ridiculing eye. The very latest in washing machines, a mangle or wringer, sink and water heater lined up under the window near the ceiling. I was sick with feelings of servitude, the contrast between my quarters and Rita's. Her dresser sparkled with perfume bottles and trinkets, and I knew the fifty dollars would contribute to an already crowded clothes closet. She lounged in a pink, puffed bed and read under a porcelain lamp. I put my back against the concrete wall, read with the help of a naked ceiling light bulb, or sat in the dark having stingy-basement-window-time, wondering if someone like me was wondering if someone like them lived on one of the lights they were watching at the other end of the universe, and often recalled how Cecil used to have similar thoughts; just as often wondered what kind of thoughts he was presently having; what he and his precious Barbara were doing. And what did Maria think about at the end of her day?

I began to dwell on those less fortunate than myself: the Blackfeet Indians on the reservation nearby who lived in makeshift shanties. I was in the basement; but I was in a house. My blankets were shrunken and discolored; but I was warm. The Indians stuffed their jackets with newspapers for insulation; I had a coat. Then there was the woman who worked behind the soda fountain at Clark's Drug Store: her son was blind. He would always be blind. She would probably always be working behind the counter; the Indians would always be stuffing their jackets. I wasn't on a reservation; or blind. I wasn't born Jewish, in Germany; never subjected to the horrors of war as a civilian or soldier. I could tolerate insult; it was only temporary. As soon as I graduated everything would improve. Someday I was going to have it all! Some people would never have anything but a small portion of the pie.

Reflections of this sort invariably brought me to the open-armed statue of Christ and turned my sights to the future, taking me beyond the magic age of 18 or 21; far, far into the future to a reunion. There was so much more than this life to anticipate. No matter what was happening at the moment, there was the future; and so much to be thankful for. If I was going to keep score, it was to my advantage to do it on that side of the ledger.

అం

There was even the possibility that Bobby Clark liked me as much as Betsy said he did; that he might even ask me to the senior prom. Now that was a thought to grab onto, and with that happy prospect came the equally mind-consuming concern that he might not; hence the decision to begin paying him more attention so he could not mistake my interest. He stood apart from the other boys. I regarded him as a noble, princely chap, and felt none of my usual aversions when he looked my way. He was the kind of boy that, if one was given to outlandish daydreams, one might expect to see him change into a cape and take to the sky. Going to the senior prom with Bobby Clark would make up for a lot!

Eleanor and Maggie were new to teaching, and with only four years separating us, it didn't take long for friendship to kindle.

Maggie said, "I feel rotten about kicking you out of your room. We're gone by seven in the morning, so help yourself to the bathroom."

Eleanor and I swapped sweaters. Maggie shared her jewelry in spite of Rita's warning. "If she loses it she won't be able to replace it, and I won't be responsible."

Rather than an intrusion, the two young women became a blessing; particularly after I started joining them for gab sessions.

"Do you have a boyfriend, Dorian?"

"Not yet."

"Anyone you're interested in?"

"There is somebody – but I'm not saying exactly who – I might jinx it."

Maggie was the more worldly of the two, so I sought her advice.

"How do you get a boy to notice you?"

"Ignore him."

"Huh?"

"It's true. Have you ever had somebody mooning over you until you couldn't stand to be around them?"

Remembering Frank Dyer, I had to agree with her.

"But if I ignore him completely, he'll think I want nothing to do with him."

"The next time you run into him, look him right in the eye, but don't say anything; just keep walking. You have beautiful eyes, Dorian; if you just keep turning them on, sooner or later he'll break down and ask you for a date. Men are like that!"

"They are?"

"And remember; always look your best, even if you just go out in the neighborhood. You never know who you'll run into. In a town this size you have to be on your toes at all times!"

"Anything else?"

"Pay attention to your walk – that's very important – like this." She glided, head up, mincing her steps, shoulders back.

"Keep your feet straight. Don't walk like a man with your feet out to the side like a duck."

My feet were perfectly parallel when I demonstrated my walk. She said, "Not bad, but you'd better work on it."

"Can you dance?"

"Just a little."

We practiced until Maggie said I was good enough to "strut my stuff." I polished my walk in front of Rita's full length mirror when she was gone. Isabel showed me what a little mascara could do for a girl, and the next time Betsy and I went to the Masonic Lodge for a Friday night dance, I felt like a regular *femme fatale*.

The local order of Masons opened their lodge for high school dances Friday and Saturday nights at the request of the town fathers. The juke box played without nickels; parent chaperones checked us in at the door. Friday night was my night out as long as it didn't interfere with something Rita and Paul had going.

Bobby Clark was an outstanding dancer, but he never asked me. Betsy still claimed he "had eyes" for me, but I was beginning to see his first day friendliness as nothing more than just that, until I considered the number of times I caught him watching me in class. Then one Friday night, just as I was sure I had all the evidence I needed to prove he was interested in me, he danced every dance with Peggy Barnes, a devastating redhead with perfect teeth and a tall, statuesque form that forecast movie star potential. It was downright discouraging to watch the two of them on the dance floor. That was the night Betsy said she'd heard they were going steady.

"Look! She's wearing his ring and everything."

Peggy was the best dancer in the school. I'd have to improve my dancing, wear more mascara, start following Maggie's instructions to the letter or give up on him entirely.

The next time Bobby looked at me, I gave him one of Maggie's carefully tutored looks, contacting his eyes for a moment, then purposely turning away, trying my best to look disinterested. Knowing it would take more than a pair of blue eyes to stir him, I mustered my courage and started adding a mysterious smile to my performance. He returned the smile. Soon we were exchanging "Hi's" on a regular basis.

My flirtatious act was drawing a variety of dance partners on Friday nights, but never an invitation from Bobby. Peggy remained his one and only. I told Maggie there was no use thinking about him anymore; he belonged to Peggy. But two months before graduation, when the boys started lining up their dates, I went back to day-dreaming about going to the prom with Bobby. I'd rather miss it altogether than go with someone else.

One afternoon he caught up to me as I was leaving the school grounds. "Hey, Dorian! Wait up! Are you doing anything Friday night?"

"I don't know. I mean I'm not sure yet. I might have to stay home with my cousins."

"Will you know by tomorrow?"

"I think so."

"If you don't have to stay home with your cousins would you go to the movies with me?"

All faculties left me. Of course I would go to the movies with him, but my mouth was twitching; so dry I couldn't answer him. I looked up into a pair of horned rimmed chocolate eyes, nodding my head, hoping he was watching my eyes, and not my misbehaving mouth. As soon as he rounded the corner I took off running.

"Rita! Rita! Bobby Clark asked me out for tomorrow night. Can I go? Please let me go. You aren't going out are you? You've just got to let me go! I've been waiting forever for him to ask me out!"

"Isn't he Butch Clark's son?"

"That's right."

"I'm glad to see a boy of his caliber take an interest in you. You'd better ask Paul what time he wants you home."

Maggie was quite pleased with herself. "Persistence always pays off."

"Not always," Eleanor reminded her. "He hasn't asked her to the prom yet. That's the real test. And with all this suspense, if he doesn't..."

"Don't even think it," Maggie warned.

"No, Eleanor, don't think about anything except what I'm going to wear to the prom."

I returned from my first date, dazed, elated, thanking God for what had turned out to be the most glorious night of my life, and waited up for Maggie and Eleanor to tell them I was going to the prom with Bobby Clark. We planned into the early morning hours; how I would wear my hair; which pair of Maggie's earrings would be the most glamorous.

"You'll need a formal."

"I know. Isn't it exciting? Hope I can get a strapless."

Rita was genuinely pleased. It was one of a girl's most significant milestones, and we were going to get downtown before the best dresses were gone. Dr. McGregor's niece was not going to the prom in anything less than the very latest. I was on my way to a strapless gown. Rita told Paul a girl's senior prom gown was second only to her wedding gown.

And how would they look if I went to the prom in less than what the other girls were wearing?

The Sunday before the dance Paul confronted me. "Who gave you permission to get into the candy I had in the closet?"

"I don't know what you're talking about!"

"Don't you lie to me!"

"I'm not lying! I don't know anything about your candy!"

He pulled me into the hall and flung open the closet door. "There! Up there! I had a full box of Hershey bars – now there's only three left."

He put his face close to mine and growled, "Now you tell me why in the hell you thought you had any right to it?"

"I didn't even know it was up there. Honest! I didn't take your candy."

Colour flooded his face and neck. "You little sneak. You lying little sneak. I'll fix you. You think you're going to the prom, do you? Well, you can just forget about that!"

I stared at him, bewildered, my mind racing for a way out of an impossible turn of events.

"Paul, I know you think you're right, but I swear, I knew nothing about the candy. I've been on a near starvation diet so I'll look good in my formal. It wasn't me! Did you ask Jimmy? I'll bet one of his friends got into it."

"I'm way ahead of you. Jimmy doesn't know anything about it; neither do his friends. And I believe him. My son doesn't lie!"

"Nobody is going to cheat me out of my prom!"

"You'll do as I say if you know what's good for you."

"You're heartless! A girl only gets one senior prom!"

"Then she'd better confess to what she's done. And I won't have any more cock-n-bull stories either. I know you did it, and that's that! Now, own up to it!"

After sobbing out my predicament to Maggie I vowed, one way or another, to go to the prom.

"You certainly will! And we'll help you. Only right now I have no idea how we can pull it off."

⊱

Monday I smuggled my shoes out of the house and gave them to Betsy, who, after confiding my case to Maude, gained her full consent to act as an accomplice. Tuesday Maggie's pearls and matching earrings were in my pocket; a strapless bra, slip and stockings under my sweater on Wednesday. It was Maggie's idea to leave the dress until Friday morning, just in case Rita happened to miss it from under the stairs. She was going to take it back for credit the following week. Fearing such an armful would give me away Maggie folded the dress under a coat and turned it over to Betsy a full half hour before Paul made it to the kitchen for his first cup of coffee. As long as Rita didn't go snooping around under the stairs everything would go according to plan.

I went straight to the Dyer house after school. Bobby and I were doubling with Betsy and her date. When we heard a car kicking up gravel in the driveway we assumed it was time to leave, until Maude gave the alarm.

"Quick, Dorian! Into the basement!"

The chief of police was at the door. "You haven't seen that McGregor girl have you, Maude?"

"What's the trouble?"

"Doc McGregor says she's run off. He's hoppin' mad. Told me to find her and bring her straight home."

"You might tell him to check with the school in Great Falls. I understand she wants to be a nun. She just may have hitched a ride back there."

"Thanks, Maude."

Cut Bank High joined with another school in a neighboring town in order to get a bigger and better dance band. It was a Cinderella evening, well worth whatever punishment Paul was going to levy. We tiptoed into Betsy's room at sunrise after meeting with classmates for breakfast at a truck stop outside of town.

When Maude roused us for lunch, she told us that she had called Paul after we were safely on our way so he wouldn't worry. He asked her to give me a message and an apology. While I was at the dance, Jimmy was caught stealing his last of the candy and confessed that he and his friends had been dipping into it all along.

I went home, made a justified entrance, announcing how I'd been up all night and needed some rest; then I retired to the basement where Maggie and Eleanor waited the details of the past twenty-four hours.

Paul's only comment about the incident was a sheepish, "I really don't know what to say except I was wrong."

৵

When Bobby told me he was planning to study Engineering at Missoula State University, I was mulling over the choices Paul delivered "straight from the horse's mouth."

"Your Dad says you should decide between nurse's training or secretarial school; there'll never be a shortage of work for either one. Personally, I think you should give some thought to becoming a dental hygienist. The day's coming when they'll be in great demand."

Any notions of entering the convent left me the night of the prom. Someday I was going to get married; but until then, I opted for Columbus School of Nursing, and looked to September, freedom, and the beginning of a bright new future. While I was planning an idyllic summer with Bobby Clark, Cecil was working on some plans of his own.

"You'd better get yourself packed up," said Paul. "Your Dad wants you in Canada for the summer." An invitation to spend the summer with Cecil? It didn't add up.

"I've made arrangements for you to spend the summer at the Prince of Wales Hotel in Waterton Lakes," Cecil said. "They take on students for the summer season. It pays $80 a month, plus room and board."

"What kind of work?"

"You'll be a chambermaid. It's probably the best job there. You'll collect some healthy tips from those wealthy tourists. If you don't have money you don't stay at the Prince of Wales! You can lay away a pretty tidy sum for school next fall.

151

Columbus is a working hospital so they go easy on the tuition. Of course I'll take care of that end of things! You'll have your earnings from the hotel for pocket money, and I understand you can work in the hospital on your days off. You should be able to take care of all your expenses quite nicely."

After cleaning up after tourists for three months I was determined to return as a guest someday. And I planned to leave a twenty dollar tip for the chambermaids when I checked out.

ॐ

Isabel and Maureen were also headed for nursing school. We met up in Cut Bank right after Labour Day. Maureen's brother, Ralph, anxious to show off a new yellow convertible, offered to drive us to Great Falls.

The excitement of finally being on my way tempered the sting of discovering the details of how Bobby went back to Peggy during the summer. She was going to Missoula University just to be with him.

"You know what they say," said Ralph, "absence makes the heart grow fonder…"

"For somebody else," Maureen chimed in.

"Cheer up, Dorian. You'll probably end up marrying a doctor and live in a fancy house in a big city someday!"

"I probably will!"

"You're certainly headed for the right place to hook a doctor."

"We all are," said Maureen. "The pre-med students have their classes with the nursing students at Columbus."

Chapter 17

"You must have a special mission in life, Dorian…"

Charlie was my chemistry lab partner, and for as long as Charlie could remember, his father had been anticipating the day he could practice medicine with his only son. I became infatuated with Charlie on the spot, and saw it as an act of Providence that he invited me to the spring dance and promised to fix Maureen up with one of his buddies.

Two hours before we were due to leave I was standing at the ironing board putting the finishing touches on my formal. I'd been pushing myself through the week in spite of severe abdominal pain, dismissing it as a bout with the flu, fully expecting it to run its course.

"The minute we get back from the dance I'll have to stop by the emergency room. Something is drastically wrong with my insides! I must have something more than the flu."

Maureen lowered her make-up mirror. "I thought you were over it."

I went from Maureen's face to the blinding light of the emergency room.

"What happened?"

"You fainted!"

"I've never done that before."

"You're on your way to surgery, just as soon as we get an authorization from your next of kin."

"But I've got a date for the dance!"

Dr. Nordstrom was a favorite with the student nurses, and when any of us needed treatment he was generally the one who attended us.

"You won't be going anywhere tonight."

"What's wrong with me?"

"A hot appendix! And I do mean HOT!"

"But the pain isn't in my appendix; it's more to the back. Can't you give me a shot and operate later?"

"I'll see you upstairs."

Dr. Nordstrom was with me when I came out of the anesthesia. "You must have a special mission in life, Dorian; you've cheated death twice tonight."

"I did?"

"First of all we removed a foot of gangrenous intestine. The appendix was as big around as my thumb; completely strangulated the bowel. I don't see how you managed to live – let alone stay on your feet with a mess like that stewing inside you. If the bowel had ruptured… and that's not all!"

"It isn't?"

"An oil tanker ran a red light and slammed into the side of Charlie's car – right where you would have been sitting. If you had kept your date with Charlie you wouldn't be alive. It's a good thing you fainted when you did. The impact would have ruptured your intestines, even if you survived the crash itself. Either way you'd be dead."

"How's Charlie? And Maureen? And what's his name?"

"Charlie's the worst off with three fractured vertebrae. Maureen has a nasty concussion and thirty stitches in her scalp. We can't be sure yet, but she may have some permanent damage to the right eye. The other fellow got off with a simple fracture and some bruises."

Dr. Nordstrom said there was so such thing as coincidence. Escaping death twice within the same night (particularly the same hour) from his point of view was due to the efforts of a diligent guardian angel who stepped in to thwart the play of circumstances against an individual life.

What would he say if he knew that I'd cheated death before? Would he say I had even more important things to do with my life? Even without the accident, Dr. Nordstrom was shaking his head days later over the timing of the events, given the consequences of a ruptured bowel and the number of people who died of peritonitis. Captivated by his theory, I shared it with Isabel who wasn't the least impressed and attributed it to fate. Charlie said it was downright spooky. He only wished he'd done what he thought of doing in the first place: given his friend the keys and stayed at the hospital with me.

Maureen made a complete recovery. Charlie was forced to drop out of school for an indefinite period of time, and in my second year at Columbus, I met Jonesy.

Robert Jones, a sandy-haired charmer stationed at Chanute Air Force Base, was given to bragging about his father's spread in Kansas the way Betsy did.

"Do you think you'd like living on a farm?"

"Why do you ask?"

"Just wonderin'."

Four months after our first meeting he said he loved me; took my face into his big rough hands and told me he loved me more than he ever thought he could love a girl.

"Let's get married."

First I said yes.

Then I said no.

Maybe we should wait until I finished school.

He pleaded; overwhelmed me with pledges of happy-ever-aftering. The potential of belonging to somebody, being loved, cherished, took command of any sensibility, and the longings of a lifetime now within my grasp far outweighed the occasions he drank a little too much; all men drank. And women naturally flirted with attractive men.

There was only one thing to consider.

Jonesy loved me!
I was that easily bought.

&

Cecil raised the question of pregnancy when I sought his permission to marry, and argued against five months as sufficient time to decide upon the person I was going to spend the rest of my life with. "Remember, once you've made your bed, you'll have to lie in it. It seems to me, if the lad really loved you he'd be willing to wait until you finish your training." We struck a bargain. I would wait another sixty days before making up my mind. "Then, if you're still hell bent on getting married, I'll give my consent. You're sure you're not pregnant?"

"How could you even suggest such a thing!"

Jonesy agreed to wait another 30 days, then "either we get married, or we call it quits!"

It was the chance of a lifetime. It might very well be my only chance. I wasn't going to let it slip through my fingers. American law required that I marry in accordance with the laws of my own country; Canadian law required my father's signature on the license. Maria just happened to be visiting Mary, and stayed over for the wedding. She took me aside to say that she and Cecil were seeing more of each other and it was only a matter of time before they would be living together again. She was teary-eyed and wished us the very best. I hugged her and told her I was happy for her, secretly counting the times I'd heard her say it, wondering how many times she would say it before it actually happened, if it ever did. And I wanted it to; for her sake more than anyone's.

Cecil approved of Jonesy; I was lucky to have found such a nice chap. He expected me to do everything in my power to make a go of the marriage, and to get us off to a good start he sprung for a two day honeymoon in Banff as a wedding present.

Promises of love and devotion went rancid our first month. A demanding, irritable personality escaped me during our courtship; his real identity clouded by an urgency to have what I felt was long overdue to me. His tenderness toward me quickly cooled, replaced by a disappointing affection toward alcohol which threatened to eat up a big portion of our military allotment for married personnel living off base. There was coarseness in his manner, and use of offending words. He thought it was high time I got busy and found a job. When he stooped to cursing me for suggesting he "lay off the booze," I was forced to come to terms with the adage, "love is blind." Jonesy wasn't acting at all like he did before we were married. He wasn't the chance of a lifetime after all.

What would Cecil say about this nice chap now?

I knew what he'd say.

"You've made your bed!"

Jonesy was resentful because Cecil didn't give us a wedding present in the form of cash. Even though he picked up the tab for a two day honeymoon, it wasn't the same. Cecil could afford more than that. The wedding didn't cost much. Evidently money was more important to Jonesy than I understood it to be.

I found work as a typist at one of the hotels, relieving Jonesy of his complaint over having "no extra money to play with." I thought if I really put my heart into it I could insure a better finish to a bad start, and make a heroic effort to please him. It appeared that things were taking a turn for the better; until he started coming home late. It all came apart in a single phone call.

"Jonesy's been two-timing you."

"I don't believe you! He'd never do a thing like that!"

"I dare you to come down to the Brass Rail. You'll get the shock of your life if you do! He's with her right now. They've been meeting here for quite awhile. She always drinks Pink Ladies."

"Who are you?"

"It doesn't matter who I am. The only reason I'm calling is because we're always the last to know. If you don't believe me get down here and see for yourself...."

What a miserable bed! What a fool! And there was no one to blame this time; not even fate. Everything I'd wanted, a home and family of my own, stolen by a woman who drank my hard-earned money; just like Graham drank my mother's.

I'd married Graham; a charming ladies' man with a drinking problem.

And they never changed.

☙

What could be more therapeutic to a broken heart than one's own child? Jonesy wasn't going to cheat me out of everything! He paled when I told him a baby was due.

"I thought you nurses knew how to prevent that sort of thing. Now what in the hell are we going to do?"

Hotel policy forbade the employment of expectant mothers. Jonesy took my dismissal at the third month with a pained expression, opened a beer, flipped on the radio and ran his hands through his hair.

"If you'd been more careful we wouldn't be in this fix."

"If you're worried about the money, we can cut back a little and live on what you make plus our allotment. And you'll be out of the service soon. You'll go back to farming – everything will be just fine."

"We won't have one extra cent. You know that don't you?"

That's right, Jonesy, I thought. And you'll have to go easy on the drinking. You won't be able to chase around with your drinking buddies because you won't have the money. And you certainly won't be buying Pink Ladies.

"You wanna baby? You can have one. But you'll raise it yourself. And there's something else you ought to know.

158

I don't love you. I don't guess I ever did. I thought you came from money."

"Money?"

"Your uncle's a dentist. And didn't you say your Dad inherited part of an oil company?"

"What difference does that make?"

"Did you really think I wanted to end up like my old man? Rotting on some stinkin' farm in Kansas? I thought your Dad could work me in at his company. But it doesn't matter anymore. I want out!"

"You can't just walk out on me. I'll go to your commanding officer."

"Suit yourself. My duty's up next year. And I don't give a damn if they bust me. They can't force me to live with you."

"I'll still be entitled to an allotment check."

"Only 'til I'm out of the service. Then what'll you do? If you can't find me you can't make me pay!"

He jumped to his feet, walked into the bathroom and slammed the door. I emptied his wallet, picked up the car keys, and fled up the stairs to find a pay phone.

"You should be calling your father, not me; we're not responsible for you. He is!"

"Please Rita, I need some advice. Let me come down – just for a day. I don't know what to do."

"You can't come down here – Paul sold out everything – we're going back to Illinois. The movers will be here the end of the week!"

"It's just for overnight. Please? Rita, I'm pregnant!"

"Now why did you have to go and do a stupid thing like that? He hasn't beaten you has he?"

"No. But he's going to leave."

Rita let out an exaggerated sigh. "All right! But you can only stay overnight – no more than that. Understand?"

"I'll never forget you for this, Rita."

It wasn't until the last of the city showed up in the rear-view mirror that the full impact hit me. Scalding tears of foolish choices blurred the road. How easy it would be to take my hands off the wheel at the next curve. I flirted with oblivion – closing my eyes – one second, two, four.

It would be the best choice I ever made.

It would be the last choice I'd ever have to make.

Replaying the early weeks of our courtship I knew I'd talked up Paul and Cecil – their social and financial positions – done it because Jonesy might see me as less of a person without family ties. After listening to him describe his family, the farm, what he had to contribute to our union was so much greater than mine. I wanted to make myself more desirable to him, and ultimately his parents. I argued aloud: for death, for life, scourging and howling in remorse and rage. When I came to a skidding stop in front of the house in Cut Bank I collapsed over the steering wheel, sobbing.

Paul sprinted down the driveway. "You'll do yourself in driving like that!" He glanced at his watch. "That was one quick trip, young lady." He opened the door and pried my fingers loose.

"Rita! Get the brandy!"

"I need some aspirin. My head aches clear down to my ears."

Rita said, "Trust a man to pull a stunt like this," after hearing my story for the second time. Paul said my young husband was talking out of fear. Once he came to terms with the responsibilities that went with fatherhood, he would once again declare his love. But then he didn't know about the woman who drank Pink Ladies with Jonesy. And my pride wasn't up to telling.

"He said he didn't love me; and he meant it."

The brandy went to work. I curled up on Rita's fat sofa. Paul covered me with an afghan then shuffled off to the kitchen for a snack. Rita was worn out after a day of packing and went to bed early. I felt the weight of a second blanket before Paul turned out the lights. He found me rummaging in the medicine cabinet early the next morning.

"Still have the headache?"

"My ears are killing me. I must be running a fever. Got any aspirin with codeine?"

He touched my forehead. "By golly you do have a fever."
The thermometer registered 103 degrees.

"A fever during pregnancy is nothing to fool with. We'd better have you checked. There's a new man in town; he's taken the office next to me. I'll give him a call."

"No! Please don't do that. The aspirin's sure to knock the fever. I'll check into the base clinic as soon as I get back."

Paul insisted. My temperature was nudging 104 when the young physician arrived and ordered me to the hospital.

"I can get free medical attention at the base. If I leave right now I can see a doctor today."

"This couldn't be worse timing," Paul said. "I wonder how your Dad is going to handle this new turn of events."

Bilateral abscess of the ears which, according to the young physician, could have resulted in complications to my pregnancy had Paul not been so diligent. Injections round the clock should soon have the infection under control. And "no" he didn't foresee any adverse effects on the baby.

Paul and Rita came by later in the day. It was an awkward visit, with Rita determined that nothing disrupt their plans to leave on time. She had great expectations over the change about to take place in their lives. Rita was finally jumping out of a little pond back into a big one.

"I've called Cecil. He'll be down directly; probably sometime the day after tomorrow."

"Was he upset?"

"To say the least."

Cecil made a blustering entrance. "I swear, girl, you must have a curse on your head!" He pulled up a chair next to the bed. "I've had a long talk with Jonesy. His folks are willing to take you in until the baby comes."

"Take me in?"

"You'll have to go to Kansas. You can't come with me. Maria and I are on the outs again. I have no idea how things will turn out."

I gave Rita a helpless look.

"Oh, no you don't. You're not coming with us. You belong with your in-laws at a time like this."

I looked from face to face. "You can't wait to get rid of me, can you? None of you ever care about how I might feel about what happens to me."

Rita shot to her feet. "That's a fine thing to say! And after all we've done for you over the years – taking you in the way we did!"

"Why did you take me in, Rita?"

She snarled, "When a stray dog comes sniffing around, you feel guilty if you don't feed it."

Paul hurried to the other side of the bed. "Don't listen to her! She didn't mean it!"

"Oh shut up, Paul, stop pretending! You feel the same way. And so do you, Cecil. For all the trouble this damned kid has caused, it would have been better for everyone if they'd tied a stone around her neck when she was born and drowned her."

"I didn't ask to be born, you know!"

I turned toward the wall; pulled the pillow over my face. A hand lit on my shoulder; I shook it off. Cecil was bending over me, explaining how everyone was just a little heated up over what was happening. "Don't pay attention to Rita. You know how short-tempered she is."

They stepped into the corridor to talk. Someone forgot to close the door all the way.

"I'm sick and tired of her myself," Cecil was saying.

I was sick and tired of me, too, and the mess I'd made by marrying Jonesy. I was going to have a baby without any guarantee of where we would lay our heads.

Rita reminded Cecil that he was the one who adopted me, not them. He had no choice but to take me to Calgary until my ears healed. Paul moved his household to Illinois two days later; Cecil and I started toward the border.

"I really have no business being away from the office. I wanted to fly you up to Calgary, but the doctor wouldn't have it; said your ears can't take the cabin pressure."

I refused to apologize for his inconvenience; it was all I could do to handle my own. Now that I knew Jonesy's heart, I had my own problems to think about: being pregnant without a husband to stand by me certainly measured up to any annoyance I'd brought upon Cecil. Oh I felt guilty enough. It *was* my fault – unless Cecil had hit on the truth when he suggested I had a curse on my head. In that case there wasn't much I could do about anything. No sense apologizing for a curse. Still I had to admit that he showed tolerance; he could have ripped me for being so stupid as to marry Jonesy in the first place; for getting pregnant in the second place. But he didn't.

"You'll get over this. Jonesy will come to his senses. He's not the first young buck to pull a stunt like this."

"Do you know what he told me? He said he married me because he thought I came from money. That's downright...."

"I wouldn't be too hard on him if I were you. After all, the truth is – economics plays a part in every marriage – whether it's brought out in the open or not."

"Why are you sticking up for him?"

"I'm just trying to clear up the facts so we can get the two of you back together where you belong."

"And what if I don't want him back?"

"That's pride talking! It's easy to take that attitude now; wait until you've got a child in your arms." He took his eyes off the road for a moment and gave me a sobering look. "Once we make our beds we have to lie in them. Your husband will have to take responsibility for his family. I'll not do it for him. I'm going to make the most of whatever time I have left. Don't be too hasty to turn away from him, even if he's hurt you."

Cecil had it all wrong; pride wasn't talking; pride was hiding Jonesy's female drinking companion. If he knew about her I wondered how optimistic he would be about a reconciliation.

His voice turned husky. "People come in pretty much the same package no matter where you find them. Sometimes it's wiser to stick with what you've got. I'd be a lot better off financially if I'd learned some of these lessons a bit earlier in life."

"Does it always boil down to money?"

He threw back his head and indulged in a hearty laugh. "You have so much to learn."

The probability of finding true love was a little like panning for gold. A person could spend years wading in streams searching for nuggets. Not everyone ended up with nuggets – probably a lot more ended up with dirt and gravel. People with curses on their heads really had no business looking for nuggets.

Cecil's apartment was in a new building overlooking a park, a far cry from his one-room efficiency days, and could have been furnished by Rita herself. Once final arrangements were in place for me to live out my pregnancy in Kansas, he was on his way to Edmonton. Jonesy's folks were sending a ticket. After the waiting period prescribed by the doctor, I was to get myself to Kansas. Cecil left money for groceries and suggested I give Mary a call.

"She'd be glad to see you."

I imagined how the conversation would go:

"Hi, Mary, it's Dorian."

"Where are you?"

"I'm in Calgary. You'll never guess what happened…."

"What are you going to do now?"

"I thought I'd give Kansas a try. I've never been to Kansas. Maybe Kansas will work out!"

And that is just about how it would go; so I never called.

Chapter 18

"How could I endure these people, this place....?"

The flight was delayed. I was off to a poor start with Freda Jones, who was nothing like Jonesy described, with her bloated body and round summer-scorched face.

"I can't waste anymore time around her. We gotta long drive ahead. There's a dozen cows waitin' ta be milked!"

There was something foreboding about the lank man carrying my bags. His narrow face suggested a tracing of the grim reaper: skin plastered to cheek bones, eyes set deep in bony cages. He wore grease splattered overalls and smelled of stale sweat.

I rode in the back seat behind Willard Jones. Every time I caught sight of his penetrating eyes dangling in the rearview mirror they were looking at me. Freda fussed over her hair with dry, hard-working hands, visibly irritated over the heat and dust of the trip, the delay, and in the absence of a spirit of welcome I could draw my own conclusions. I wasn't welcome!

We split from the highway three hours out of Wichita onto a country road leading to a two storied porch-skirted farm house. The place conjured a host of trepidations, as if once I stepped through its doors it would never release me; as if I were about to play a part in a sinister movie in which the heroine was done away with. The day was all but gone. It was difficult to assess the place except for a barn and odds and ends of machinery. Freda's cows were complaining nearby.

Willard reached for an outside switch. An amber light grabbed his face, accentuating his grim bone structure.

"It certainly is deserted out here, isn't it?"

"Yep. Nearest neighbors 'bout two miles in all directions. It takes a good 20 minutes to make it to town. I 'spect it'll be too quiet for your likin'."

He took my luggage to the only upstairs bedroom in use, and stood at the door like a bellhop expecting a token, staring at me. Then he suddenly stepped forward and put his hand on my stomach. I froze.

"Five months?"

I stepped back. "Yes. Now, if you don't mind, I'm awfully tired."

My initial aversion to him intensified. I felt violated, threatened because he felt free to touch me. He meandered toward the door and turned for a last look before going downstairs.

After a disturbing night of country noises and reflections of a man's face, I woke to Willard's figure framed in the door.

I clutched at the covers. "What do you want?"

"Nothin'. Just checkin' on ya."

He grinned. "I'll say this for my boy, he sure can pick 'em. He could always pick 'em."

The sight of my father-in-law poised at the door came as introduction to his true self. I turned over, giving him my back; a move to hide my uneasiness and induce him to leave, and only after I heard the sound of his stocking feet padding down the stairs did I dare to move and close the door again. Feelings of helplessness and resignation at sharing a house with another disturbed individual was more than I could take. Either something was wrong with me because I seemed to have an affinity for these types of situations or something was wrong with a lot of men. Either way, it was something to cry about. So I did.

Freda assumed I'd want to make myself useful while I waited for my baby. "I don't 'spose ya know how ta milk a cow, do ya?"

"Sorry."

Willard showed his teeth and said, "I'd like ta see ya teach her ta ketch lunch."

She snickered. "I don't expect a city girl ta be any good at ketchin' chickens."

Freda stalked the birds, eyeing one, then another. Once she made her selection it was over in a matter of seconds; a hen caught; a neck wrung. With a magician's flourish she produced an ax, flung the fryer onto a stump, lowered the ax and tossed the bird to the ground, sans head, to thrash and spew blood in all directions. It was hot. I was still prone to morning sickness. The experience of watching her kill, pluck, dismember, fry and serve up the bird sent me running to the bathroom.

"If you're goin' ta puke every time a chickun' gets killed, you're goin' ta be in trouble. We eat 'em six outta seven days."

I passed on lunch and sat at the table nursing a cup of weak tea. Freda described the choicest parts of the bird: the feet and "the part that went over the fence last."

"I like ta save the feet 'til last."

She picked up a curled foot and riveted her teeth up and down the toes corn-on-the-cob fashion, finishing with one long, rude sucking of each of the digits.

How could I endure these people, this place, until my body gave up the prize? I was repulsed by their habits, lack of manners and coarse speech. The anxiety of Willard's face at the bedroom door kept me on edge. I closed it before I went to bed; it was always open when I woke up. Sometimes he was there when I opened my eyes; sometimes he wasn't. I pushed a chair under the door handle, a futile attempt to discourage a determined man. His visits brought with him others of his kind: the kind that lived in the chronicles of a child's worst fear.

I bought a hook and eye lock my first trip into town, along with my own screw driver and small hammer and installed it on the bedroom door; then hid the tools under my pillow, so distraught and defensive over his spying presence that I felt it necessary to be prepared for every eventuality. The handle turned the morning after; a few moments later Willard's feet were padding down the hall. At his first opportunity to get me out of range of Freda, he said, "What's the matter sweetie? Afraid the boogie man is gonna git ya?"

It would be easy to force the lock. I counted on his not wanting Freda to discover his morning habit of loitering at my bedroom door to look at me while I slept. He always took off his shoes before he sneaked upstairs, so if worst came to worst I was going to go to her. When I told him as much he laughed at me, but to the best of my knowledge he never tried the door again. There was no way I could prevent his ogling during the day.

Letters from Jonesy started to arrive near the end of my seventh month, begging forgiveness. He really did love me. He was arranging leave time to coincide with my delivery date. I wasn't falling for anymore promises; I would not have him around when my baby was born. But his letters persisted until I began entertaining their potential.

If he was sincere….

If he had changed….

Maybe we could redeem our marriage.

He made his entrance five days before David was born, as though we were never estranged; as though our life was set in order for the next 50 years, suggesting we let bygones be bygones and start over. I was willing to try, for the sake of pride that longed to say I'm not a fool after all. And I was willing to try for the sake of the baby – but only if we moved away from the farm.

Chapter 19

*"I finished the day on my knees;
counting my blessings…"*

"I am sorry to have to tell you that your son was born with a cleft palate. Are you familiar with the term?"

I shut my eyes, and thought, "Dear God! Why?"

"Then you understand that the roof of his mouth is open into the nasal passage. Feeding will be difficult and crucial. He can't nurse or take a bottle, so we'll have to train him to drink from a glass. You have a real challenge on your hands; an open palate is every bit as much a hardship for the mother as it is the child."

He laid a fatherly hand on my shoulder and explained the surgical options for children like David.

"You can thank your lucky stars he doesn't have the hair lip which generally goes along with this. Your son will never have a scar on his upper lip like the majority of children with this birth defect."

It wasn't my stars – lucky or unlucky. What a stupid thing to say! Didn't he know who was in charge of things? Things like birth defects and broken hearts? There was absolutely nothing to be thankful for.

It wasn't fair!

Nothing about life was fair!

The Someday Kid

The first time I got my hands on David I gave him a thorough going over. It took all I had to look into his mouth when he cried. The sight of the gaping hole provoked bloody images of what it would take to close it. Why God? Why? Then a strange submission came over me. I had to look to the future – the remedy that would correct what was wrong; look to it with such determination that it crowded out any notion of curses, or of passing them on to my offspring.

The initial anger and sense of injustice over the cleft palate was tempered by a surprising acceptance and determination to make the best of the hand that was dealt me. The doctor was right – it could have been worse. A hair lip would have been much worse. How many mothers would gladly trade places with me? Maybe one of the babies sharing the nursery with David couldn't have surgery; what was wrong would stay wrong. Determined as I was to hold to this line of thinking, I was still prone to vacillating between being spared and accusing God, depending on the strength of my perspective at the time over what David escaped; what he could not escape.

While other babies were delivered to their mothers' arms, David stayed in the nursery, fighting for nourishment, resembling a baby bird with tiny flailing wings; opening his mouth as the glass was pressed to his mouth, trying to nurse from a cold, comfortless glass. At the end of his trying arms, angry baby fists quivered in frustration. He sputtered at the glass, struggling for food, while I strained at the nursery window, working my mouth in support. When he appeared to have a good mouthful he gagged and lost the formula through his nose.

David fought the glass feeder.

I fought God and the suggestion of curses.

Getting formula into David was intimidating and exhausting. He choked and screamed through his feedings, unable to

170

retain but a small portion of formula until I experimented with a variety of nipples and bottles for a better system. Cross cuts in the nipple allowed a steady trickle of formula, and prevented much of the gagging, as long as the bottle was tilted at just the right angle. I sat on the floor with my knees bent and propped him against my thighs to brace him in an upright position to prevent choking. David took the nipple eagerly and learned to work his gums so that he was actually chewing the formula from the nipple.

Jonesy never counted on a "defective child."

"He is not defective! He has a cleft palate. Surgery will correct that."

"Where's the money gonna come from? I'm getting out of the Air Force soon. We can't take him to the base clinic. And Doc told me it'll take three or four operations before he's right."

Freda whined. "We're just poor farmers. Where we gonna come up with enuff money…."

"Maybe your folks?" Willard piped in.

"Folks? All I've got is a bunch of relatives who aren't really my relatives. I can't depend on them! If we start saving right away, and you get a job as soon as you're out of the service, we'll have enough to swing the surgery when the time comes. We can do it!"

"You're nuts, do ya know that? Nuts! We don't have a chance of getting enough money to raise this kid. I'm not sacrificing the rest of my life. You wanted him – you take care of him. He was your idea! Remember? You tricked me!"

He was right. I had tricked him. The decision to have a baby was mine alone, knowing he would be an unwilling father in the beginning, that a child would prevent my working and curtail his drinking, yet I'd never really relinquished hope that once the baby was born Jonesy might mend his ways and become what I needed him to be, to both me and our child. But then he'd also tricked me by proposing under false pretenses, courting the security he thought he was marrying into, just as determined to escape a predictable future on the farm as I was to escape a discrediting past; and for me to announce to the world that there really never was anything wrong with me after all. I had the ring to prove it.

It was too late to argue rights and wrongs. This time Jonesy was walking. Whatever happened to David from now on was up to me. I was 21 years old; swamped with responsibility in a hostile household. I suspected Jonesy's letters and offers to let bygones be bygones probably stemmed from Cecil's prompting him to be a man and go back to his wife and child. If David were born a normal child Jonesy might have done just that. But David wasn't normal – Jonesy wasn't going to do the manly thing – and I had to find a place to live.

Stray dog or no stray dog, I risked a call to Rita. It was close to Christmas. She couldn't turn me down at Christmas.

"Your Dad was right! You are cursed!"

She was not the least surprised at Jonesy's parents. "I didn't think they'd be anything to shout about. You know what they say: the apple doesn't fall far from the tree. We'll let Cecil know what's going on. I'm sorry things worked out the way they did. We'll do what we can."

Rita's compassion brought me to tears. Cursed or not I had a place to take David. Thank God she reacted the way she did. I would forever be in her debt. There were so many problems to work out. How was Rita going to take it after she found out I exaggerated? I did have money laid aside, but never told her that my allotment checks would soon be cut off now that Jonesy was about to become a civilian. I could find work; find someone to watch David during the day. We could get by with a single room. How much could that cost? And Rita did say we could stay for awhile; that was all I needed to establish myself in Illinois.

We intruded on the Christmas party Rita and Paul were hosting for all the neighbors who went "overboard" to make them feel at home when they moved in. They had a lot of catching up to do to repay all the invitations extended to them.

After the party Rita started cooing over David.

"He's not very filled out, is he?"

"He lost some ground in the beginning because I couldn't get his formula down him. He's starting to pick up now."

I turned to Paul. "You've lost so much weight. Have you been ill?"

Paul opened then closed his mouth, deferring to Rita. "Oh, you don't know what we've been through. It's been one thing after another since we got here. They took out most of his stomach. He hemorrhaged one night. It was terrible! I thought we'd lose him. And when they opened him up he was full of ulcers. It happened just as he was due to open up his new office."

Moving to the Midwest had apparently sweetened Rita. She ran a caring hand over Paul's balding head and said, "In a year or two we'll be back on our feet, won't we honey?"

Paul's face divided into a broad grin. It was heartwarming to see them that way.

"I haven't heard from Cecil since I left Calgary. How is he?"

"Oh, you don't know about that either. He spent some time in the hospital. He recognized the symptoms and got himself into treatment before it got out of hand. He's in Lethbridge with Maria. They've finally patched things up."

Maria's blue and white storybook house came to mind. I was happy for her; happy for me. Evidently there was good reason not to hear from Cecil while I was in Kansas.

"Does he know about David?"

"Paul gave him the news. He took it well, but compared to what happened to Bill…."

"What happened to Bill?"

"We only just found out ourselves. His first child, a girl, was born retarded. He didn't say anything until recently. They've had another one, a boy, and he's fine. But nothing can be done for the little girl."

I was stunned, overcome with sympathy for Bill, and gave myself a mental dressing down for ever feeling sorry for myself, knowing a cleft palate could be repaired. No operation would ever change the outcome for Bill's family.

"Cecil took it very badly. We're hoping it doesn't bring on a relapse."

I finished the day on my knees; counting my blessings. And at the top of the list was that all David had was a cleft palate; that Rita and Paul were willing to take me in one more time; that they refrained from throwing my mistakes in my face.

∂

Rita ordered me to place David in a foster home and start looking for a job after I revealed my true financial picture; and do it "ee-mmediately!"

"I can't put him in a foster home! Do you have any idea what could happen to him in a place like that? I'll never do that!"

"I've arranged for a few interviews. I checked these people out myself. We can't have the baby crying every three hours during the night. Paul needs his rest. It won't hurt to meet a few of these women...."

At the third house I refused to get out of the car. "This won't be any different than the others. Did you count the children at that last place? David is very susceptible to infections. He isn't going into a foster home. He isn't an orphan! I'll find another way."

I was back on my knees, pleading for someone to take care of David; someone who didn't need a lot of money.

I could understand Rita's reluctance to step up and offer to relieve me of my problems by taking care of David and letting us stay where we were. I didn't belong in her home. I wasn't her daughter. I was old enough to take responsibility for myself, and the child I was so determined to have; but knowing the facts didn't give me the grace or stamina to face them.

Cecil called to say he was sorry and urged me to get an attorney to make sure Jonesy paid child support. I offered my sympathy for Bill's daughter.

"That's life! There is nothing we can do about it. I'm glad to hear there is something they can do for David."

Chapter 20

*"There would eventually come an accounting for my time
on earth.... I decided life deserved one more shot...."*

Alice, a trim, high-energy little woman in her late forties,
lived directly across the street. Her children were married; off
living in other states. She and her husband were members of
the Baptist Church and believed in "serving the Lord through
service to others." Alice had the entire day to herself, and as
her husband was "one of those neat, tidy men, who never
makes a lick of extra work," she was only too happy to be of
help, considering it a pleasant diversion to her otherwise tidy,
tedious life to have an infant to occupy her time. Her husband
could sleep through anything; David would be no bother.

"Feel free to come over anytime. And at night, if you see
a light on, you're more than welcome."

My impulse to throw my arms around her and plant a
kiss on her cheek followed on the heels of her offer to assume
the mothering of David for a manageable $35.00 a month
which would then be passed onto the church by way of a
contribution.

On David's first night with Alice, I sent up a prayer of
thanksgiving and put in my bid for a second break; a job.
Then I remembered that Paul needed an office girl.

Expenses were high after Paul's surgery. It would be the perfect solution for everyone if I worked for six months, without salary. Of course Paul would provide room and board. This would serve as a thank you for "taking me in." I was not prepared to brave the world on my own, or willing to tamper with a workable plan for David through any premature act of independence.

"That's a good idea, Dorian. I'll take it!"

"You realize, of course, I don't know beans about dentistry except what I've picked up listening to you."

"You'll learn quick enough! All I need is someone to handle the phone, make appointments and take care of the billing. I'll train you to assist at the chair as we go along."

Rita was beaming. Six months gave Paul a change to get on his feet without the drain of a salary. "And it will give you some time, too, Dorian. Have you thought about how you'll manage after you get out on your own? It isn't going to be easy."

With money enough to pay Alice for the next several months, the extended future could keep for awhile. One thing I couldn't put off facing was a series of upper respiratory infections, common in cleft palate children, which led to pneumonia and a number of hospitalizations for David. His pediatrician, Dr. Randolph, suggested I pay him a visit.

"I don't know where to begin, Dorian. I've put it off as long as I can."

It was with premonition that I took a seat opposite a man who was looking at me with such intensity that I began to perspire.

"Haven't you wondered about David? Or asked yourself why he isn't able to hold his head up and roll over like babies his age?"

"What can you expect with so many infections? He no sooner gets a few pounds on him and he's sick again."

He reached for a book on the corner of his desk. "Listen to this…." He spoke directly from the text, describing a series of symptoms; a syndrome. I started to rise, but toppled back into the chair, staggered by what I'd been told. David was mentally retarded with certain other unique physical weaknesses. He would never grow up. At the best he would live seven or eight years; probably six.

"You'll need time to adjust. I admit to putting it off longer than I should have. After speaking with Paul we both agreed to wait until you were stronger before we broke it to you. I understand you're going through a divorce. We all thought it best to wait."

"You mean they knew about it all along?"

"I've only recently confirmed it with Paul. He thought it best that I told you. I've always suspected it, but I wanted a second opinion before I said anything. Paul feels very badly for you; we all do."

"I'll get another opinion!"

"All parents go through the denial stage. You can get dozens of opinions – the diagnosis isn't going to change."

"I can't take this! I don't know what to do!"

"There's really only one avenue open to you. David's father is an American. If you take the child to Kansas where he was born, he'll be eligible for the state programs."

"You mean give him up?"

"Paul tells me you are not a citizen; you don't qualify for assistance. Moving back to Canada will do you no good either because the child is an American. David is old enough now for an artificial appliance to facilitate feeding; the prosthesis will be modified as he grows. He has so many other medical needs in addition to the prosthesis; far beyond what you could possibly afford. Take him to Kansas where he can be properly looked after. And don't take too long.

"I referred Paul to an attorney I've worked with in the past; he has experience with this type of situation. He can arrange a court hearing. My advice is that you move on this as soon as possible, for David's sake, before he has another setback."

Was it the fever during the third month? And what about Bill's little girl? Could it be hereditary? Dr. Randolph had no answers.

I was afraid it was more than a cleft palate that held David back, and I dreaded the moment of truth. Still, when the moment fell upon me, I never suspected it would be so harsh a revelation. David didn't look retarded; it never entered my mind.

&

I would have thought, if grief had colour and consistency it would be pitch black. But grief was dazzling; a brilliant, pervasive intrusion of suns to prick my senses; a blinding spectrum of agony, from which there was no rest, no shade to be found.

Jimmy complained that I was turning into a grump.

"Then stay away from her," Paul said.

"What's the matter with her?"

"Never mind, Melissah."

"I don't like her anymore."

"Me neither," echoed Jimmy.

Paul lightened my office duties, never probing for a decision. Rita badgered me to make up my mind.

"You'll have to do it sooner or later; you might as well get it over with."

When I told Paul I was prepared to do the sensible thing, I knew I lacked the courage to manage the trip, court proceedings, and make it back under my own power, and once again went begging to Rita to see if she would be willing to make the trip with me.

Paul agreed. "I'll get in touch with your Dad and have him send the train fare."

Cecil's reaction incensed Paul. He wasn't sending money for train fare. He suggested we contact the Jones family. And why was it necessary for Rita to go with me?

Paul swore to "find the money somewhere." He swore again because he was short of funds himself. A third cursing resulted over "that irresponsible Kansas bunch!"

"You do have a time of it, don't you? Never mind; I'll see that you and Rita get to Kansas. You won't have to go through this ordeal by yourself."

From the very outset, Rita encouraged me to do what was best for David, but as time for the hearing approached, she turned judgmental, telling Paul, "I don't think I could give up one of mine."

"Use your head, Rita. You know this isn't easy for her!"

"I haven't seen any tears yet."

"She's always been one to keep things corked up. You know that!"

"But Paul, to give up your own child…."

"What other choice does she have?"

"All I'm saying is that I don't think I'd handle it quite the same way if I were in her shoes."

"Well you aren't, so you'll never know, will you? And while you're at it, you might consider how fortunate you are that you will never *be* in her shoes!"

I asked Rita to stop lending her opinions one way or another. But that was Rita; willing to allow me asylum from Kansas; unable to open her heart to the toll I bore.

"It wouldn't hurt you to be a little more tolerant of the children. They had nothing to do with this. You can't spend the rest of your life sulking in your room."

"I am not sulking! I'm on edge. I need to be alone right now."

Fearing I was approaching the stray dog status again, I took a stab at self-sufficiency and told Paul I was going to make the trip alone. "I don't need Rita. I'll do just fine by myself!"

Paul asked Rita to stop picking at me.

"I just think she's making a big mistake. How's she going to feel a year from now? Five years from now?"

"What else can the girl do?"

"Well…."

"Then leave her alone. And no matter what she says, she needs you in Kansas – and you're going with her."

"Of course I am. I never said I wouldn't. She's the one who said she didn't need me."

"Now don't tell me you can't figure out what that was all about!"

శ

The judge called for the medical reports at the opening of the hearing. Rita marched up to the bench and slapped the envelope down with a flare, and directed a condemning look at the Jones gathering before she returned to her seat.

The judge admonished Jonesy for failing to provide child support, promising, that while the State would provide medical treatment, he would be expected to contribute to those expenses according to his income. There would be no free rides for an able-bodied father.

"You ignore the court, boy, and I'll garnish your wages."

Jonesy tugged at his tie. I had no sympathy for his position as an unwilling father.

The physician who delivered David approached me. "I owe you an apology. I knew when he was born this was likely to happen. I just couldn't bring myself to tell you at the time. I never expected you to leave the state. It would have been far easier for you if I'd told you in the beginning."

Three court appointed pediatricians examined David and agreed he should go directly to the University Medical Center.

The judge invited me to his chambers after the hearing. "You'll have full visitation rights, and should you ever find yourself able to provide for the child on your own, the court would probably rule in your favor."

I clutched his final words as a drowning man to a life preserver. It was possible that I might be able to find myself able someday. The court might – and God might – still rule in my favor.

I focused on the possible future to deflect the idea of David at the University Hospital, knowing he faced medical tests at the hands of strangers in a pediatric ward where he would get only as much attention as the nurses had time to give. Once I scraped enough money together I would move to Kansas City. First I had to pay Paul for the trip. We already agreed on the status quo until my debt was settled. I couldn't save any money working for my room and board.

For all its modern speed and power, the Kansas City Chief, like all my trains, had a mean voice: a-curse, a-curse, a-curse.

The fall of 1952 was endured the way one endures an illness: striving toward the time when the debilitating loss of what might have been was lifted; the fever of guilt broken; waiting for the return of emotional and financial strength to get me to Kansas City; closer to David. I considered taking a job at a nearby convalescent home from 7 to 11 after I finished up at the office to accelerate the move.

Paul put his foot down. "How could you possibly handle two jobs and get enough sleep between the two to be of any use at either of them? I'm concerned for your health. You're run down, far too thin; a bundle of nerves. You'd better put off anymore notions of two jobs and concentrate on what you're doing for the time being."

What I was doing for the time being was wrestling with remorse and depression and the debilitating "If's":

If I'd never married Jonesy….

If I'd never been so selfish as to bring a child into the world….

If only I'd gone back to St. Thomas and become a nun….

Would God be kinder if I'd given Him a life of service?

Rita fanned my guilt. "I guess when you're young you get over things a lot faster than you do at my age."

"I'm not over it, Rita. I'm trying to deal with it. And it doesn't help if we have to talk about it all the time!"

"How do you feel about having him so far away?"

How did I feel?

Guilty!

I took it upon myself to play God; created myself an image – looked to a child to atone for the insults of youth – to my own flesh and bone for revenge. The burden of David's life was entirely mine. I was whipped by guilt, and anger, seeing the outcome of David's birth as an indictment from the Supreme Court of the universe – a cosmic slap on the wrist. I even went so far as to go outside one evening and shake my fist at the heavens.

"I'm tired of always being on the short end of the stick! It isn't fair. What did I do to deserve this?"

I bellowed with all the conviction of one who fully expected Heaven to justify itself with an answer, sobbing, waiting in the sultry darkness that wretched summer.

The shadow people crowded me with accusations and neurotic solutions: you were a bad child and you are still bad. And bad things always follow after bad people. It will always be the way it's been. Don't you understand, Dorian? You've been cursed – what chance do you have? Go ahead – give up. You've wanted to, several times, haven't you? Nobody would blame you. You're entitled after all you've gone through. Why don't you do what Elizabeth did?

I wrestled impressions of an inclement childhood, the disastrous outcome of David's birth, and wanted to give up. But to do that would mean that on top of everything else I was a coward; the shadow people would have beaten me once and for all. Death was something you couldn't change your mind about. And there was my immortal soul to consider. What if I blew my eternity like I blew my life? There would eventually come an accounting for my time on earth, and life, no matter how disappointing, was no more than a blink of an eye compared to forever. With that perspective for a foundation, I decided life deserved one more shot; I was prepared to start over, if for no other reason than to be satisfied with my story when the books were opened in Heaven. A final impetus sprung from a timely remembrance of Dr. Nordstrom's words the night of my operation: I had something important to do with my life because God had spared it twice in one hour. If God was willing to pull so many strings in a single hour, it didn't seem logical he would then turn around and curse me. And anyone who could create and maintain a universe would have to be logical.

Chapter 21

"We know that in everything God works for good with those who love Him, who are called according to His purpose." Romans 8:28*

Beginning again included reaching out to others through a season of copious letter writing. The first fruits of harvest came from Bill. He wrote a brief, appropriate note of sympathy; he understood exactly what I was going through. Alma reminded me there was always a higher purpose to our suffering, and instructed me to memorize Romans 8:28*. Maria reported that Cecil was traveling again. She hoped I was "bearing up under it all." Mary was happy to be back in touch, and asked that I keep writing so she could keep track of me. Maude Dyer answered in place of Betsy.

"Rita! You are not going to believe what happened to Betsy! She was in a train accident; her car got hung up at a railway crossing. Betsy's lost her legs! Oh, Rita. Poor Betsy!"

Betsy was attending business school in Tacoma, Washington. About the time I was swept away by Jonesy, she was swept away by an accounting student. She was eight and a half months pregnant at the time of the accident, and gave birth to a six pound boy in the ambulance.

"Betsy's living at home now. Her husband walked out on her. Rita? Does anything ever turn out the way we want it to?"

She started to cry.

Betsy had everything when we were in school. I assumed that those who grew up with advantages got to keep them. I wasn't the only broken-hearted girl in my graduating class. Broken hearts were one thing; amputations quite another. When I weighed the loss of my legs with my own life, my life wasn't as severe as I once judged it. At least I was in one piece, independent of wheelchairs or artificial limbs. I had a new appreciation for the mechanics of walking. In the past, I'd been critical of my legs because my ankles were not as finely boned as I would like them. I vowed never to criticize them again, and suddenly wanted to dance! I was enjoying a surprising sense of celebration over what I had rather than the sadness over what I didn't have. David was still alive. And as long as he was, the possibility existed that he would improve – always a chance the doctors could be wrong.

It wouldn't be the first time. As long as I kept Dr. Nordstrom's remarks handy, I was convinced that something good could eventually come out of everything; including David.

తు

There was one more letter I needed, but before I could expect to get it, I would have to locate Duncan. Paul said Mother McGregor might know; she said the Canadian Government might know. Duncan was probably in the service like a lot of other Canadian boys. An official letter confirmed that he was serving in the army in Korea. I was apprehensive writing to him. How did one go about introducing oneself to a brother who probably had no recollection of you?

Rita called the office when he answered.

"I can't wait 'til I get home. Open it up and read it to me."

The letter was three short lines: he thanked me for writing; he had absolutely no recollection of me or our parents; and he would be in touch after his tour of duty was up.

I was disappointed because he didn't seem very excited about being found; equally disappointed because he failed to include a return address.

"After all, how could he possibly remember you? You better get used to the idea that he may never want to see you. Paul should never have encouraged you."

I might have shelved the whole idea if not for Ted Ford, a lieutenant stationed at Rantoul Air Force Base. We were introduced by one of Paul's patients and started going out together. Ted had orders for Korea and said he would do his best to locate Duncan; and when he did he gave Duncan my photograph. Two months down the road Duncan wrote to say he was on his way back to Canada. I could expect to see him within six weeks.

"What do you think of that, Rita?"

"I'll believe it when I see it!"

Paul said Duncan probably got "cold feet" and that was the reason he never showed up.

"I'm still glad I found him. And I'm not giving up. He'll probably show up someday – when I least expect him."

Paul was pleased to see I wasn't going to let it get me down.

"Things don't get me down the way they used to – not after what happened to Betsy."

Betsy never answered my second letter. But I understood why.

Chapter 22

"The greater inheritance was still in my possession....
I was introduced to the eternal life to
come through Alma's confirmation Bible...."

My debt to Paul was retired by the spring of '55. A secretarial position with the University of Illinois Health Service put me in touch with two other secretaries in need of a third roommate to share an apartment on campus. It was time to move on; but not to Kansas. Kansas would have to wait a little longer.

Rita took me into her confidence that same year. She didn't feel comfortable talking to her friends; it was embarrassing to admit that her husband wasn't what their husbands were: he wasn't as successful as his colleagues; never made good his promise to let her design and build their own home. He paid her little attention; the Chicago Cubs rated higher than she did. Rita cried a great deal that year. In some respects, so did Paul.

It was impossible to make Rita happy. He was unappreciated. She had no idea how draining a profession dentistry was. He resented her "to-do" lists; he deserved a rest on weekends. It was important to exercise, and he enjoyed his golf cronies. I gave them each an ear and tried to stay neutral.

Alma McGregor had her first stroke and started saying goodbye that summer. Paul asked me to dinner when he returned from a visit with her in Vancouver.

"Cecil was in Vancouver the same time I was. I can honestly say I've never seen him looking better. It appears that he and Maria have mended all their fences."

He reached into his pocket. "Mother asked me to give you this. She said you may have forgotten all about it. It was important to her that you get this before she dies."

I had forgotten; laid the promise aside for more pressing concerns over the years. I recreated the scene in the bedroom the night she promised me her engagement ring. Paul was visibly moved.

Melissah and Rita inched to the edge of their chairs when I slipped the ring on my finger.

"Isn't it beautiful? I can't believe she remembered. I never thought I'd ever inherit anything! I can't believe it's really mine. What an honor!"

"Mother's never gone back on a promise as long as I can remember. She thinks very highly of you, Dorian; she says you've got starch!"

Melissah wanted to try on the ring. "Why can't I have it? Why did she get it?"

Rita raised the same objection. "I think the ring should go to Melissah. After all, it does belong to her grandmother."

"Mother wanted Dorian to have it. She has plenty of other jewelry. Melissah will be well remembered. Give the ring back, Melissah," Paul ordered.

Melissah turned to her mother. "I want my grandmother's ring!"

Rita insisted that it was only proper that the ring go to Melissah. "It isn't as if Dorian is in the family. She's only a shirttail relation."

"No I'm not! I'm a cousin!"

"Four times removed! That hardly counts when it comes to something as important as an engagement ring!"

Rita's darts were well placed. "I think you'd be the first to agree that Paul and I were always there for you when you needed us. We did take you in when your father asked us to, and when you had no place to go with David. And Paul did pay for the trip to Kansas."

"And I paid him back – every cent!"

Where would we have been if she had turned me down when I needed a place for David and me? It was an uncomfortable choice; give up the ring or my allotment of family security, and shirttail or not, it was terribly important to be related. In the same way the needy are subordinate to those who hold what they need the most, I needed to belong. Charity always had a string attached to it. Rita's favours demanded payment. Obligation was the currency by which I could settle my accounts.

Melissah lost the ring the first time she wore it. Rita treated the loss as if the ring were a prize in a Cracker Jack box. "It must have slipped off her finger somewhere in the theatre. I'll call the manager. Maybe somebody turned it in. There are still honest people in the world. It may show up yet."

When it never did, Paul shrugged his shoulders. Rita said, "It was just a ring.'

I answered her in thought only. No, Rita, it wasn't just a ring. It was my inheritance; my only inheritance. If it was just a ring, why was it so important to bribe me out of it?

Alma died at the end of the year without learning the outcome of the gift. I wrote often, lying to a dying woman who honored a promise of so many years; ashamed because I allowed a gift of such integrity to be stolen. Losing the ring was more than a loss, it was a defeat, until I came across her confirmation Bible in my box of belongings carried from place to place through the years. The cover was brittle, its pages bonded by neglect.

I was looking for a particular verse: Romans 8:28

> *"And we know that all things work together for good to them that love God, to them who are called according to His purpose."*

I understood that Rita could never deny her own flesh. Melissah would always come first, but no matter how badly

Rita wanted the ring for her daughter, she knew in her heart that she could never honestly claim the endowment. It was mine, and I reclaimed it despite the loss of the ring itself. Someday a jeweler would make me one just like it: a diamond, emerald, ruby and blue sapphire side by side in an old fashioned setting. The greater inheritance was still in my possession. I was brought into this world through Graham and Elizabeth, to live a limited time, but I was introduced to the eternal life to come through Alma's confirmation Bible; a gift that surpassed the sentiments expressed in a ring.

ॐ

My plans to relocate to Kansas were scuttled when the teeth Paul saved during my high school days started to crumble again.

"You have lousy teeth!"

I ended up in hock to the University Employees' Credit Union for the awesome sum of $610.00. Paul couldn't use silver anymore. "We have to go to gold." A molar was too far gone. "It has to come out! You need a three-unit bridge."

I'd no sooner turned over the credit union funds to Paul when a medical report from a doctor at the University of Kansas arrived, containing new evidence on David; it would be worth my while to come to the clinic and meet with him personally. He was contesting the original diagnosis. I had just enough put away to cover a bus ticket and one night in a hotel. Before I even saw David a higher ranking physician explained that I should never have been called to the clinic in the first place. It was simply the case of an overzealous young doctor with a lot of highfalutin theories that just didn't stand up. I was due an apology for the distress the trip and false hopes may have caused. The original and dismal diagnosis stood.

One excruciating afternoon with David and I knew I could never see him again. It seemed the only thing to do:

to let him pass into the shadows where painful people and events could be tolerated. It was what I always did; it was the only thing to do again. And if I pretended he was already dead, had the funeral then and there, had my time of grief, it would be over with. But David wouldn't stay in the shadows; he followed me back to Illinois, looking up at me with his peaked little face as if to say, "Who are you?"

Even Betsy couldn't help me; waiting for "someday" wouldn't cut it anymore. It was a solution born of desperation: pour yourself into others – help others get what they want – leave your wants out of it. Maybe that was my problem; I'd always wanted too much. I'd be better off to approach life from another angle; from everybody else's angle.

Then I met Martin.

A quick wit and a pair of horned rimmed glasses gave Martin Hahn the same wholesome appeal that attracted me to Bobby Clark, although he could more readily have been taken for a professor with a head of prematurely gray hair and a pipe between his teeth. I was surprised to learn he was only 26; eight months my senior.

Martin attended the University of Illinois. He worked rotating shifts between the blood bank and pathology lab at City Hospital, and showed the drive and grit that comes with high aspirations. To make the most of his G. I. bill he shared a house near campus with three pre-dental students who made light of their shoestring existence and monotonous diet. Girl friends that were at home in the kitchen were always welcome. We were introduced by mutual friends. I was drawn by his humor. When he invited me to church after our second date, I was all the more drawn. Paul took an immediate interest in Martin upon learning he was preparing for dental school.

"I'd like to meet him. Why don't you bring him for dinner?"

By the time we got to dessert Paul was offering to write a letter of recommendation to Northwestern where he served on the faculty prior to meeting Rita.

Martin said, the night he proposed, that if there was any chance for David he was willing to drive to Kansas to get him. I was moved by his tenderness and relayed it to Rita.

She cautioned me. "You can't marry a man just because he's soft-hearted. Do you know what a struggle you'll have with five years schooling ahead of you? You'd better hold off; make sure he is all that you think he is. Remember, you've been fooled once. I think you should wait until he's out of school before you get married."

Paul made up his mind the first night he met Martin. "Marry him! He'll be good for you. You'll have a great life together. That young man is going places. And don't worry about the struggle. Hard times can bring you closer together; they may even be some of the best times you'll ever have."

Martin was the only child of Mildred and George Hahn, a God-fearing couple who retired from farming and moved to town when Martin was sixteen. George was an amiable man, quick to congratulate us, and the initial objection over my previous marriage on Mildred's part was short-lived. We had a small wedding on a Saturday morning and were back on campus on Monday. Wednesday night I had a disturbing dream.

Jonesy was engulfed in flames, screaming, "I'm sorry, Dorie, I'm sorry." Then the flames shot up over his head, hiding him, but his screams continued. The dream was so vivid and unsettling it woke me. I was afraid to shut my eyes for fear of slipping back into it again. Ten days later Rita called to say there was a letter from Freda Jones. She was sure I'd want her to read it to me.

"I don't know how to tell you this, Dorian, but…"

"Jonesy's dead isn't he?"

The words popped out of my mouth before I considered how foolish they were going to sound.

"How could you possibly…."

I told her of the dream.

"I can't believe it! The hair on my arms is standing straight up. Dorian, he did burn. Evidently he'd been drinking and ran into a bridge abutment. The car caught on fire."

It was instant replay. I was bathed in chills.

"I hope he was dead before he burned."

"His mother said he was probably killed on impact. But then how would anyone possibly know for sure? What a horrible way to die."

"Horrible!"

"Do you want to talk about it?"

"No. And I don't think I ever will."

Martin was skeptical about the dream; sorry that anyone would have to die that way. I couldn't cry over Jonesy, but I knew I would never forget him, or that I had the dream on the very night he died.

We moved to Chicago to begin a four year stint at the University of Illinois Medical Center after Martin completed his B.S. Degree. Northwestern was far too expensive for us. I transferred from the Urbana campus into the College of Dentistry as secretary to one of the clinical heads. We depended on student loans to see us from one semester to another and Martin worked full time during the summers. Married students gravitated to each other, especially those married to wives employed within the dental school. We got together with classmates for end-of-the-month potlucks, and those who had no children offered relief for the odd night out for those who did. We moved four times in four years; lived in some decent parts of town, and in some not so decent.

Six weeks before Martin graduated I retired to await the birth of our first child. Student wives received preferential treatment at the clinics by the very nature of our friendship with the interns who went out of their way to assure me the chances of having another child like David were unlikely. Martin and I poured over textbooks after Christine was born, comparing her progress against the danger signs; three months later we put the books away.

Martin took over a practice in suburban Chicago. Jenny came into our lives three years later, and in her third year we sought the sunshine of California after a warning that another winter of respiratory infections which kept her dependent on antibiotics since birth, placed her at risk of long term consequences. The consequences of three years of illness was an alarming sixty percent loss of hearing. Corrective surgery, followed by six years of speech therapy, reversed all but ten percent of that loss; we would not dwell on the remaining ten percent, considering what might have been.

The consequences of a celebrity practice in Beverly Hills was a four-day work week for Martin; the country club golf course any one of the three remaining days of the week, and a house, once inhabited by a movie queen, in the more than decent part of town. We were all very much aware of our blessings, and while David remained my perennial thorn, I was consoled with the knowledge that he was in Heaven.

I was given to comparisons of life before Martin and all we accomplished together with those of my formative years. If we were confronted with difficulty it was easy to put things in perspective. No matter what the problem, it never compared to growing up. If any of us got to grumbling, I reminded them, "We've nothing to complain about; we aren't blind, or deaf, or crippled," which was always followed with, "Oh, Momma," or "If you say that once more…."

Other lives were not as well ordered. Paul finally made good his promise to let Rita build her own house, but it came too late. They divorced in '64. He died two years later. Rita maintained her striking figure and classy appearance, attracted a man considerably younger than herself and remarried.

Cecil continued his sporadic rounds of depression and passed away in '61. Poor investments and illness depleted his inheritance from Ben Whyte, but one wise decision, the construction of a duplex in Calgary, provided security for Maria. She proved herself the one with the head for business, maintaining her own investments. My affections remained, and after Cecil left us, our relationship took on a pleasantness enjoyed by Martin and our children. One tearful afternoon during one of her visits, she told me how sorry she was for withholding my milk.

"Your father was so tight – always yapping at me because I could never stay on the budget. I really don't understand how I could have done such a thing. Please forgive me."

I understood how her need for financial security super-seded my needs. Her background had a lot to do with it; being married to Cecil probably had a lot more to do with it. Of course, I would forgive her. I forgave her years ago. I acknowledged the difficult situation she inherited when she married Cecil and assumed the management of a child with my history. It was a healing conversation; our first honest conversation about such matters.

Chapter 23

*"It wasn't human nature for people to invest their hearts
in what was forced on them."*

It was an ordinary Sunday in the spring of '72. The girls were working a puzzle at the dining room table. Martin was puttering in his greenhouse when the telephone rang.

"Hello. Is this Dorian McGregor? I mean were you ever known as Dorian McGregor? The one who's related to a Bill McGregor in Peoria?"

The caller didn't have to identify himself. I knew who it was.

"Duncan? It is you, isn't it?"

"How did you know?"

"I just did. How on earth did you find me?"

"Remember that Lieutenant? The one that looked me up in Korea?"

"I remember."

"He gave me your picture. I've been running it in all the Canadian papers. Then I remembered you went to school in Montana so I put the ad in some of the papers down there. You had a friend in nurses' training by the name of Isabel. She recognized your picture and called me. She said she'd lost track of you years ago, but thought you had a cousin or an adopted brother who was a dentist. So I traced him through the American Dental Association. I just finished talking to him.

"I want to apologize for not coming to see you after the war. I got cold feet at the last minute. I didn't have the nerve to visit a complete stranger. I'm sorry about standing you up like that. I never used to think much of myself – never had much confidence – but I'm getting over that. When I came back from overseas, I had some problems; they put me in the hospital for awhile."

"You needn't apologize. I understand."

"Now don't get me wrong – I don't want you thinking your brother's a nut - I'm as sane as the next guy!"

"Please, Duncan, you have no idea how much it means to me to find you again."

"When do you think we could get together?"

"Gee, I don't know. But we will. I'm going to have to work that out. You could come down here too, you know. We'll work on it. Okay?"

"I get my holidays in August. I could do it then."

We exchanged addresses and promised to get pictures of each other and our respective families, including dogs and cats.

Much of the information I'd passed along to Martin about my brother had slipped his mind. He had only sketches of my history; only what I felt comfortable in telling him.

"It must be a real shock to talk to him after all this time. I think you should plan to meet him sometime in the future – when it's convenient, of course."

Sunday evenings were scheduled around favorite television programs. Once Martin and the girls were settled in the family room, I excused myself and went into the bedroom to call my best friend.

"Kay? You are never going to believe this but…."

Martin was studying me for long periods of time.

"Why do you watch me like that?"

"Can't a man look at his wife?"

"You don't look at me – you scrutinize me."

He was concerned over the change in me; I was distant. Chrissy told him I was ignoring her. He shared her feelings.

"I'm sorry. I guess I have been a bit preoccupied. I don't expect you or the girls to understand what an impact this has had on me. I'm not so sure I fully understand it myself. I have a great deal on my mind now that I've found my brother. We're all that's left of the original family. And as wonderful as it is – it's got its downside too."

"How so?"

"I'm thrilled that he called, and I can't wait to see him, but I'm uncomfortable about something. Things are a little out of whack. Maybe it's just too many rotten nights lately. I'm having a real problem with insomnia again."

Poor sleeping habits were a normal occurrence. Martin had no trouble falling asleep, but he was a light sleeper, and my tossing interfered with his rest. Out of consideration for him I was sleeping on the couch more often than not, flanked by our two cats. What little sleep I caught was invaded by dreams of Duncan and my parents during the time we lived in the flat above the drug store.

Kay told me I didn't need to worry about the extra ten pounds I'd been so obsessed about, and asked if all was well between Martin and me.

"Martin has nothing to do with this. It's all happened since Duncan called. I can't turn my head off – all this stuff is coming back to me – things I haven't thought about in years. And some of it's pretty disturbing."

"Want to talk about it?"

"Not today."

"You certainly haven't been your old easygoing self, that's for sure!"

"You'd be pretty ragged, too, if you were managing on 3 to 4 hours a night. And I can't sleep in the day time. I never could."

Kay was digging in her purse. "Why don't you give my therapist a call? You'd like Adam. He's easy to talk to."

I looked at the card. "He's a marriage and family counselor. There's nothing wrong with my marriage."

"He handles everything: phobias, insomnia."

"Thanks, but I don't think so." I made a move to return the card. She refused it.

"You keep it; just in case you change your mind in the middle of one of your sleepless nights."

"I've come this far without a shrink; I guess I can make it the rest of the way. I've had these spells before. They run their course; then I'm fine for awhile. Did I tell you I'm planning to meet Duncan this summer?"

"I wonder what effect that's going to have on you?"

A fat envelope arrived from Winnipeg. I'd carried two vivid memories of Duncan since our separation: on my mother's lap, asleep in the crook of her arm that last night, and afterward, in the hospital, in the next bed before he vanished. Now, I looked into the face of a 39 year-old man, held him in my hands, traced his features with my fingers: a strong, squared jaw, cleft chin and bold blue eyes. I ran to the mirror and held the photo beside my reflection. Did I favour my mother? My father? I chilled at the sight of family likeness, striving for a hint of my parents.

I told Martin that I didn't think anyone felt complete without photographs. "You have pictures of yourself, all your family, from the time you were born, and back two generations. I've never had any. I never will. It's terribly important to know who your people are. At least now I can look at these pictures of Duncan and know that between the two of us there's at least a resemblance of those we came from."

At thirteen Christine was excited over the discovery of four cousins, and wanted to know more about how Duncan and I were separated than I felt comfortable in telling. Jenny, age ten, shared her sister's curiosity. Martin paid perfunctory attention to any news from Winnipeg.

Duncan and I agreed to meet in Calgary as it was a mid-travel point for us. Maria had no qualms about my staying at her place the three days Duncan and I would be together; she did question that I was coming at all. "Are you sure you're doing the right thing? Don't be surprised if things don't work out the way you expect them to."

"Duncan was the one who found me this time, Maria. I'd all but given up ever seeing him"

"He'll have to stay in a hotel. I don't want strangers in my place."

"He plans to do just that; he doesn't want to put you out, and neither do I for that matter – would you rather I stay in a hotel as well?"

"Oh, you won't be putting me out. I won't be here. I've planned a few days in Lethbridge with my sister, Angie. She's practically blind you know, and it's been far too long since I made a trip to Lethbridge. You and your brother can have the place during the day, but I don't want him staying overnight. We don't know what sort of a person he is."

"Maria! He's my brother!"

It was her position, brother or not, I knew nothing about him, and kinship in no way guaranteed him to be a man of sterling character.

❧

Duncan wanted to prepare me before we actually met in Calgary.

"I have trouble walking at times, and I never know when it's going to hit me. Sometimes people step aside when they see me coming. They probably think I've been drinking. I thought I'd better tell you that I have multiple sclerosis. It can be pretty embarrassing."

"I won't be embarrassed, Duncan."

"I didn't want to shock you, so I thought it best to let you know up front."

"I'm so sorry! How terrible for you. I can't imagine any-thing worse. You need never worry about me. I'll never be embarrassed."

"Well, the way I look at it, as long as I'm not confined to a wheel chair I'm not going to complain. There are a lot of people worse off than me. I've been in remission for quite awhile now, and who knows, I might get lucky and not get any worse."

࿊

Getting to Calgary a day ahead of Duncan gave me an evening to visit with Maria. She brought out a box of pictures and offered me a portrait of Alma and her four boys taken shortly after Maria and Cecil were married.

"I thought you might like to have this. And, by the way, here's one of me when I was young. Would you like it?"

"Thank you, Maria. What a lovely picture."

Fifty years earlier, at age 22, Maria's face was downright beautiful, budding with promise, a touching contrast to the bitter years etched into the expression she now wore.

"They used to call me the pretty sister. Do you think I was pretty then?"

"You were a beauty, Maria! Cecil used to say that – and he was right. I always thought you were beautiful, and you're still very attractive. You don't look anywhere near your age."

Her hands moved nervously to her hair. "Do you think so?"

"Absolutely!"

"I am a little worse for wear. Still, I do my best."

"I'm a little worse for wear myself; we all are. And we'll be a lot more the worse for wear before we're done!"

Maria brought up "the woman in Edmonton," and how despondent she was over the affair.

"The only reason your Dad came back to me was because she didn't want him anymore. He knew I'd take him back. I was proud. I didn't want the scandal of a divorce. It was different in those days."

"But you did love him, Maria, I know you did. It was more than just pride."

She shrugged. "I don't think he ever loved me. He certainly didn't go out of his way to show it; not after we were married."

"But he never was much for sentiment was he? Besides, he would never have come back to you if he didn't love you. He'd never do that. Not Cecil!"

Tears came to her eyes; her face dropped into her hands.

"Don't cry, Maria. He never told me he loved me either, but that doesn't mean he didn't. I always felt he didn't want me either, but...."

Her face popped out from behind her hands. "That's because he never did. He only adopted you because Mother McGregor talked him into it, and it was easier for them to adopt you than to live with the guilt she'd heap on them if they didn't take in their little cousin. He always resented her for that, especially after Beatrice died. He always resented being stuck with you. But you always knew that! Didn't you?"

In a frantic attempt to salvage what remained of my own pride, I came back at her with a convincing, "I always suspected as much! It doesn't come as any great shock to me! That's why he sent me to Cut Bank."

"That's right. Cecil made a deal with Paul and Rita. When Paul borrowed the $5000 for his move to Montana he was supposed to pay it back within five years. Cecil felt as long as he wasn't getting what was due him, the least he could do was get you off his hands. Paul was supposed to support you from then on."

"And I was supposed to pay my way doing housework and taking care of the children. So in the long run, Paul wouldn't actually be out any money."

"So you did know!"

My first thought was that Maria had been waiting for years for just the right moment to spring the facts on me. I was so stunned by the cruelty of her words, I went rigid on the couch beside her, as if the revelation had no effect on me; when I was tempted to rescind any suggestion that Cecil loved her; when I really wanted to retaliate and tell her that as long as he didn't want me he probably never wanted her either, and no doubt married her for the reasons I'd eaves-dropped on as a child: for convenience. I'd like to be able to say it was out of a magnanimous spirit that I didn't. It was only that I refused to join her ranks of indifference.

"I'm pretty tired, Maria. We've both got a big day ahead of us...."

I digested the outcome of staying up late; uneasy at the prospect of spending the night in Cecil's bed. What a differ-ence it would have made – the difference of a lifetime – had we gone to bed a few minutes earlier; before the conversation took the turn it did.

Cecil's dead eyes were looking straight at me from a picture on the dresser. I stared back – engaged in silent self-talk – trying to put myself in his shoes. What must it have been like taking on a child he never wanted just because his mother insisted? Mother McGregor played her role as head of the clan to the very hilt, and maintained authority to the very end. How many times did he look at me and wish that I was the one in the grave instead of Beatrice? I had to acknowledge his heartbreak; I'd seen it. How he must have suffered, not to mention chafe under the aggravation of living with me after the love of his life was gone. It wasn't human nature for peo-ple to invest their hearts in what was forced on them. How could I expect him to do otherwise? And let's face it; you were a pretty mixed-up kid. Remember all the trouble you caused?

It was futile to try to get into Cecil's shoes as over-whelmed as I was with my own. Being forced on him wasn't any easier on me. If I'd been able to read the signs in his dis-tance and reserve so long after he acquired me, I would never have wasted all those years chasing after his affection. He was free of me now, but I would have to accommodate him for the rest of my days in a relationship based on the brutal truth. The more I remembered, the more power emanated from the portrait; power to hold me responsible for something I wasn't responsible for, bringing me to the point of embarrassment for myself and pity for Cecil because his mother forced my adoption. It had all been a lie. That year with Beatrice was a lie; Friday afternoon teas in the sunroom another lie.

I reached for the lamp on the night table, pulled the chain to escape the condemning picture, and immediately switched it back on. Afraid of the dark at your age? Pull yourself together. He's dead. Remember?

I might just as well have flown in for his funeral; stood over his open grave a few hours ago. Maria was clutching her coat, rolling the collar around her neck. The air was still brisk on the 27th of May. The wind lifted the loose dirt around the grave site. Maria said he planned his own funeral, choosing what she termed, "his favorite hymns," which surprised me at the time. He never changed his mind about organized religion, but at his request, "The Old Rugged Cross" and "Rock of Ages" were delivered by a portly tenor. People do not cling to the old rugged Cross without cause or faith. I took it as a sign that he came to see Heaven and hell as something to reckon with before he died, and was comforted. Even Mary said it was good to know he was "right with God when he went over."

Maria was composed the day of the funeral. Later, at the house, passing out refreshments, she had given no hint of a widow bereft. Their marriage was never entirely ironed out; she'd never got what she bargained for. But all that was sixteen years ago, when the loss was not as severe as it was now; the mourning not as raw. In his room, racing back in time, I could interpret Maria's performance the day of the funeral in a different light. Perhaps she had been simply relieved that he was gone; she could give up pretending everything was right between them. Or she might have pretended for the reasons I was pretending now: denying how much she loved him so she could tolerate the loss.

His portrait challenged me. How I wanted to go on as before; making allowances because he was a manic depressant – because he never got over Beatrice's death – because he probably did the very best he could. What could I say now? Thank him for putting up with me? Maybe I really owed him an apology for being the millstone that I was.

I peeled back the sheet and went to the kitchen. Today I was going to meet my brother. It would be a joyous occasion. Nothing was going to spoil it; certainly not a dead man. I downed a cup of hot milk and fell asleep on Maria's newly upholstered Chesterfield because I didn't want to share the night with his portrait. Maria muttered over a snag in one of the cushions the next morning; I pretended not to hear.

Duncan walked with stiff, deliberate steps. I approached him with caution and put my arms around his neck, finding it difficult to meet his eyes – to look at him full face. And later, in the taxi I had to keep looking away. If this was a dream come true, why was I afraid? It was equally difficult to come up with anything other than superficial remarks about the weather; how much the city had grown since my last visit. We were both in need of aspirin when we reached Maria's, and agreed that our headaches came from neither of us wanting to make a bad first impression.

Duncan had no memory of our parents; he did have a bank of information from the Welfare Department. Graham received an engineering degree from the University of Minnesota. He was born in Winnipeg in 1906, married Elizabeth in 1929, and moved to Vancouver when I was two, a year before Duncan was born. As of late 1939 he could no longer be located.

We both admitted to being extremely fatigued; Duncan left early. I took another dose of aspirin before retiring and turned Cecil's picture face down on the dresser. Lying down intensified my headache; I scrunched up the pillows to elevate my head and closed my eyes. Seconds later I was sitting up, alarmed. Something in the room sent me running into the living room panting in fear, into the arms of a chintz-covered chair. I cowered with my feet tucked safely under my haunches, shivering; seeking protection from the bulk of the chair against whatever was sharing the house with me.

The place was riddled with late night noises. My head throbbed with pain and questions birthed by the discovery of how I became a McGregor. An awakened, illumined child told her elder sister that she always knew she was a nuisance to him; it's impossible to fool a child about some things.

A child and a woman cringed in that chair, yielding to truth, the grown woman thinking that this was probably the stuff that nervous breakdowns were made of. It would no longer serve my purpose to defer to the good fortune of recent years. There was no comfort for the child in the accomplishment of the woman; not now. Not since the reunion with her brother, whose very presence brought back the handsome mustached father, the beloved fair-haired mother; all that transpired since the dissemination of that unit. Brutal truth heaped upon brutal truth. I finished the night where I was, dozing, snapping awake as my head fell to my chest; only after the first hint of daylight could I give up the security of the chair.

Duncan was interested in what I knew about our mother's suicide. He'd been plagued with the memory of being tied in a chair when he was very small; now he had the facts to back it up.

"Duncan, do you know why she killed herself?"

"I heard it was because Graham was playing around. She was going to have another baby. She didn't see how she could take care of us. I guess we didn't have much money."

"That's what I heard too. Do you ever wonder where she is? Or how she must have felt when she realized we weren't with her?"

"I don't understand what you mean – when you're dead, you're dead – you don't know anything."

"I disagree. I believe in life after death. I think she knew we got left behind."

He appeared uneasy and directed the conversation toward himself. After he left the army he went to work at an aluminum plant. In fifteen years he could burn the mortgage.

He planted a garden every spring; his wife, Dorothy, canned every fall. He was proud of his children, and if it weren't for M. S. he'd have everything anyone could possibly want out of life.

"Most of the men I work with are looking forward to the day they can retire; I'm dreading the day I can't work anymore."

"I've been so lucky, Duncan. I've been healthy most of my life. And when you've got your health…."

"There's another way of looking at it though. I'd rather have this than a lot of other things I can think of."

"Like being blind?"

"Right. Or like some of the guys who left their legs in Korea. Mine may not always work the way I'd like them to, but at least they're still attached to my body!"

"I had a friend who lost her legs in a train accident. I can't tell you how many times I've thought of her over the years."

As Duncan related his history, I paid divided attention; jostled between his story and my private deliberations on the brutal truth. I was here to reunite with my brother, but Cecil's memory contested for first place until all I wanted was out of his house; back to my own safe ground with Martin and my children. The extent to which the dead could influence the living was staggering.

Chapter 24

"The past came at me like a dragon out of a pit…"

Martin was baffled by Maria's disclosure. "She could have kept it to herself!"

"I've had more time to think about it, and as long as I keep it in perspective it really doesn't bother me all that much. After all, I have so much to be thankful for. There isn't much sense in living in the past."

At the time I never considered that professing so nonchalant an acceptance of such an emotional time bomb would be so convincing as to free Martin of any obligation to console me. But he never saw me handle unpleasant situations any other way. Why would he think I needed any special attention? Logically, I knew it was unreasonable to expect him to see through the mask, but at the same time I was hurt because he didn't. What I really wanted to hear was, "You've got me now, and I've always wanted you."

Without getting specific or giving away my situation, I asked Kay how Alex responded when she needed an emotional boost.

She sighed, "If a woman's looking for understanding, the last place she should look is to her husband."

"Now that's a pathetic statement if I've ever heard one!"

"What do you think caused the rift in my marriage? Alex can't be bothered with what's happening with me, and I thought a wife was supposed to be the most significant person in a man's life! We have to talk it over with the girls, or find ourselves an Adam."

"Don't you find it difficult to open up to a stranger?"

"That's just it – a stranger is the only one you can confide in. You're my closest friend, but there are things I would never tell even you. You'd be surprised how quickly you can get comfortable with a therapist when you're at the end of your rope."

"What does he charge?"

"Fifty."

"Fifty?"

"It's the going rate."

"That lets me out. It's too expensive. I don't think Martin would stand for it."

"How do you know? Have you asked him?"

"You don't know Martin."

"Is he cheap?"

"I wouldn't go that far, but we stick pretty much to a budget; that comes from growing up poor. His folks didn't have much."

"You really love him, don't you?"

"Of course I love him!"

"I envy you that much."

"You don't love Alex?"

"Not always."

"Really? How does that work? Do you love him on alternate days of the week and just put up with him the rest of the time?"

She laughed. "You're not far off."

"Either you love him or you don't; otherwise you're just fooling yourself."

"Women do that all the time. You do it too."

"I beg your pardon!"

"You don't complain like the rest of us. You're always talking about how lucky you are. It's not normal. I've always felt you had a lot pent up inside. You don't like to talk about it, do you? Whenever I asked you about your childhood you act like you never had one."

"I've told you quite a bit about my childhood."

"Not really. You talk in circles. You act as if you live under a protective covering; nothing ever wipes you out like it does the rest of us. You said you were adopted, that your mother died, but that's about it. I know there's a lot more you don't talk about."

"My! My! Do I get this advice for nothing or can I expect to be billed?"

"Hey! We're friends! Okay? I'm concerned about you, that's all!"

"As a matter of fact, I have been giving some thought to calling Adam. I've been having some very disturbing dreams lately. And they don't go away when the sun comes up. I'm going to tell you something that's been eating at me for years. Martin and I haven't discussed it since Christine was born. I'll try to get through it without crying."

Kay gave me a very hard stare. I stared back, wondering why I was talking about David instead of my own childhood. It was as if the pain associated with him had been waiting for that precise moment to escape the coffin of denial.

"How long have I known you, Dorian?"

"About ten years."

"And you've never said a word about this before today? And we're supposed to be best friends."

"This is hardly the kind of thing you share openly. Besides it happens to thousands of people, and I don't think they talk about it either. You just have to accept it, that's all. Life goes on."

"There you go again – acting as if it doesn't hurt – as if you're strong enough to handle anything!"

"I never wanted anyone to pity me. And I don't want you to either. Tragedy is a part of life."

"But you could at least react. Get mad! Something!"

"Oh, I've been angry enough, but that didn't change the way things were."

"What ever happened to him?

"He died."

"When?"

"That's what's bothering me. I never knew exactly when. I don't even know where he's buried. And every time I think about it… I gotta' go, Kay. I feel a migraine coming on."

I might never have found out, if not for Alex. With a friend in Administration within the State Welfare system there were ways to cut through red tape even when it stretched as far as Kansas.

Martin asked, "Why do you torture yourself like this? Does it make any difference where he's buried, or when he died?"

"It makes a big difference to me. I'll never have any peace until I know."

"I didn't realize he was on your mind all these years; you never talked about him. I assumed you'd come to terms with this a long time ago."

I considered driving to Martin's office when the letter arrived; it would be better to have support when I read it. I held the envelope to the window for a clue; my stomach knotted with the threat of impending answers. Then I made the decision to open it.

Dear Mrs. Hahn….

Oceans roared in my head.

They told me he would never grow up.

Dear Jesus, why didn't he die?

The experts made a mistake.

I made a mistake.

I believed them.

David was alive!

Martin's building was ten minutes away.

"What's the matter?"

I handed him the letter. "How am I supposed to live with this?"

Martin scanned the report, looked up, and went over it a second time. A familiar pressure was building behind my eyes; flashes of white lightening signaled a headache. I moaned. "On top of everything else, I'm getting a migraine."

The letter floated from his hands onto the desk. "I don't see why you're so upset. He's probably very happy where he is – probably a lot happier than you are."

He moved toward the door. "I have a patient waiting. We'll talk about this when I get home. Do you want something for your headache?"

I stumbled out of the office.

One would never count a migraine a blessing, but it was the very excuse I needed.

"Got one of your headaches, Momma?"

"Uh-huh."

"We'll be quiet."

The shutters were closed; a pillow covered my face. Against a throbbing, inked screen, a parade of skyscraper-sized figures passed before me. Nine men-children on a farm outside Kansas City – and one of them belonged to me.

Was it possible for a child like David to feel abandoned? Would he wonder who he belonged to? Why he ended up where he did? Would he ever have felt like I was feeling since Maria dropped the bomb? That I wanted to get rid of him?

Martin suggested that I use a little common sense. "You were only 21. You had no money or family support. What else could you do but turn him over to the State? He needed specialized care. And what about the court hearing? All those medical experts had a lot to do with your decision, didn't they? Don't forget, you weren't the only party with responsibility in this. Why must you persist in assuming all this blame?"

"You don't understand."

"I guess I don't."

Neither did Kay. "I would have done the same thing in your place. What else could you do?"

"I could have gone back one more time. I didn't have to give up on him. I was only thinking of myself."

"What difference would that have made?"

"Oh, Kay, you don't understand. Nobody understands."

"No, I think you're the one who doesn't understand! And unless you get some professional help you are never going to snap out of this. And don't forget – there are others to consider." She hesitated, "It's affecting the girls. I was making small talk with Chrissy the other day. She's unhappy because her mother's sad all the time. And Jenny feels the same way. And what about Martin? How do you think he feels?"

"All right! All right! I'll call Adam."

"Good!"

"You don't happen to have another card on you, do you?"

She fished a card from her purse. "The girls don't know about David, do they?"

"No!"

"Are you going to tell them?"

"Not until I have to."

Adam's office was located in the inner triangle of Beverly Hills, on the second floor of a charming older building situated in the midst of a wave of redevelopment. The suite was out of character for the professional community, furnished in an eclectic, homey style reminiscent of second generation furnishings; his boy-next-door image in khaki trousers and bulky blue pullover equally out of character. I questioned Kay's faith in one so young, and glanced at a grouping of diplomas in a last ditch search for confidence.

"What can I help you with?"

"I've got this problem….from a long time ago…."

Could he possibly suspect me of holding back out of guilt? Guilt for wanting a baby in the first place; for giving him up in the second place; guilt because I wanted him dead?

"Now, about your guilt…."

What affected one family member affected the entire family. Adam asked that Martin and the girls be present at the next session. He would support me as I revealed the "secret" to my children, and prepared me for possible resentments on their part.

Kay was eager for my opinion of Adam.

"You never told me he was so young!"

"You never asked. He's thirty-four. Alex had him checked out – and you know Alex. Adam has a very impressive following. Doesn't he remind you a little of Alan Alda?"

"More like William F. Buckley, Jr. if you ask me! He wants to see Martin and the girls. Everyone in the family needs to be included. Do you have any idea how difficult it's going to be telling Chrissy and Jenny about David?"

"There's no use going to an expert if you're not going to take his advice."

⁂

Adam started the session by addressing the girls.

"Your mother has something to tell you. It will be difficult for her so I want you to listen carefully; don't interrupt. You can ask your questions after she's through."

All eyes were upon me. I looked to Adam for reassurance.

"Take your time," he said.

"I don't know where to start."

"Take a few deep breaths."

Martin went to the window and stood with his back to us. The room echoed with the change in his pocket. I couldn't get started.

Martin was growing impatient. "For Heaven's sake, just tell them! Tell them you were married before; that you had a son."

The girls jolted to attention, looking from me to Martin, to each other. I focused on a spot a little above their heads to avoid their stricken faces and told of another time and how it came to pass, hedging where I could; no need to tell them everything. Martin kept his post at the window, stirring his coins while I spoke.

Adam asked the girls to tell us what they were feeling. Jenny ran to the back of my chair and stood quietly; she had nothing to say. Christine was disappointed now that she no longer was my first born. Robbed of this enviable position, she felt unimportant and turned an icy shoulder when I reached out my hand to her.

Martin said we wouldn't be going through this if I'd left the past where it belonged. Adam said the past has a way of catching up with us sooner or later, and no amount of effort on my part would have prevented it.

Revealing David to my children was only part of the problem. The children they might have someday could be a greater problem. Bill and I were fifth cousins; both our first born were mentally retarded; both with an uncommon, rather than common, Down's Syndrome, suggesting a genetic link.

When Adam coached me against leaping into the future, the past would be work enough, I had no idea just how involved the process of coming to terms with David would be; how interwoven David was with everything that transpired before his birth; no idea that what I was feeling went back as far as my own childhood, or that it would take months to uncover.

The past came at me like a dragon out of a pit, daring me to do my puny best, and while I sparred and jabbed at the thing, it laughed and hissed in my face. I swayed and teetered out of its reach, retreating, advancing, retreating again behind the shield of counted blessings. Adam kept digging for truth. I dug for comparisons; compared to x, y and z, I had it pretty good.

"But Adam, you can't deny that there is always something to be thankful for; always those who are far worse off."

"For instance?"

"I had a friend in high school that lost her legs in a train accident. I don't think I could survive something like that. What about the Jews, and the soldiers imprisoned during the second World War? They went for years on end, suffering; living on the edge of every minute. Right here in L. A. some people are living on the streets. It all boils down to this: no matter how much we've been disappointed…."

"Try not to speak for the entire human race. Speak for yourself. Speak in first person – no matter how much I've been hurt...."

"No matter how much I've been hurt – or disappointed – I'm not the only one. I'm not blind! What if I was blind? Now that would really do me in. It's not just a case of comparing poisons, Adam; I feel very strongly that you have to take stock, excuse me, I have to take stock of what I have instead of what I didn't have."

"It's all well and good to recognize your advantages, but not to the extent that you deny the emotional wounds you have accumulated since childhood; to deny that you are in pain and in need of healing. There is no substitute for the grieving process, or for honestly facing your losses and your anger."

"Are you telling me that examining all of this stuff is like taking the medicine that's going to get me better?"

"In a manner of speaking, yes."

"I'm afraid, Adam. So afraid that once I open up these wounds I'll never be able to close them up. I'm not sure I can go through this. I feel a lot worse now than I did when I first started coming here!"

"Dorian, you've plastered those wounds with philosophical band-aids to the extent that you can't see them as plainly as you used to, but they're still open – they still smart. What do you suppose keeps you awake at night? And the migraines?"

I couldn't argue against him; but being right wasn't the law; I didn't have to take on more dragons if I didn't want to. Rather than offend him I asked for a break, insinuating, so as not to come across as a disgruntled client, that I would call when I felt up to pursuing the "rest of my life."

He confronted me: now was the time to continue. "There is much more to do with the issue of David than David himself. We've only touched on the problem. You need to understand how your history contributes to the remorse you're experiencing today. But I can only advise you. I won't try to coerce you into coming back; that's your decision. You know where to find me when you're ready to clean house."

It was so much easier to crate it all up again, look to the bright side and count my blessings. Life wasn't perfect. Nobody's life was perfect. My life was perfect enough. My marriage was perfect enough. I was really a very fortunate woman.

Chapter 25

*"Unconnected sequences from the mystery dream
of kittens, a school yard, and
the drug store got in my way…"*

It was another ordinary Sunday afternoon. Duncan was calling to tell me about his vacation.

"We spent our holidays in Vancouver this year. I wanted to see if I could find our mother's grave, and I found it! She didn't even have a marker. All those years with no marker! The superintendent said lots of folks didn't get markers during the 30's. But I know where she's at. I stood on the very spot. And I told them I wanted a marker. They'll have it installed in about six weeks. I want proof, though, so they're sending me a picture. I'll get a copy to you."

"Duncan, please let me split the cost with you. It would make me so happy to be a part of it."

"That's fine."

"You'd think that after all this time Graham could have put a stone on her grave. She was his wife."

"I'll feel much better when we get that marker in place."

"Me, too! Just think, Duncan, if you and I weren't here, it would be as though she'd never existed."

Jenny and Christine wanted information about their grandmother's death, having gained enough of my end of the conversation to arouse their curiosity.

The "accident" (as I had previously tagged it) that took my mother was presented as factually and as completely as I had the information to tell it. They asked to chip in with their allowance toward the marker.

Christine wanted to know if there would be any more surprises.

"Have you told us everything, Momma?"

"I think so, dear."

I told Martin that it was going to be one of those nights.

"I'll take the sofa so I don't disturb you."

My thoughts were in Vancouver, hovering over a patch of ground that covered all that was left of her. Those precious bones, once wrapped in flesh, cradled the womb that was my passage in. I went from the cemetery to the flat above the drug store to recall my last night with her; the feel of her body holding me. I was a child again. Suffocating.

Thirty-seven years without her, yet grief was as fresh as that very afternoon; as if Duncan had called to say that Mummie died today; as if I'd just lost her. The psychological trenches put in place immediately after her death could not defend me from the onslaught of feelings over growing up without her; the painful shocks that followed because she wasn't around. Grief mixed with anger at the loss of her – at the reasons why she turned on the gas. Graham and Marian stepped from the shadows, holding hands, sharing the same secret smile they shared when he painted her portrait.

Why did you do it, Daddy?

And why did you leave Mummie without a marker?

Have you been so busy all these years?

So poor, that you couldn't give her that much?

Or did you guzzle all your money so there was nothing left for grave stones?

Did you die before you could get around to it? I hope you did. That's the only way I can forgive you for leaving her there; without as much as a name to identify her remains.

&

I never should have stopped going to Adam and told him in as many words when he agreed to work me in between clients.

"You said you'd had a bad night. What happened?"

I spoke just above a whisper."My brother called me yesterday afternoon. He's found our mother's grave. She's been dead 37 years but it wasn't until last night…."

"You don't cry easily, do you?"

"No."

"But you were able to cry last night? Good!"

"I also had a very unusual experience last night. There is another person inside my skin with me. I think this little person has been asleep for quite some time, but she's wide awake now. And she remembers everything!"

"You were aware of her before last night?"

"She popped up last year, too, when I met Duncan for the first time, only I didn't recognize her as clearly then, not like I do now. There is this real sense of her standing on her tiptoes, peeking through my eyes, as if she were looking out a window with her little fingers on the lower rim of my eyes, hanging on to the window ledge. She would like to come out; she's tired of hiding. She wants to do more than peek, but it isn't safe outside. What if she can't get back inside again? I think what's happening is that for the first time she is feeling – and realizing the tragedy of Mummie's death. And I think I'm finally seeing the real effects of her death and the chain reaction it caused."

Adam asked that I set aside some time each day to record my thoughts and feelings. I didn't have to share it with anyone if I didn't want to; not even him. The first time I tried I felt foolish. When the little girl got hold of the pencil, it was no longer a foolish exercise. I couldn't shut her up. And I couldn't wait to share it with Adam.

"I've always blamed Graham for Mummie's death. They said he was extremely good looking – that was probably his main problem. Some people mobbed us for his autograph once when we were on the ferry on our way to Victoria. The steward told them he wasn't a movie star, but he still had to take us to a place on top of the ferry so we wouldn't be bothered. Odd that I should remember that!

"After I was adopted, I'd hear them talk about him; that he resembled Clark Gable. Beatrice told me that, so did Alma. I used to collect pictures of Clark Gable from movie magazines when I was growing up. I had a whole box of them. When he died, I actually cried. There's one thing that always troubled me. I never understood why we lived and Mummie didn't. You'd think two children would be more susceptible to gas, wouldn't you? I could never get it settled within myself. I thought he murdered her so he could be with Marian. Now isn't that a terrible thought to hold against your father?

"I was suspicious as soon as I woke up in the hospital. There were these welts across his cheek – so who put them there? I'd seen Mummie scratch his face before. I was certain they must have had a fight that night. They were very fresh marks. You can tell the difference between a fresh wound and one that's a day old. It never made sense, at least not to the kid part of me, that if he managed to pull me and Duncan out in time, why he couldn't pull her out too. I used to imagine how it happened; as if he held her down in the chair and she clawed his face. I don't know where that comes from, but it's always been with me.

"Common sense would say somebody would have found him out if it really happened that way. But common sense isn't convincing the kid in me; she keeps carrying on about the welts on his face. I've seen that face - the way it looked when he was bending over me that night in the hospital - so many times: in my dreams; sometimes when I'm out driving the car – with my mind on idle – you know how it is when you're driving."

"I would expect that you were afraid of him."

"Yes, but I did love him, and when he didn't show up that Christmas like he said he was going to I was devastated. Of course now I realize there may have been any number of reasons why he didn't."

"Such as?"

"Maybe it wasn't just Marian who couldn't deal with children. Maybe because of his alcoholism he couldn't cope – or he didn't have the money to make the trip. I remember making up a story, just for myself, that he was killed in an accident. And for all I know, that could very well be the case. But no matter what I, as a woman, can rationalize, this little kid in here is still hoping it will turn out the way she wants it to."

"Which is?"

"That he'll show up someday. That he'll say 'Yes, Dorian, there was a good reason, and here it is.' And the kid can say, 'Gee, Daddy that really is a good reason.' And after he tells her he really did love her, and has never forgotten her, even after all these years, they can sit down and swap stories about everything that happened to them since they last saw each other – except he's have to come up with a good reason as to why he never put a marker on my mother's grave before things would be right for the kid."

"What do you remember of your mother?"

"I get glimpses of her – in the kitchen mostly. She was troubled much of the time; even when she was singing; and she sang a lot. At least that was how I remember her. She had a timid side to her, except when she and my father got to fighting. Sometimes it came to pitching dishes, or she'd take off her shoe and heave it at him. One of their fights keeps coming back to me: the time she threw a pie tin at him. He picked me up and held me in front of him like a shield. He was dancing around trying to dodge her finger nails. She was slashing at my head, trying to get at him."

In relating the incident I was thrust beyond mental imagery to the physical perception of hands around my rib cage; the sensation of dangling in mid air before my mother's combatant face; thrashing above the floor; twisting from side to side to avoid her nails.

"I don't think I was ever clear at whom she was the most angry – me or my father. She cleaned houses, so I looked after Duncan. I don't know where my father was. I could give him the benefit and assume he was working someplace instead of off drinking. Before she left she'd point her finger at me and say, 'Take care of your little brother. Don't let anything happen to him.' I was always afraid that something would go wrong when she was away and it would be my fault.

"I felt guilty for a long time because I was angry with her for leaving us, but I worked it out as I got older. I realized she wasn't really a coward. I used to judge those who committed suicide as cowards for taking the easy way out because I see living as the real challenge. But she was only 25 years old. We lived on welfare, and she was pregnant again. Graham was having an affair at the time. It was more than she could take.

"We're getting her a gravestone. Then when anyone walks by her spot at least they'll know who's buried there. They might even wonder about her; what her life was like. That's what people do in cemeteries; at least I do. I'm always curious about the lives of those buried under the ground I'm walking on. Now they'll see her name and know she belonged to somebody once. It's terribly important that they know that she belonged to us; just as important, maybe more important, that they know we belonged to her. Strange how much I can love a person I spent such a short time with. Maybe it's the idea of having a mother that I love; or the vision in my head when I go back to when I was little. I'd give anything for a picture of her, but that can never be. She was so pretty, really she was. A lot of kids think that, I know, but she was. She was Swedish. If I had a picture of both her and Graham I could back up what I say about them. I remember people saying how beautiful she was – how handsome he was – too handsome for his own good – certainly for her good.

"She did try to take us with her, so she must have loved us, and that's what really matters. I've wrestled with that one, too. I fight the idea that she was just trying to get even with Graham, and even if she did, it isn't important anymore.

"And then there was Beatrice…."

"You've carried the burden for every bit of it," Adam said, "for your parents' arguments; your mother's death. And with your adopted mother's untimely death so soon after you came to live with her, well, it was just too many traumas too close together. A child naturally assumes the blame when things go wrong. Tell me, how do you handle arguments in your own marriage?"

"Martin and I don't argue because I've learned how to handle him. He has a very short fuse! I decided a long time ago not to subject my children to what I saw my natural parents doing. Couples aren't always going to agree, but I try to see that we settled our differences in a civilized manner. Besides, when Martin gets ticked, he puts me in knots, so I work at keeping the peace."

"You must have some disagreements. I've never known of a couple who didn't admit to having some dissension."

"We've had a few and it's not that I can't get angry. And I can do a pretty good job of it when I do! But I try to control it. Getting angry makes me sick. I don't handle temper well; mine or Martin's."

"And you don't want to relive the same feelings you had as a child?"

"Probably. I have no problem admitting to the anger. It's more like rage. If I could convert it into electrical power, I could light up all of L. A. I've always been afraid of it though; afraid to let it out. I don't want to be like my parents, so I don't think I really want to get in touch with it!"

"Start using your journal. Begin with the little things first and work up to the big issues. Put it down as though you never had to share it with another soul; as if you and the child are the only ones who ever need to know."

Adam leaned forward over his desk. I knew the signal. He was about to probe deeper.

"Were you ever molested as a child?"

"How did you know?"

"I'm paid to notice what others might not. Tell me how you're feeling right now."

"Like you just noticed a sign I've been carrying around my neck all my life. I'll chalk it up to professional know-how, but I am very uncomfortable now that you know. And I'm not going to open it up for discussion!"

"You don't have to tell me anything you don't want to. Be aware, however, that you've also assumed the responsibility for that as well. And it is never the child's fault."

"I know that! I think I have more understanding of how that affected me than anything else. I've done some reading. I'm okay with it now."

"Exactly what does that mean? You're okay with it now?"

"Adam didn't you just tell me I didn't have to tell you anything unless I wanted to?"

"I did."

"Well then, I'm not discussing it. I'm keeping the lid on that can of worms!"

"Do I detect some anger?" Adam asked.

"I'm sorry if I sound sarcastic. You took me off guard."

"You never have to apologize for your feelings in here. But I have to tell you, this issue is responsible for a great deal of stress. It's probably your major issue; one that affects all your other issues."

"It affects me at times, when I run across a certain kind of man or set of circumstances that brings it back to me, and I get hit with a flashback and relive it again. Then I panic. Like right now – telling you how it is! I don't want to get into it!"

"Then we'll move on to something else."

When Adam raised the question of molestation it amounted to his opening a file drawer and scattering the contents. Nothing was in the right place, and I wasn't up to sorting and filing again. Unconnected sequences from the mystery dream of kittens, a school yard and the drug store got in my way as I drove down Wilshire Boulevard. Only it wasn't a dream anymore, and something was added.

There was blood.

And a little girl on a bridge, looking for a way home.

I went to bed early after taking the strongest medication I could find and prayed for dreamless sleep. My only salvation was to put it back in the file again, unsorted. There was more than enough time to discuss with Adam. These files could keep; perhaps for a lifetime.

I didn't get what I prayed for. The dream hit with terrifying force; it was no longer a mystery. I couldn't deal with it lying next to Martin so I eased out of bed and went to the living room. The dream and all its painful sense went with me. I sat on the sofa – detached from a reply of what I'd experienced in sleep – seeing without feeling – aware of a precious little child inside myself scrambling to get back into hiding. I told her I understood why she had to put it away right after it happened, but we were going to have to talk about what took place before Mummie died. I just wasn't sure when.

Chapter 26

"It isn't so much that dreams don't come true…
it's people that don't come true."

"Adam, you once compared therapy to cleaning house. Now I see why. That's exactly what this is all about – cleaning house! I'm going from room to room dragging the child with me. And she's none too happy about it most of the time because she's got no choice but to look at it again. I tell her it's for her own good, then I get mixed feelings and think I'd like to get rid of her again; put her behind the windows and pull the blinds because what she sees, I see; what she feels, I feel. So then I have to admit that it's for my own good too. We're making one discovery after another.

"Take yesterday: I was thinking, or I should say, we were thinking, about stoves. It won't come as any surprise when I tell you the smell of gas makes me nauseous. I'm extremely sensitive to it. I can smell gas when nobody else notices. When Martin and I bought our first stove it had to be electric. Now, it seems to me that every time I walk into the kitchen it's a little like socializing with the thief that stole my treasure, no matter what kind of stove it happens to be.

"If you had a shotgun hanging above your fireplace, and it was the very gun that killed your mother, you'd get a jolt when you looked at it, wouldn't you? At least subconsciously? I've never had an affinity for cooking. It boggles me that I never saw the connection before. I didn't realize there was a legitimate reason for disliking the kitchen; or maybe I'm just super sensitive to stoves right now. Am I making too much of this?"

Adam didn't think so.

"I feel like an actress in a dual role. First the child, then the older sister, talking it over."

"I'd like your opinion of the child."

"This is one extraordinary kid! The closer I get to her the more I see what a brave little trouper she's been – growing up without security, feeling abandoned, unwanted. It isn't so much that dreams don't come true, Adam; I think it's people that don't come true. And her people never came true; none of them. What a trauma to lose two mothers so close together – and she also lost two fathers when it comes right down to it. And the men who hurt her…. I told her she was really a little heroine to come through it the way she did."

Adam smiled and nodded.

"I want to take care of her. She's never felt safe a day in her life. Somebody has to make it up to her!"

"And who do you suppose that's going to be?"

"Me?"

"Exactly."

"How?"

"The 'older you' and the child are getting acquainted; learning to appreciate and validate each other."

I was seeing things differently now – understanding that it was possible for the big me to put my arms around the little me and love her into a safe place. She was out of my reach during her hidden years, locked up because I was afraid to look at her pain. As long as she was out of the way I didn't have to.

"Sometimes I'm overwhelmed by it all – as if it couldn't have happened. That's why I can't tell you everything. I'm not sure you'd believe it, and if you didn't it would hurt her all over again."

"Have you tapped into the anger yet?"

"Do we have to get into the anger today?"

"Only so far as to give you some instructions. Next time come prepared with some of the things that anger you. You'll probably list the most insignificant first, and work your way up to what angers you the most. And bring it up to the present time."

"How would you feel if I told you that I'm going to put your name at the head of the list?"

He laughed.

"That's the first time I've ever heard you laugh."

"I rarely have much to laugh about in here during the course of a day."

"It must get depressing."

"It can – if I don't keep my perspective."

Journaling flushed out the effects of dysfunctional parents; the stormy relationships between Cecil and Maria, and Paul and Rita, bringing to light the conditioning which patterned the decision to avoid confrontation in my own marriage.

"So I pretend things don't bother me? I'd rather stifle it than let it out? Because what might happen would be worse than putting up with it?"

"You've quite an inventory stored up."

"I remember showing my temper a few times when I was younger. I was somewhat of a rebel. I was expelled twice!"

"Rebelling out of frustration and processing anger in a constructive way are two different things. Give me an example of a time you reacted in anger."

"Just before Martin and I were married Rita was giving me advice, needling me because he had so much schooling ahead of him. We were getting dinner ready; I was chopping vegetables. She wanted me to postpone the wedding. I told her to stay out of it, but she kept pushing. I snapped and threw a knife at her."

"Humph!"

"It was a big one, too. The blade passed right next to her head, close to her temple, in fact, it even took some of her hair. It landed with such force that it knocked down a spice shelf and went into the wall. If I'd been an inch or so to one side I'd have put out her eye."

"What did she say?"

"Nothing."

"Nothing?"

"Absolutely nothing. I pulled the knife out of the wall, waved it in her face and told her to keep out of it. It was my wedding. Neither of us ever brought the incident up, and haven't to this day. I tossed that knife like I'd trained with the circus. Ever see one of those knife throwing acts? I've never forgotten the sound of it. *Thwaup*! It scared the daylights out of me afterwards; scared the daylights out of her, too, I'm sure!"

"How do you blow off steam now?"

"About the most I'll ever do is slam the kitchen cupboards. I did throw a hairbrush at Martin when we were in dental school. He was preaching at me because I put a ding in the car. He wouldn't let it drop. I was brushing my hair at the time and tossed the brush at him, too. Of course I felt terrible about it. Martin was livid. He warned me never to try a stunt like that again."

"And what did you say to that?"

"I told him he'd better never talk down to me like that again."

Adam laughed. "It doesn't pay to badger you when you've got a weapon in your hand, does it?"

"I broke a perfectly good cup and saucer not too long ago."

Adam wanted the particulars on what drove me to break the china, which brought up an evening out with Kay and Alex. We met at their home for cocktails prior to setting out for a new restaurant Alex was touting.

Martin took a *Playboy* magazine from the coffee table and he and Alex began ogling the centerfold, exchanging typical masculine expletives. I walked out onto the patio to look at the lights in the San Fernando Valley, offended by their remarks. Alex criticized the anatomy of a well-known actress featured in the centerfold.

"Careful what you say about that one," Martin said, "I've always had a crush on her. That's one actress I'd like to add to my practice. I think she's terrific! I have got to have a copy of this."

"It's the way he said it, Adam. It cut right through me. How would he feel if I took pictures of naked men and drooled over them? It turned my stomach."

"Did you say anything to him?"

"You bet I did!"

"And?"

"He called me a prude. Then Alex said something to the effect that women who took offense at *Playboy* were either menopausal or just plain jealous."

"Humph," said Adam.

"I could have smacked him on the spot. I was in a foul mood the entire evening – still put off on the drive home. He wouldn't discuss it. He said he'd forgotten all about it."

"I'm guessing – but you slept on the sofa?"

"Good guess! The next day he said I was making a big deal out of nothing."

"He probably didn't know what to say. I doubt that you've showed disapproval of him very often."

"That's true – I haven't."

"It's a step in the right direction. And I hope you noticed that nothing terrible happened as a result of it."

"Nothing positive came from it either."

"That will show up in the future; the next time you're angry."

"As you can see, I'm still upset. I've seen Martin act like that before – you know – the boys-will-be-boys routine. But it never affected me to the extent that it has lately. And when he actually bought the magazine and brought it home – well,

I told him he'd have to keep his pinups at the office. I don't think it's a very healthy influence for the girls.

"I even got into a harangue over this with Kay. She thinks I'm getting terribly judgmental. Maybe I am. And I'm also upset because my best friend isn't as worked up over this as I am; as if what bothers me should bother her to the degree it does me. Not that she approves; she's just resigned to it.

"I don't understand why an actress would sell her body like that. Does she put so little value on herself that she's willing to offer sexual favours to any man willing to pay the price of the magazine? And what is most disheartening about this is – the man I love is buying what she is selling!

"I told Martin these types of magazines gave men an acceptable way to cheat on their wives, and that it was pretty insensitive on his part. He accused me of a holier-than-thou attitude. He sees nothing wrong in appreciating a beautiful woman, anymore than if I noticed an attractive man. That's hardly in the same category as drooling over a woman's naked body; actually buying a picture of her so you could have it on hand whenever you wanted to look at it! I wonder how many times he looks at her. Granted she's a lot prettier than I am; her figure is sensational, but you'd think a man would stop and think about how his wife feels knowing what he really wants is the woman in the centerfold! I haven't actually caught him in bed with another woman in the flesh, but he's there in his mind every time he looks at her!"

Mine wasn't the first complaint of its kind to strike the walls of Adam's office. And what he said to others he said to me. "Keep communicating with your husband. Tell him exactly how you feel about what he's doing, and how it affects you."

"He knows exactly how I feel. But that didn't stop him. He still bought the magazine. He still looks at her. And God only knows what's going on in his mind when he does."

"And you feel…?"

"Devalued! Belittled! Betrayed! About how he would feel if I was devouring a male centerfold. You're right, Adam, telling myself how fortunate I am to live where I do – that my children are healthy – all the standard stuff doesn't work any-more. I've got to get rid of this ache – no matter what it takes! I'm sick to death of it!"

Adam nodded. "When did you smash the china?"

"The day he brought the magazine home."

Another effect of the magazine was that it dredged up the memory of a man who used pornography before he used me. Everyone who ever used my body against my will moved from the shadows into the spotlight when Martin dis-covered his favorite actress in the centerfold of *Playboy*, and somewhere during the procession of ugly memories I'd lost respect for him; and I'd always had that. The thought of him engrossed in a woman's body, knowing he was fantasizing, trying to separate what Martin was doing from the flashbacks of my foster father arousing himself through pornography before he sodomized me had separated me from Martin. I couldn't let him touch me. And I was in such pain it is beyond telling.

The threat of the by-products of examination kept me from revealing it to Adam; compassion for the wounded child and what it would mean if she had to go through it again.

Chapter 27

"It made sense now.... I was never really alone,
and that same Companion was still with me. "

I limped into Adam's office with the anxiety of childhood stabbing at my throat, talking under my breath: "I can do it! I have to do it!"

If it had been entirely my decision, I might have held to my chicken-hearted thinking. But the child accused her older sister, pointing to a woman who preferred the shades drawn, fearing that someone might see into the disorder of her rooms. Cleaning house meant more than delving into basements and attics.

"Adam, I'm prepared to admit to what's really going on at home."

The dusting off of a marriage revealed a cracked and peeling veneer. I had no choice but to acknowledge the damage. It can happen in a marriage: when a woman throws herself into balancing everything to compensate for what used to be off kilter – to prevent a similar situation for her own children. It can happen: when two histories clash, when two kids living inside two adults can't work it out, and everybody loses. A man can easily take a woman for granted if he follows his father's lead. And if, as a boy, a man is subjected to the tyranny of criticism, there will be no pleasing him. A woman can tolerate criticism (and being taken for granted) if she was never the apple of anyone's eye.

"I've been looking at Martin through the eyes of the child who spotted the child in him. He's living with his own diary. Then we have all the others: Martin and I weren't the only ones at the altar when we took our vows. His parents, my parents, all my caretakers, were consummated into this marriage. Martin is what Martin is because he's been shaped by those who raised him according to how they were shaped, just like I was.

"Jenny has a stack of wooden figures with removable heads in her room. When you unscrew the top head there's a smaller figure inside, and a smaller one inside that one. They get smaller and smaller, but they are identical figures. Aren't we like that? Aren't we all stuffed with smaller and smaller selves? I'm really trying to understand the different ages that make up my husband. I'm not living with a 44-year-old man. I'm living with all the Martins, and he's living with all the Dorians. Some of the Martins are difficult for me to understand and live with; as I'm sure some of the Dorians are for him."

Adam threw up his hands when I told him how Martin reacted to my suggestion that we had serious problems in our marriage.

"He said what?"

"He said there was nothing wrong with our marriage; he was perfectly happy."

"And how did you react?"

"I was too shocked to say much of anything except suggest we get into counseling together. He wasn't at all receptive to that. Maybe he tuned me out. He didn't seem to understand what I was trying to tell him. But there isn't any doubt as to where I stand as far as he is concerned. I've had a nagging feeling for quite some time that the only reason I am still married to Martin is because I did what was expected of me. I think I've finally learned to be a good girl so I can stay! When Martin's happy, I'm a success. I know how to manage his moods like Beatrice did Cecil's. And I set myself up for this! My sole aim and purpose in life has been helping Martin get where he wanted to go. I've been devoted to that end."

If Martin's response was his only way of deflecting a threatening move on my part, I could understand that. But it came as a witness as to how he perceived my position in our relationship, and proved my suspicions: Martin didn't love me. Martin needed me.

"The way I see it, Adam, is that I keep his world in order. I helped him through school; took care of his father when he was old. I fill in at the office. I'm up to snuff socially. I'm not sure Martin ever fell in love with me. I think he fell in need of me!

"Now I realize I can't look to Martin to cushion whatever I went through growing up; that would be unfair. But if a man really loved a woman it seems to me he wouldn't have the habit of saying, 'I should have married a rich woman so I don't have to work so hard,' or 'I've always had a thing for taller women. I don't know why I married a shrimp like you.' He's been saying that for years. I tried to see it as a joke. I'm not willing to write it off as a joke anymore. He says it too often. And it hurts. It really hurts! It always hurts!"

"Have you said anything to him about it?"

"It doesn't matter anymore. It's like *Playboy*! He's going to keep right on buying *Playboy*, and I expect he'll just keep on telling me how sorry he is that he didn't marry a woman with money – why he didn't marry somebody taller. He does it because he wants to. Nobody could be that unaware of what they say."

"What is it you want most from Martin?"

"To be loved; to be the most important person in his life. That's my whole problem, isn't it? I want to come first! I think I've always wanted to come first – just once!" "Everyone fits that category! Most of us enjoy that position at some time during our lives; those who don't, continue to search for it. It's a basic need in every child."

"When you get right down to it, though, it's a ridiculous need, given that Martin would naturally be the most important person in his life, wouldn't he? Isn't that what it boils down to?"

"Some are more considerate and giving than others. You were forced to defer to the needs of others because you lived on the verge of another abandonment or relocation. Then when you married Martin you wanted to avoid another failure; if you lost yourself in him and didn't think about your own needs, you reduced your risks. You could never have survived another blow. You had to shut down after you lost David. It was your only means of survival. Your experience was predominately negative – without healthy relationships – you've been conditioned to believe you couldn't expect much from people. And you lived accordingly."

"I see how my girlfriends work their husbands to get what they want. But I can't operate the way they do. I can't take the dissension. For example, if I threw a tizzy because Martin was playing too much golf, it would amount to my asking him to choose between me and a mistress."

"And who do you suppose is afraid of the outcome of such a request?"

"The insecure little kid of course!"

"Exactly!"

"Kay told Alex that she never remembered hearing that a man was to cleave to his golf clubs. She makes sure he spends a certain amount of time with her."

"Have you suggested that you and Martin spend more time together?"

"Yes, once, and he invited me to the golf course. I drove the cart. I enjoyed the course; it's beautiful. Then I tried to take up golf, but I just don't care for it. So, if I were to bring it up to him now, he'd say, 'Why don't you learn the game so we can play together?' Then where's my argument? We've always had our own interests. And I'm glad he has his, but…."

"But?"

"This is going to sound so typically housewife, but there isn't any other way to put it: I feel that my only function is to hold things together. In fact, Martin even said it himself; he said I was the glue that holds everything together; the one he can always count on to fill in at the office. Then there was his father – now don't get me wrong, his father was a sweet old man most of the time, but he was also a lot of work as well as worry, and I'm the one who looked after him. I am so perfectly functional! That's what I've been. Functional! And I don't think Martin has ever seen me any other way. He needs me! But need is not synonymous to love! He said as much when he said there was nothing wrong with our marriage because *he* was perfectly happy!"

Martin had no inkling of the effects of my history; no idea how his own history motivated him; how he viewed our individual positions within the marriage. He was so seemingly innocent of the emotional climate of his home. We started therapy together; he saw Adam privately.

Understanding does not promise forgiveness, nor will it guarantee willingness for long-suffering in hopes of reconciliation. It was too late for counseling; too late to dress the wounds; too late for good intentions; pleading children or tears; so late that sacred vows were no longer sacred.

A year later, after the final meeting with our respective attorneys, Martin and I stood side by side facing the Hollywood hills from a 14th floor conference room, affirming to each other that the past 21 years were not necessarily a complete failure. We'd accomplished a lot together; raised two fine children who honored us with exceptional courage and understanding. My eyes never left the Hollywood hills when Martin said goodbye. Tears at a time like this were just as unbecoming to a grown woman as to a grown man. I could save face for the both of us.

Guilt took Martin's place at the window. How could I do it? How could I break up a family? Would it have been so difficult to leave it the way it was? I argued aloud in the room, professing, as I did to Martin, that I was willing to own my 50% of the responsibility, but no more.

Martin was involved with Judith now. He would probably marry her. He said he was "thinking about it." She was a good match for him. She was attractive; very attractive. She ran in all the right circles; came from a wealthy family; the perfect match for him. Judith even played a respectable game of golf. But she wasn't tall. She was an inch shorter than I was.

&

"It's amazing how quickly a man can bounce back from a divorce," Kay said, after learning that Martin was serious about Judith.

"I'm glad she's in the picture. He needs to know that he's still got what it takes. Besides, this wasn't one of those ugly divorces. I don't hate him. I'd like to see him happy. Martin is the sort of man that needs to be married."

"Well, he certainly has everything going for him. He's nice looking, in the right profession, in the right town, and being 45 never seems to hinder a man at all. In fact, it's probably in his favour."

"It's the gray hair that gets them."

"It's the country club," snapped Kay.

"She's got her own membership, she doesn't need his."

"That's my point. Do you think she'd be interested in him if he weren't in the club?"

"She happens to be a very nice woman. He couldn't have found a more ideal person."

"Well, now that Martin's taken care of, what about you? If you ask me, I think you've thrown yourself to the wolves with this divorce. Look what you settled for. Most women would have...."

"You give me more credit than I deserve. I took what my attorney said the judge would give me. I wanted it over with. The whole thing was very hard on Jenny and Chrissy.

Besides, I have to live with myself. You don't tell a man you can't live with him anymore, and then ask him to take care of you the rest of your life."

"If you ask me, you had a lousy attorney. You helped Martin build everything he's got. Do you have any idea how difficult it's going to be to find a job at your age?"

"I've had plenty of work experience. I can always go to work for a dentist. I'll get by. I've always gotten by. I'm different from you, Kay. I didn't grow up the way you did. I've never had any pampering. I'm only 45. I do have a few years left on me."

"Have you decided where you're going to live?"

"No, but I have to get moving on it right away. We have a buyer for the house. I have exactly 60 days to find a place that will take two teenagers, two cats and an unemployed woman."

"I don't suppose you'd give up the cats?"

"Not a chance!"

&

I managed to sell the owner of an eight-unit building on the idea of letting me move in with my brood in exchange for managing the building in addition to paying rent. He was skeptical in the beginning; not much for cats. There were plenty of people looking for three bedroom units, and a bricked-in patio running the length of the apartment was hard to come by in Westwood. He really didn't need anyone to oversee the place; his son could do that. When I offered to upgrade the carpeting at my own expense, the cats no longer posed a problem, and as far as two teenagers, he guessed that girls were never as bothersome as boys.

Kay said, "Nobody in their right mind would improve the property, collect the rent, give up their weekends to show a vacancy and pay top dollar on top of it!"

"They would if they'd been turned down for two solid months, they were living in a house that was being sold out from under them, and the only decent apartment in the right school district came with bright orange carpeting. Are you forgetting that I promised the girls they wouldn't have to change schools? Actually, I think it was very resourceful on my part."

"That's what Alex said."

"So did Adam."

☙

Christine was approaching her sixteenth birthday. She often alluded to how "it was all for the best." She was supportive, never stooping to judgment, or forwarding Martin's resentments. Adam spoke with her at length and assured me I could take her at her word, not that she wasn't suffering; everyone was suffering.

Jenny chafed under the brunt of decisions out of her control. At twelve, she had no understanding or patience for a world turned upside down because her mother decided she couldn't stay married to her father, as she habitually reminded me.

"It was all your doing, Momma. You were the one who broke up the family."

"Yes," I'd tell her, "I broke up the family. And I'm sorry. I would much rather have been able to keep us together, but…."

Jenny was having a difficult time of it; so I was having a difficult time of it. When I lucked onto a small, affordable house and told her we were moving again, only the promise of the big dog she always dreamed of owning made the proposition of another move just eight months after we took the apartment tolerable for her.

According to Jenny the house needed a lot of work; to Christine it had potential; to me it was the right price.

246

There was also the reassurance of friends in the immediate neighborhood.

"Momma? What are you going to do about this icky carpet?"

"I used to live in a house with hardwood floors. It would be nice to have them again. What do you think girls? Take a look at what's under the carpet."

A crew of gracious friends helped pull carpet, staples and tacks. When the final varnish dried I kicked off my shoes and showed the girls how I polished floors at St. Theresa's. They followed suit and skated after me, giggling. It was a marvelous sound; a marvelous sight. Ten noisy toes belonging to a sweet-faced German Shepherd, rescued from the pound, tapped across the floors behind us.

Jenny didn't think the cats were ever going to adjust to having a dog in the family. Christine said they'd just have to learn to be flexible "like the rest of us."

"It's a cute little place," Kay said. "Alex and I feel a lot better having Roger and Meg just a block over, just in case. You never know what might happen. It's not that we don't think you're capable, but you have to admit, this is not the best part of town."

"This is what we can afford. And there is nothing wrong with this part of town. I feel very secure with this dog. She's a beauty, isn't she?"

"Don't you think she's awfully friendly for a Shepherd?"

"She was a stray. Once she realizes this is her home her protective instincts will take over."

"Whatever made you decide on a name like Chauncey?"

"You'll have to ask the girls – they picked it out."

"Are you going to keep working at temporary jobs?"

"I need something permanent now; something that fits the girls' schedule. They can't take a bus from here, so I'll be hauling them back and forth."

Kay wanted to know if I had any regrets over the divorce.

"Of course! Anyone in their right mind regrets divorce. It's been very hard on the girls. I hate that part of it more than anything."

"I don't see that you're any better off. You've simply exchanged problems. I couldn't stand to live the way you do!"

"She isn't you, Kay," Alex said, "and it looks to me like she's doing just fine."

"Thanks, Alex, I appreciate that."

"But knowing what might be down the road for you," Kay said, "doesn't that terrify you? Martin would never bail you out!"

"The trick is not to look too far down the road, but wherever I'm headed, it can't compare with where I've been."

"What if you never remarry? It isn't easy for a woman in her forties to find a husband. They all want younger women."

"I may very well never get married, and if I don't, it won't be the end of the world."

"It certainly isn't going to be easy for you if you don't."

"Life isn't easy, Kay, married or single."

"She's got you there," said Alex.

Chauncey made a show of charging the front room windows when a couple slowed down in front of the house for a glimpse of the new neighbors.

"That dog is going to be hard on your new floors," Kay warned.

"She's going to be a great watch dog," said Alex.

Throughout the night, Chauncey's feet clicked off her rounds. She pressed her snout to the windows, sniffed and moved on to the next room. Each time she patrolled my room I praised her, "good girl, good girl."

It took the better part of a month before the house was in order and a feeling of home greeted us when we walked through the front door. A chip of guilt fell from my shoulders after the girls told me how much they liked our little house; another when Martin and Judith announced their engagement.

I confessed to Adam that while I was more at peace than I'd ever been, there was always the blame for the dissemination of the family lurking in the wings.

"Will I ever get over it? Will I ever stop digging up the guilt?"

"You haven't learned the difference between real and misplaced guilt. Martin played as much a role in this as you did. And you know it. But you are making progress; more than you think."

"Once in a while I have a day where I think I am, too. Then it sneaks up on me again."

"These things take time."

"It's like a piece of lint that's stuck on the end of my finger. I can't shake it loose."

"It's tied up in your feelings of self-worth."

"I'm not in touch with much of that lately."

"You have more of it than you think. At sometime during your growing years you gained some degree of worth – at least enough to see you through. If that weren't the case, I don't believe you would have made it. And strange as it may sound, I think it was your father – either Graham or Cecil – who gave it to you."

Adam's statement came as a display of professional incompetency and thoroughly riled me. Evidently he wasn't paying attention to what I'd been telling him over the past 18 months. My father? My father, indeed!

When I thought about it later, after the source of my self-esteem was revealed, it seemed more plausible to expect it to come at a less common time, and in a less common place; during Sunday worship services at my own church, or on one of my visits to the Catholic Church near Adam's office; at least when I was praying or thumbing through Alma's Bible. But that wasn't the case. It came when my mind was cluttered with trivia and plans for the day. When I was bent over the sink brushing my teeth; when I could not mistake the still small voice, as it is so often described, because a voice that imposes upon thoughts so far removed from the message it delivers is heard with such startling clarity it prohibits doubt.

"It was me – it was your Father – your Heavenly Father."

Awareness fell on me like a net – catching me up at age eleven and my year at St. Theresa's. It made sense now, such perfect, beautiful sense. I was never really alone, and that same Companion was still with me.

Because God so loved the world….
Because God so loved me….
He sent His only begotten Son….

The supernatural is truth to those who experience it; more likely to be taken for foolishness by those who hear of it, and the one relating such an experience will be suspect by reason of motive or stability. I had judged others by the same standard. It stood to reason I might expect the same. It was unfair, better still, naïve, to expect Adam to see it my way. The experience was too precious to risk; still I wanted him to know to whom I could credit my self esteem.

"Do you remember what you said to me about my father giving me a sense of self worth? Well, I was pretty upset with you – scratch that – I was extremely upset at the time. It seemed so ridiculous to suggest that either of my fathers gave me any confidence in myself. But you were right; at least partially. It was one of my fathers all right, only it was my Heavenly Father.

"When I went to St. Theresa's it was really tough on me, yet it was there, in spite of my unhappiness, that I acquired the faith that was going to sustain me. I saw a movie on the life of Christ and started going to the Chapel every day. It was the only place I ever felt worth anything. I always came away feeling better. I got my hope and encouragement from Him. His life and His face as I remembered it from the movie kept coming back to me. It was the story and the face that wouldn't go away; the face and the story that sustained me."

Adam's voice was flat, condescending. "Faith can be a very powerful influence in a person's life."

"I understand now that while I didn't grow up with a physical handicap, I was handicapped emotionally. I was thinking about Betsy. She probably went through physical therapy to help overcome her physical limitations. Now please don't interpret this as a putdown of your efforts, Adam, but I feel emotional handicaps are handicaps of the spirit. Of course psychological counseling has its place – but it can only do so much. It's given me understanding of why I am the way I am – why I think and react the way I do much of the time – and why things turned out the way they did between Martin and me. But I need more than understanding. I need relief! And I'm not sure therapy can give me that. But I know Who can."

When Adam straightened himself against the back of his chair I knew my remarks had landed uncomfortably.

"You've helped me so much – I could never have uncovered it all without your help – please don't take what I said personally."

He half smiled and said, "I won't." I didn't for a minute believe him; so I never told him that only God offered complete healing.

Chapter 28

"God has a record of everything that hurt you…
He promises to take whatever was bad and
make it into something good…"

"You'll never guess who I talked to last night?"

"Duncan?"

"Yep! It's me."

"You're right… I'll never guess."

"Graham!"

"Graham?"

"Yep!"

"You're sure it was him?"

"One hundred percent sure."

Duncan learned that if he took a letter to the Canadian equivalent of our Social Security office with Graham's last known address (which he got from the welfare office in Vancouver) it would be forwarded to his current address. They would not divulge his whereabouts, but they would mail the letter. If the letter was not returned, Duncan could assume that Graham received it.

"What did he say, Duncan? Tell me everything."

"I'm having a problem trying to remember it all. He called pretty late. I was already in bed, asleep. At first I thought I was dreaming."

"Did he say anything about your letter?"

"He said he knew I wanted to know if anybody in the family ever had MS – that's what I asked him in the letter. I'm afraid it might be hereditary. I worry about my kids getting it."

"And did he?"

"No."

"What else did he say?"

"That it was a nice thing we did for our mother at the cemetery."

"And?"

"That was about all. I asked him where he lived. He said in Winnipeg, but he goes to Vancouver quite often. He told me the area he lives in. I know the district. He didn't give me the address though."

"What else?"

"To tell you the truth I think that was about all. I got kind of tongue-tied – I didn't know what to say to him – guess I was in some kind of shock."

"Do you think you'll hear from him again? Did he say anything about calling again?"

"No."

Duncan's next report on the whereabouts of Graham came a few months later.

"I think he was here yesterday – outside my house. A car drove up with two men and two women in it. A woman in the front seat rolled down the window and asked if I was Duncan. I said I was, and asked who wanted to know. When I walked down to the car, a man in the back seat rolled down his window and warned me not to come any closer. Then they drove away – in a hurry. I never did get a good look at them. But I'm sure it was him. Who else could it be?"

"Who else?"

"Don't you think it's strange that he would take the trouble to come over here and then take off when I came up to the car?"

"Sounds very 'cloak and daggerish' to me. I wonder why he would do that! Keep me posted. Who knows what might come of all of this."

Graham showed up just before Christmas that same year in a toy store while Duncan was doing some Christmas shopping.

"This guy walks up behind me and called me by name, and when I turned around and asked him who he is, he looked at me for a minute then took off. I recognized his voice. It's the same guy. It must be him!"

"Oh, Duncan, it had to be him. But how did he know where you were? Winnipeg is a good-sized city. It doesn't seem likely that he would just happen to run into you in a toy store does it? Do you suppose he could be following you?"

"I don't know."

"Can you describe him? How tall was he? What was he wearing?"

"He was pretty tall; I'd say about 6'2, maybe a little better than that – of course he has gray hair. He was wearing a hat, and an overcoat, but I think he was probably pretty well built when he was younger, probably pretty handsome too. He sure didn't hang around long."

"What I can't figure out is, if he isn't going to let you talk to him, why would he come up to you in the first place?"

"It's a mystery to me."

"Me too, and that's just what this is beginning to sound like; a mystery. If he ever comes up to you like that again, would you tell him we just want to talk to him? That we'd like to have a picture of him – and our mother."

"I will, if he ever shows up again and I can get him to hang around long enough."

"On second thought, I think I'll write him a letter. If I send it to you will you take it to the place you took yours, and have them mail it like they did your letter?"

"Good idea! Maybe you'll hear from him."

"Maybe!"

Mulling over Duncan's encounters with Graham led me to speculate that if Graham knew about the gravestone it was a very good indication that he had been there; further indication that he would be drawn to her grave for reasons of guilt or remorse over the outcome of his life; perhaps for the outcome of all our lives. I was the only one who had never been to our mother's grave. It was time to attend my mother's funeral. Adam encouraged me to go.

I was finally going to do it! Go back to where it all started – finish it up once and for all – fill in the gaps and find enough of me to make a whole person again, in spite of the emotional price I knew it was going to cost. And it was going to cost! The most threatening of all eventualities would come if I could locate our building.

I went directly to Chinatown my first evening in Vancouver to hunt down the drug store. In mid July there was ample daylight to go on. It was all so painfully, exquisitely familiar; mountains, bridges, oriental restaurants, markets. I went from street to street searching corners for a building to match the one packed in my head since 1937, and took a picture of one that was similar, thinking that if it wasn't the exact place, it was close enough; better than going back empty-handed. Then I noticed a street car moving one block up. This was not the building I was looking for. People caught the streetcar at our corner. It was foolish to continue the search without an address. Unless – unless I could get some information from the cemetery. Surely they would have a record of the address of the deceased.

I explained to the gentleman at the cemetery office how I came all the way from California to find my mother's grave; that I was trying to trace my family history. Could he check his records for an address that could tell me where my mother died? I so wanted to be able to go back there, for old times' sake, to take a picture. Would he be so kind as to do that for me?

He wasn't sure; records that far back were in another building.

I prayed and asked again.

"You have no idea what it would mean to me. You see I have nothing of my childhood – absolutely nothing, and my brother and I were separated after her death. I lost track of my father, too."

"In that case, I'll see what I can do. I'll have to go to the basement files. Stop by after you visit the grave site. I may have something for you then."

Self-talk said: "You sure played that like a real ham." More self-talk said: "The end will justify the means if I can just find the drug store."

The child was anxious. *"I don't want to find the drug store!"*

The gentleman made a swipe on a map with a yellow highlighter. You'll find her in the Oak Section."

This is it! This is finally it! I'm going to my mother's funeral!

"This is going to hurt, kid."

"Did you bring Kleenex?"

I opened my purse. I had plenty of Kleenex.

"We don't have any flowers. We should have brought flowers."

"I suppose you're right. I wasn't thinking flowers, I was thinking Kleenex. Be a good girl and don't give me a bad time about this – all right?"

"Do you think she'll understand?"

"She would if she knew we were here. She isn't here, you know."

"Then what are we doing here?"

"Paying our respects."

"Wouldn't it be wonderful if Daddy showed up too, while we're paying our respects?"

"He won't."

"But wouldn't it be wonderful if he did?"

"You've seen too many movies, kid. Things like that only happen in the movies."

"I know, but it was nice to think about it. It's okay to think about it, isn't it?"

"Of course!"

*"What if we can't find it? What if we've come all this way and
we don't find her grave?"*

"We'll find it," I whispered, "even if I have to go back to
the office and get somebody to help."

The 20-foot pine stationed at the foot of her grave must
have been a seedling when she was buried. It was the only
tree in the area. It seemed fitting that she had a tree for a
marker before she had a stone. At least she had a tree. How
very fitting that the tree was where it was.

How many people visited the grave besides Duncan and
me? I wanted to believe that Graham had been here, holding
to that as an explanation for his knowing about the marker
rather than through any second-hand information, because it
would also suggest he came for reasons of "second thoughts."

Where did he stand? Here? Or here? Did he sit on the
bench located some 8 feet away? Standing on the grass at the
foot of her grave I was as close as I could get to either of them
in this lifetime. I sank onto the bench and ran my hands over
the stone. Graham's hands might have done the same.

Of course she wasn't here. She couldn't hear me. But I
had to release the words; speak them aloud. Perhaps there
was a Divine provision for those like me – a way for the intent
of my heart to reach her.

"I don't blame you for what you did. And I don't think
you were a coward. I only wish you could have stayed because
if you had been here a lot of things would never have happened; but I can understand why you wanted to die. Some
people miss their mothers part of their lives – I've missed you
most of my life."

Emotion swelled like the waves of the Pacific outside the
city; the Kleenex wilted. I couldn't sit on the bench much longer; stand over her spot, or cry much longer. I was empty. But
I couldn't leave her there alone again. We stayed at the bench,
yielding to the bolts of memory that pounded and pressed us
dry.

"Dear God, let her know that we were here to pay our
respects. Tell her how sorry we are that her life was so short;
so difficult; that it ended the way it did. Tell her we are going

to do something with our life, for her sake, so her life will count for something. We can do that much. Dear God, let us do that much!"

The grass was encroaching upon the face of the stone marker. I knelt and swept it away, tenderly, the way I would brush the hair from the face of a daughter. A small oblong stone was nestled in a portion of the grass in the exact center, a few inches below the rim of the marker, so perfectly centered it could have been deliberately placed. I plucked it, along with a few blades of grass, folded them in my hand and started back to the cemetery office, anticipating the information I hoped would be forthcoming from the nice gentleman who was taking the time to go into the basement to check the records.

The gentleman wasn't available, but he left two papers with the receptionist. Two papers: one with a piece of Graham on it, the other with a block of history. Line ten of the burial agreement indicated the plot cost $20.00. Line twelve showed a burial fee of $10.00. My heart leaped. No need to walk up and down the streets of Chinatown now. It leaped again at line seventeen. I finally had something of my father: his signature.

It was the child who stroked the signature line as if some of him might be preserved in the ink; the child who clutched the paper as the car turned onto her street, and recognized the building before the address was compared with the death certificate.

A band tightened around my head when I took the stairs to the apartments. I recognized the linoleum covering the stairs; it proved its age with just the right amount of wear. I turned at the landing and looked down the stairs that once echoed the sound of my child's feet, and was taken back to a day when she skipped into the street with a pair of roller skates in hand and ran to a church at the end of the block, entered and ran down a hall into a room resembling a scaled-down gymnasium. She put on her skates and skated around the room, swinging her arms, laughing. Then the door flew open. A woman was shaking her fist because the child was marking up the floors. The child made a dash for the door, but the woman landed a smack on her backside as she went by. The woman looked very familiar; she's run the child out before.

I continued to the second floor, and stopped in front of door #3. The band around my head cinched tighter. To my left another door was locked, no doubt intended for non-residents from the street. The bathroom was there; Mummie did the washing in the bathtub behind that door. The last time Duncan and I came through that door we were unconscious.

Memory provided a key to the flat; to the upholstered chair where Marian posed for her portrait; the sink with the mirror above it where Graham shaved because there was always somebody taking too long in the bathroom. I saw the stove, the rocker, the black and white squares of the linoleum. Then the air in the hall went thin and I had to escape into the street. I was gulping the outside air, looking at the fire escape and the window where Duncan and I sat on the ledge. Two tow-headed children were swinging their feet, watching the people passing underneath; waiting for the street car that brought Mummie home.

Most of the buildings were as they were in the 30's, with a few signs of renovation. I peeked into oriental restaurants and shops, very much aware of the child at the end of my hand, peeking with me. Some of those behind the counters could be the very children she went to school with.

My heart picked up when I rounded the block and came to a school. Suddenly it turned cold; my body was pounding with adrenaline and fear. It was the school of my mystery dream! I steadied myself on the schoolyard fence; frantically fighting the flashes of recall exploding like the Fourth of July. I could almost hear the voices of the boys; almost feel the hand of the one who led her away. I saw the look of innocent expectancy and trust on her face as she went, like a lamb, to the slaughter.

I raised my hand to blind out the drug store side of the building, walking head down back to the car, not daring as much as a peek into the place.

So much happened within these two city blocks.

So much to twist and mold a little girl to fear and mistrust.

So much to brand a child's soul.

"How are you doing, kid?"

"I'm scared. Can we go back to the hotel now? I think you're going to get a headache. I hope you brought your pills. Your headaches are terrible!"

"I did."

We drove over a bridge several blocks from the drug store.

The child was in distress. *"This is where the police picked me up and took me home to Mummie. She was mad at me because she couldn't find me all afternoon. Daddy spanked me for running away. Only I didn't run away. I got stolen from the schoolyard. But he spanked me anyway. I guess he didn't know about the boys."*

"No, he never knew about the boys. He should never have spanked you. It wasn't your fault, you know."

"Did Adam tell you to say that?"

"Children are never at fault when that sort of thing happens to them."

"I don't want to talk about it. I don't want to cry anymore. It hurts to cry. I thought we were going back to the hotel!"

"Then we won't talk about it. You've really done a wonderful job of holding up, kid. I'm proud of you. I'm so sorry you were hurt – so sorry. And so is God."

"He is? How can you be sure?"

"Because he recorded every one of your tears in a special book. He saved all your tears in a special bottle – that's how much he cares about what you went through."

"Who told you that?"

"It's in the Bible – in Psalm 56. God has a record of everything that hurt you, and He promises to take whatever was bad and make it into something good. And there's something else you ought to know."

"What?"

"I love you very much. And I'm not going to let anyone hurt you again."

"Thank you."

"You're welcome."

We went back to the hotel, and took our pills. We had our headache and our window time. And we cried; grieving our loss and the atrocities of three school boys and a man. We were going to share our deepest wounds with Adam now - life was far too precious to spend it managing files.

Chapter 29

*"Dorian, as a person, you are the most convincing
proof of the existence of God."*

"Remember that can of worms I said I was never going to open?"

"I remember," said Adam.

"Well, the lid blew off in Vancouver. Emotionally, I feel like Humpty Dumpty. Everything is moving a lot slower than it normally does – including me. When I took the girls to school this morning everyone was honking at me, and I ran a red light. I didn't even see the light. I almost called a cab to bring me here. I didn't know if I could make it here on my own, and the only reason I didn't was because I couldn't handle being trapped in a car with a strange man. The past two nights I think I've averaged about two hours of sleep. I almost phoned you – several times."

"Why didn't you?"

"I was afraid."

"Of what?

"That you wouldn't believe me if I told you what happened; how often it happened. And I knew I couldn't get the words out."

"Are you prepared to talk about it now?"

"Not exactly – you'll have to read it. It was difficult enough to write, let alone speak it out loud. And I had to do it in third person. I needed the distance."

Adam took the papers. Only the night before, I opened the door to the room of horrors. The child pleaded to stay behind; the wiser-sister-of-herself insisted. It was the last room in the house, and while I was every bit as terrified, those who hid behind the doors had to be evicted, otherwise they would pollute the house again. I summoned the shadow people from the room of horrors and submitted them – one by one – to the conviction and condemnation of the pen. They had no right to my body; no right to steal my childhood; no right to haunt and damn me to years of torment. Had they ever given me a second thought? Ever wondered how it affected me? I wrote and bawled until the residents of the room of horrors lay as helpless and pitiful wretches exposed for what they were: victims of another kind. There was something drastically wrong with those who could use a child to such an end. And how many others had fallen prey to their appetites? How many Dorians spent their precious lives contending with these same shadow people? How many casualties?

I shifted my eyes from Adam onto the buildings outside the window behind his back, tracing the unspeakable words in my mind as he turned the pages.

….She was in the first grade the day the older boys from the neighborhood lured her from the school grounds under the pretense of giving her a kitten if she played a game with them. One of the boys lived in her building. They showed her a box of kittens; she picked out the black and white one. She had to promise to keep the game a secret. They took her to a field, covered her eyes and mouth, tied her hands and put her on the ground. She can still remember the feel of the dry grass under her back, the pain of burning thrusting sticks, their filthy mocking language. Then one of them untied her; another said, as if in a moment of remorse, "Don't cry; don't cry." Another one said "Run, run!" Then it was quiet.

She took off the blindfold and uncovered her mouth. She found her panties and used them to clean herself, but there was blood, so she hid them in the bushes, afraid of what her father would do if she came home with soiled panties. Two policemen found her wandering on a bridge. One of them asked "What's your name, little girl?" She couldn't find her voice. The second policeman said, "She fits the description," and put her in the police car.

She tried to keep her dress pulled down so her father wouldn't notice her panties were missing, but he did. He demanded to know what she'd been up to. What happened to her panties? He was angry because she wouldn't answer him. She must have done something terrible because he was disgusted with her. He gave her a good talking to before he spanked her. She was very ashamed of herself, very sore, and sad because she never got her kitten.

The man who owned the drug store kept candy behind the counter for children in the neighborhood. Graham smoked cigarettes with him on the street corner. What happened behind the counter has to stay a secret; she is too ashamed to tell. But Graham knows. He must have been looking for her because he came behind the counter, snatched her away, tossed her over his shoulder and ran up the back stairs, scolding her because she knew she wasn't allowed in the drug store. She was a bad girl to disobey him. He had to punish her again.

What happened in the foster homes was on page four; all about Peter on page six. Adam collected the papers, mumbled a hoarse, "You'll have to excuse me for a few minutes," and left the room. He returned some ten minutes later, stuffing a handkerchief into his jeans.

"Forgive me for running out on you like that. I've been in the john all this time. I almost lost it in there."

He cleared his throat and retrieved his handkerchief. I groped for the box of tissues on the table in front of me.

"You do believe me, don't you, Adam? I know it could sound pretty far-fetched. I was so afraid you might not – sometimes I can't believe it myself. How could I have come across so many people like that?"

He moved to the chair next to me, took my hands and stared into my eyes. "I believe you! I believe every word of it – and I can't tell you how much it grieves me that you were subjected to it – that you've had to live with the effects of such abuse for so long."

Pain pooled in my eyes. "I actually used to bang my head against the wall when I was growing up – trying to get it out of my mind. And after the girls were born it was worse! I can't tell you what it's been like – living with the fear that somebody would get a hold of my daughters the way they did me; that somebody might rape them. It's worn me out. Bad enough that they stole my childhood – that they have my peace of mind as a woman.

"Why didn't my father stand up for me in the drug store? Why didn't he defend me? How could he blame me for what happened? I had no reason not to trust that man. I thought he was my father's friend! I played with his kids."

"Maybe your father was afraid of him. We like to see our fathers as the hero when the truth is, some of them are cowards, or overly concerned for their own reputation. Even if he and your father were just casual friends, the friendship may have been more expedient to his needs than those of his own daughter. Please understand that this is only a stab at an explanation.

"You didn't have anyone around to watch out for you. There are a lot of disturbed people in the world; you ran into more of them as a child than most of us will in a lifetime. The economics of your family had a lot to do with it. I don't think either of your parents was around much of the time. Child molesters are always on the lookout for children who aren't well supervised; they know how to bribe a child into their confidence. They also prefer blonde, blue-eyed children, and you would attract attention in an Oriental community. And foster homes were not as closely monitored in those days as most of them are now."

We spoke of the majority of decent men incapable of sentencing a child to so damaging a history, and as a woman I could agree with him; but not the child. An abominable succession of betrayals left her floundering in a private world where men were always suspect. A violated child listened to

the conversation of two adults, never for a moment believing any man or boy could be trusted because of those who made the choice to do it, knowing as they did that it was wrong; as wrong as any human act could be. They deliberately spun a web of promise and trust to trap and then betray. They committed the crime; she served the sentence. They should have paid! With the right punishment she was sure a lot of sick people would get well – in a hurry!

Adam gathered the papers, tenderly, respectful of the painful outpouring of a child's soul. "Would you like to keep these?"

"No."

He tore the unspeakable into pieces, then, rather than tossing them into the wastebasket, he bent over and carefully laid them to rest.

"There's a part of me that still feels ashamed – still feels it might have been my fault."

"Is there also a part of you that knows it wasn't?"

I was fighting tears again and could only nod.

"The time will come when the little you will be able to let go of the shame."

"I'm feeling very uncomfortable right now, Adam. I'd like to leave now."

"I understand. But before you do, there's something I'd like to say. Knowing your history as I do, particularly with this new information, I really don't know why you're even sane. With all that happened during the first 12 years alone – not to mention the continued rejection – Jonesy – then David – your survival is a miracle. And I must confess that I'm not as skeptical about your Heavenly Father as I was the day you told me about Him. It would take something, or somebody pretty extraordinary to get you to where you are today in spite of all that happened to you."

After promising to call him at his home later that evening, I left the building, plugged the meter and walked two blocks to the Beverly Hills Catholic church and fell on my knees and wept, mourning the years of flashbacks, ugly dream visitations, the strain of living on red alert for the next mental

explosion of pictures that forced me to relive the molestations. I was past striving for healing now; I had to surrender; give myself over to the Encourager of my youth; accept His timetable, however He wanted to do it and for however long He wanted to take.

Healing came in increments over a grueling span of months; a metamorphosis as a result of consistent visits in that quiet, holy place; times of solitude in my room engrossed in the Bible. One by one the splinters of betrayal and loss worked to the surface until all that remained were the barbs of revenge.

"Lord, I want to forgive."

"Lord, help my Unforgiveness."

I ached with the need and desire to forgive, for a prescription to kill the pangs of Unforgiveness, knowing I was fair game for another dragon; the scavenger I invited to pick my bones and prolong complete healing because I could not shake the need to punish those who damaged my child. I was uncomfortably aware that forgiveness came cheap when I wanted it for myself; it carried a far higher price tag when it was my turn to extend it to others, particularly these "others." I could not pardon the acts themselves, or discount the outrage over what was done to my own child, but I could not have compassion for the inner child in them, what might have happened to twist and bend them as adults to become a party to such an evil.

So I waited, knowing He would have to prepare the ground of my heart as He prepared it for faith. The day I cried aloud saying, "Dear God, do You realize I've spent two-thirds of my life paying for other men's crimes?"- the still small voice spoke a second time.

"I understand what it means to pay for other men's crimes."

The face of Christ never blazed more brightly than on the day the dragon of Unforgiveness was slain. I would never again see the Cross in light of my sin alone, but also in terms of sins perpetrated against me and others like me. Father God demanded payment for those offenses; they were grievous in

His sight. He shared in my suffering; to the extent of the death of His only Son. Would I wound Him further by not accepting the sacrifice and the love that provided it? An awareness and compassion for the heart of God relieved me of the anger and brokenness over wasted years, and I could forgive, not the acts themselves, but those who committed them. I could even feel compassion for them because of what might have fashioned them into doing it. There was only one appropriate target for the outrage over the damaging evil of molestation – the roaring lion that went about seeking whom he could devour. I could pin it on him. And that is where I left it.

Misplaced guilt and shame stepped aside for recognition of the child for who she really was: a remarkable little girl, a brave little soldier who endured and overcame through faith. Seeds of expectation took root and flourished in newfound confidence, overgrowing the terrors established in the garden of her childhood.

"Remember how you used to go to the Chapel when you were upset?"

"It was right after I saw the movie."

"The movie really affected you deeply, didn't it?"

"I cried."

"Why?"

"Because He didn't deserve to suffer like He did."

"Any other reason?"

"Because He loved us."

"You and me?"

"Yes. No! It was just me then. You weren't there yet."

"How did you feel after you found out He loved you?"

"I didn't want to share Him with anyone else."

"Why do you suppose you felt like that?"

"Because it was the first time anybody loved me."

"What about Mummie?"

"She wasn't here to love me!"

"Did you love Beatrice?"

"I'm not sure. I liked her very much. But then she went away too – so I'm glad I didn't get too close to her – as long as she was going to leave like Mummie."

"How did you feel when she died?"

"Like it might be my fault again – that I might have done something wrong to make her go; just like I did Mummie."

"It wasn't your fault."

"You asked me how I felt. That's how I felt!"

"Tell me about Cecil."

"I really loved him, but it didn't do any good. He was always trying to get rid of me. And he finally did, too. He sent me to live with Paul and Rita."

"But Cecil was sick."

"He wasn't too sick to be with that woman in Edmonton and all her kids. He liked being around them."

"And Maria?"

"She didn't like me either. But I loved her. I still do. But it wasn't very nice of her to say what she did when you went down to visit Duncan in Calgary."

"Maria was hurt very deeply. She's bitter. We have to overlook what she said. And we need to pray that God will heal her, too. What about Rita and Paul?"

"What about them? I didn't live with them; you were the one who had to get along with them. I went to sleep then. Did you ever love them?"

"I came to in my own way; or maybe it was just loyalty, or appreciation for helping me out when I needed them. I'll have to think about that for awhile. I can tell you one thing, I always felt obligated to them."

"Maybe you should visit Rita. It might help to talk to her."

"Maybe it would."

During my final session with Adam I told him, "So many times, if I come across a certain kind of man, the child reacts and I have to reassure her, remind her that her big sister is in charge, and nobody can touch her without my permission. It works every time. The kid isn't looking over her shoulder like she used to. And that's a good sign."

"A very good sign," echoed Adam. "And how is the adult you feeling about David these days?"

"He'll always be tugging at my sleeve, but I've let go of the guilt and turned him over to God. Someday we'll be together. He'll be whole then. He'll know who I am and none of this will matter anymore."

"So your faith is still holding?"

"Stronger than ever!"

I never told Adam about the day the Father slipped it into my mind that He understood my heartbreak over David. He knew what it meant to give up a Son. That insight brought instant healing and peace, and from that day on I could no longer access the pain associated with David; it simply wasn't there anymore.

"And Martin?"

"What is this? 20 questions?"

"You're graduating! Call it a final exam."

"Martin? Well, I'm still tender about him. You can't love a man for 21 years, have his children and then say he isn't a part of you. I don't suppose that will ever change. I know so much more about Martin now than I ever knew while we were married. I know a lot more about people in general, now that I know myself.

"I think people are a lot like puppets, Adam. We don't see the people standing behind us pulling our strings. I found out who was pulling mine. And I'm not going to let them do it anymore!"

"And you're feeling better about your mother now that you've been to Vancouver?"

"Much better. So does the kid. We brought back a little stone and some grass from her grave. It's in a china box on the coffee table. Every now and then the kid opens the lid and takes out the stone and holds it awhile."

"Graham?"

"There's always a chance he could contact Duncan again; or he might even answer the letter I sent him. He's in his 80's now so the odds aren't too high. He may already be gone. We'll just have to wait and see. I've stopped needing him, so whatever happens is all right. I've lost the sadness that went with him, too.

"What still bothers me, though, is that what I remember most about my parents is their anger and discontent with each other. They must have had some tender moments – at least in the beginning. I hope I can dig up some of those someday. I do wish I had their pictures. I still feel cheated in that respect. I've had some very tender times trying to visualize them as children. They must have had their own struggles. As I told you before, it isn't dreams that don't come true, it's people. How many people didn't come true for them? I'll never know their backgrounds – how it was for them when they were growing up. They did the very best they could, I'm sure. I've made my own mistakes with Jenny and Christine, and I'd like to think it was out of ignorance. I've never made good on all the promises either, not because I didn't want to. Graham deserves the same understanding I would like from my daughters for the times I didn't, or couldn't come through for them."

"It would appear that Humpty Dumpty is back in one piece again."

"Thanks for working through it with me."

"Dorian, as a person, you are the most convincing proof of the existence of God that I've ever come across. I'll never forget you."

"I'll never forget you either, Adam."

The shadow people were gone. The pain was gone. But healing, like life, is an ongoing process, and the child continues to react, less frequently with time. We couldn't erase the history; we could manage it so it could no longer rule the present or foul the future.

"How are you feeling, kid?"

"Better, much better."

"Good."

"Can we go back to Vancouver someday?"

"I don't see why not."

"After we pay our respects at the cemetery, can I take you some-place instead of you always taking me someplace?"

"Sure, kid, where would you like to take me?"

"To Stanley Park. You'll love Stanley Park! I remember Mummie taking us there once."

"I'm sure I would."

"Could we stay all day?"

"If you like."

"And could we bring a picnic, and put a blanket on the grass and sit as long as we want to?"

"We'll take a picnic, and a blanket, and we won't be in any hurry to leave."

"We could take the ferry to Victoria. You'll love Victoria, too."

"Of course."

"Could we stay at the Empress Hotel? It's the most beautiful place you could ever wish for."

"I can't promise you the Empress. That might be a little out of my reach, but we will definitely go to Victoria someday."

"The next time we visit Vancouver do we have to go to the drug store?"

"No, we've finished with the drug store."

"Will we ever get back to Calgary?"

"Would you like to?"

"It would be nice to see the Centre Street lions, and walk across the bridge one more time. And I'd like to see how tall the willows are now. And we could take pictures so we'd always have them after we leave."

"We have a lot of adventures to look forward to, don't we?"

"And what about Heaven? Are we really going to go to Heaven someday?"

"You can count on it."

"What an adventure that is going to be!"

ॐ❧

*"And God will wipe away every tear from their eyes; there shall
be no more death, nor sorrow, nor crying. There shall be no more
pain, for the former things have passed away."*
Revelation 21:4 *NIV*

ॐ❧

Epilogue

The King's Tears

Once upon a time, in the City of Disappointments, there lived many known by the name of Broken-and-Wounded. And high above the City was the Kingdom of Peace – ruled by the King of all that ever was or ever shall be. No one became a citizen of the Kingdom of Peace except by choice, and no one willing to pledge allegiance to the King was ever turned away.

Next to the King's great throne was a vessel of translucent pearl. An angel, known as the Keeper of Tears, stood beside the vessel. His was a very sacred duty indeed, for the vessel contained the tears shed by those known by the name of Broken-and-Wounded in the City below. Since the beginning of all that ever was or ever shall be, there was never a day when the angels failed to gather tears for the King, and never a day when He was not present as the tears were measured and recorded.

And the King grieved for the people. It was never His plan that they should suffer so. Suffering entered the City after the angels of darkness, led by the Deceiver, were banished from the Kingdom of Peace. From that time on their only ambition was to interfere with the destiny of the people. And so it was that the enemies of the King became the enemies of the people.

Then it came to pass that the King came to the City to teach the people how to live according to the Kingdom of Peace. Some would not listen, but those who did preserved His truth for all who would come after them. With every generation there were those who loved the King and accepted His plan for the good of all. Those who scoffed at the King's ways fell under the rule of the avenging angels of darkness and walked in *their* ways.

The avenging angels, being wise to human behavior, continued to prey upon the people until the Kingdom of Darkness began to manifest within families. Husbands were harsh with their wives. Women were provoked to anger. Children became discouraged, fearful, and rebellious. Indifference and pride gave way to anger and violence; families were torn apart as the wounds of one generation were handed down to the next generation.

Those who remained loyal to the King told and retold all He had accomplished during His time in the City. One of these stories concerned a young woman whose heart was hardened against the King because of the many abuses she had suffered. One day the King spoke to her, saying:

"Listen my child! My words will be as life to you if you will heed them! I hear your cries for justice, but you must leave justice to Me. Why do you judge Me for what *man* has done to you? Have you not heard how the avenging angels work their evil through those who harden their hearts against Me?

"You long for peace, but you will never find it apart from Me. My love is far more powerful than any sorrow that has befallen you; My hand many times stronger than the evil that manipulates you. I offer refreshment for your soul and a reward for your sorrow that is far greater than what you have suffered.

"Do not think that because I ask you to forgive those who have harmed you that I regard your wounds lightly. I have recorded and saved all of your tears. I have grieved for your afflictions and suffered them with you. It is for *your* sake that you must forgive. Bitterness holds you hostage to the past and continually stirs up your pain."

As the young woman stood in the presence of the King, her hope was restored. No longer would she measure the King's love by her circumstances or blame Him for the cruelty of others. Never again would she question His ways, but trust Him to transform what was meant for evil into something beautiful for His purpose and her eternal benefit; for this was the promise to those who put their trust in Him. She treasured the King's words in her heart and went about the City to encourage others known by the name of Broken-and-Wounded. It was in the telling of such stories that the people learned of a King who saved tears in a beautiful vessel.

The battle for the destiny of the people continued until it appeared that an entire generation would be swept into the Kingdom of Darkness, for just as some served as agents of hope for the cause of the King, there were those who served as agents for the Deceiver. So it came to pass that there came upon the City a time of great fascinations with angels, with no discernment between the two Kingdoms in which they operated. More and more people were intent on doing what was right in their own eyes, with no regard for the danger of living by the law of the Kingdom of Darkness.

From age to age the Keeper of Tears carried out his duties, knowing that as surely as he had witnessed the beginning of evil, he would witness the end of evil. How often he longed to inquire of the King as to the hour of reckoning, but he kept his silence for only the King knew the day and the hour when all who would choose to live in the Kingdom of Peace had made their decision. Only then would he take up his sword.

Then there came a time of such evil that the Keeper of Tears sensed the new beginning and began to measure the days by the condition of the City. Fathers deserted the home. The preborn and the elderly were no longer valued. Perversion of every kind was published and practiced openly. There was no honor to be found in those elected to govern the City. Violent children roamed the streets, the prisons were filled, and there was little room left in the vessel for the King's tears.

Surely the appointed time was at hand! At any moment the heavens would echo with the thundering of horses as the angels of justice, led by the King, descended upon the City. Soon the angelic hosts were speaking in hushed voices about the coming battle. Excitement spread to every corner of the Kingdom. Even the King's horse, set aside from the very beginning, grew restless and ran at increasing speeds. He reared high into the air, eyes fierce with anticipation, sensing that his hour was close at hand. Never had there been such a horse as this – a brave and noble horse – fit only for a King. And none but the King of all that ever was or ever shall be would sit upon the back of this dazzling white steed, the very one foretold in the final pages of the Record of the King.

To this very day the angelic hosts are poised and ready for the signal that will bring an end to the Kingdom of Darkness. On that day the Deceiver, along with his avenging angels and those who served with them, will be taken captive and banished to the Land of No Return. Then the King will proclaim the end of evil and the end of sorrow and tears. Once again He will live among the people in the City, and there will come a time of peace such as has never been known before. All these things have been foretold in the Record of the King. They shall come to pass!

And after the old things are passed away, the Keeper of Tears will seal up the vessel and place it in the center of the Kingdom of Peace – where it will remain for all eternity – as a reminder of the love of the King for those once known as Broken-and-Wounded.

‌⮀⮀

We are born into conflict, but not without resources. God has made provision for us by way of an arsenal of truth, which is readily available to those who will honestly seek it. How encouraging it is to know that God grieves with us, that our circumstances are no indication of His love, and that in Him we find all we need to face any situation.

If you are living with regrets and the grief of *what might have been,* it is never too late to give God the broken pieces of your past and ask Him to make something beautiful out of them for His glory and your eternal happiness.

The King's Tears is taken from *If I'd Known Then What I Know Now*

Appendix

The Voice of the Abused

We have chosen to walk the road to recovery
You may have known us for years but you probably know very little about us. We grew up without confidence, security or a sense of our value. We had to learn how to keep ugly secrets, deny our feelings and assume the blame for the cruelty of others. We became expert at disguise, denial and pretense. But we no longer allow the effects of our past to manipulate us.

We have chosen to learn new skills
The survival skills of our childhood can now be put away. We will come out of denial, stop hiding behind our false selves, and risk trusting others with who we really are. We have chosen to respond rather that to react to all people, at all times, in all situations. We will learn how to recognize the truly loving people in the world and know that we, too, are worthy of love.

This won't be an easy journey for us
The journey to wholeness may at times drain our courage and strip away our confidence. We will run into traps and setbacks. We will get frustrated and angry.

281

We may cry. At times we will even feel the way we felt as children: terrified and helpless, unable to trust or feel safe again.

Please be sensitive to the struggling child within us
We are mourning the betrayal and cruelties of our youth. We know the full extent of our brokenness. We know, too, that some of our pieces are missing. But please do not label our grief as self pity, for our tears are long overdue. They flow in sorrow for our wounded inner child. They fall silently for the loss of our childhood and for the adult years stolen by our offenders.

Please don't tell us to forget about our past, to count our blessings or to get on with life
We've all tried that. It doesn't work. We know we must learn how to put the past to rest now. But healing the scars of an abusive childhood is a long, difficult process. We don't know just how long it will take. We need to learn how to establish safe boundaries, how to find the confidence to manage our new life; and how to put away the survival skills of the old one.

We realize that you may frequently resent the effects our past abuse has had on us – as marriage partners or as friends
We know too that you may feel threatened by our decision to seek healing because at times, you may have to take this difficult journey with us. No, life isn't fair. You don't deserve this anymore than we deserved the abuse. But we need to be liberated from our anger and our resentment. They keep us bound to the pain of our past.

At times we may pull away from you when you reach out to help us
But please keep on reaching. And you may feel shut out by the walls we erected as children, trying to protect ourselves when we were growing up. But try to be patient. We

can only take down our walls one brick at a time. We don't expect you to make up the wrongs of our childhood. Nor do we ask that you assume the responsibility for our healing. This we will do for ourselves. Just affirm and support us as we seek healing for our wounded child.

And finally please don't try to "fix" us
We don't need your pity. We need your prayers, your encouragement and your understanding until we can take our place beside you, as whole persons. When we have completed our journey, when we have finally closed up our wounds this much we promise:
That we'll be able to look up with trust, to share new strengths and feel safe expressing our love as we begin the celebration of the rest of our days.
Together.

19231056R00156

Made in the USA
Charleston, SC
12 May 2013